EX AUDITU

An International Journal for the Theological Interpretation of Scripture

VOL. 28   **2012**

Ex Auditu is published annually by Pickwick Publications, an imprint of
Wipf and Stock Publishers, 199 West 8th Avenue, Suite 3, Eugene, Oregon 97401, USA

SUBSCRIPTIONS

Individuals:
U.S.A. and all other countries (in U.S. funds): $20.00
Students: $12.00

Institutions:
U.S.A. and all other countries (in U.S. funds): $30.00

This periodical is indexed in the ATLA Religion Database, published by the American Theological Library Association, 300 S. Wacker Dr., Suite 2100, Chicago, IL 60606, Email: atla@atla.com, www: http://www.atla.com/; *Internationale Zeitschriftenshau für Bibelwissenschaft; Religious and Theological Abstracts; and Old Testament Abstracts.*

Please address all subscription correspondence
and change of address information to Wipf and Stock Publishers.

©2013 by Wipf and Stock Publishers
ISSN: 0883-0053
ISBN: 978-1-62032-609-1

EX AUDITU

An International Journal for the Theological Interpretation of Scripture

Klyne R. Snodgrass, Editor
Stephen J. Chester, Associate Editor
D. Christopher Spinks, Associate Editor

North Park Theological Seminary
3225 West Foster Avenue
Chicago, Illinois 60625-4987
USA

Tel: (773) 244-6243
email: ksnodgrass@northpark.edu
Web site: http://wipfandstock.com/journals/ex_auditu

EDITORIAL BOARD

Terence E. Fretheim, Luther Seminary, St. Paul, MN
Richard B. Hays, The Divinity School, Duke University, Durham, NC
Jon R. Stock, Wipf and Stock Publishers, Eugene, OR
Miroslav Volf, Yale Divinity School, New Haven, CT
John Wipf, Wipf and Stock Publishers, Eugene, OR
David Kersten, Dean of North Park Theological Seminary

THE EDITORIAL BOARD MEMBERS AND CONSULTANTS represent various disciplines and denominations. Theological interpretation of Scripture is a task to be taken seriously by scholars who are committed to the Christian faith and tradition. However, as one editorial consultant stated: "Let people gradually get used to the idea that a sane hermeneutics is both oriented in advance toward agreement/consent and is simultaneously exigent, discriminating, critical."

EDITORIAL CONSULTANTS

Richard Bauckham
University of St. Andrews, Emeritus
St. Andrews, Scotland

M. Daniel Carroll R.
Denver Seminary
Denver, Colorado

Jan Du Rand
Emeritus, University of Johannesburg
and Extraordinary Professor, North West University

Willie Jennings
The Divinity School
Duke University
Durham, N. Carolina

Robert Johnston
Fuller Theological Seminary
Pasadena, California

R. Walter L. Moberly
University of Durham
Durham, England

Kathleen M. O'Connor
Columbia Theological Seminary
Decatur, Georgia

Iain Provan
Regent College
Vancouver, B.C.

Anthony Thiselton
University of Nottingham
Nottingham, England

Augustine Thompson
University of Virginia
Charlottesville, Virginia

Marianne Meye Thompson
Fuller Theological Seminary
Pasadena, California

Kevin J. Vanhoozer
Trinity Evangelical Divinity School
Deerfield, Illinois

Geoffrey Wainwright
The Divinity School
Duke University
Durham, N. Carolina

Sondra Wheeler
Wesley Theological Seminary
Washington, D.C.

William H. Willimon
The Divinity School
Duke University
Durham, N. Carolina

N. T. Wright
St. Mary's College,
University of St. Andrews, Scotland

EX AUDITU

CONTENTS

Announcement of the 2013 Symposium	v
Abbreviations	vi
Introduction *Klyne Snodgrass*	vii
Finding Happiness in Family Life: Biblical Reflections *Stephen C. Barton*	1
Response to Barton *Luke A. Powery*	17
Imposter Happiness or the Real Thing? Marriage, Singleness, and the Beatitudes in the Twenty-First Century *Jana Marguerite Bennett*	21
Response to Bennett *Jo Ann Deasy*	41
Jesus, Paul, and Family Values *Julie Hanlon Rubio*	45
Response to Rubio *Michelle Clifton-Soderstrom*	70
Tyranny, Authority, Service: Leadership and Headship in the New Testament *Lynn H. Cohick*	74
Response to Cohick *Dennis R. Edwards*	90
Revenge, Forgiveness, and Sibling Rivalry: A Theological Dialogue Between Scripture and Science *Dennis Olson*	94

Contents

Response to Olson *Jack R. Lundbom*	120
Wives and Daughters: Women, Sex, and Violence in Biblical Tradition *Caryn A. Reeder*	122
Response to Reeder *Christopher B. Ansberry*	142
Generativity, Covenant Witness, and Jesus' Final Discourse *Jim Dekker*	147
Response to Dekker *Linda Cannell*	160
The Use of Scripture in Catholic Social Teaching's Vision of the Family *Mary Veeneman*	165
Response to Veeneman *Erica Olson-Bang*	177
Family Worship (Isaiah 58:1–12) *Luke A. Powery*	180
Annotated Bibliography on Family	187
Presenters and Respondents	203
Ex Auditu – Volumes Available	205

ANNOUNCEMENT OF THE 2013 SYMPOSIUM

North Park Theological Seminary in Chicago, Illinois, is pleased to announce that the twenty-ninth Symposium on the Theological Interpretation of Scripture will take place September 26–28, 2013. The symposium will start at 7:00 p.m. on September 26 in Nyvall Hall and will extend through a Saturday afternoon worship service on September 28. The theme in 2013 will be Urban Ministry. The following persons have agreed to make presentations:

> Vince Bantu, Catholic University, PhD student of Semitic and Egyptian Languages and Literature
> Danny Carroll R., Denver Seminary, Old Testament
> Soong-Chan Rah, North Park Theological Seminary, Evangelism
> Dennis Edwards, Senior Pastor of Sanctuary Covenant Church, New Testament
> Amy Laura Hall, Duke Divinity School, Christian Ethics
> David Leong, Seattle Pacific University, Missiology
> Efrem Smith, Superintendent of the Pacific Southwest Conference, Evangelical Covenant Church, Preaching
> Paul Trebilco, University of Otago, New Testament
> Chanequa Walker-Barnes, McAfee School of Theology, Pastoral Care

Persons interested in attending the sessions should write before September 1 to:

> Ms. Guylla Brown
> North Park Theological Seminary
> 3225 W. Foster Avenue
> Chicago, Illinois 60625

Meals may be taken at North Park and assistance can be provided in finding nearby lodging.

ABBREVIATIONS

All abbreviations are as specified in Patrick H. Alexander et al., eds., *The SBL Handbook of Style* (Peabody, MA: Hendrickson, 1999). Abbreviations not listed here can be found there.

BTB	*Biblical Theology Bulletin*
BZAW	Beihefte zur Zeitschrift für die alttestamentliche Wissenschaft
ET	English Translation
HTR	*Harvard Theological Review*
JBL	*Journal of Biblical Literature*
JSNT	*Journal for the Study of the New Testament*
JSOT	*Journal for the Study of the Old Testament*
JSOTSup	Journal for the Study of the Old Testament: Supplement Series
MT	Masoretic Text
NICOT	New International Commentary on the Old Testament
NIV	New International Version
NRSV	New Revised Standard Version
NTS	*New Testament Studies*
OTL	Old Testament Library
SBL	Society of Biblical Literature
TDNT	*Theological Dictionary of the New Testament*
TDOT	*Theological Dictionary of the Old Testament*
USCCB	United States Council of Catholic Bishops
VT	*Vetus Testamentum*
WBC	Word Biblical Commentary
WUNT	Wissenschaftliche Untersuchungen zum Neuen Testament
ZAW	*Zeitschrift für die alttestamentliche Wissenschaft*
ZNW	*Zeitschrift für die neutestamentliche Wissenschaft und die Kunde der älteren Kirche*

INTRODUCTION

Everyone has a family—or at least a history of one, and few realities are as valuable as our families, dysfunctional as they may be. Even disrespected politicians can gain a hearing by speaking of the importance of the family. Erosion of the family is one of the alarming fears of our time, and justly so. Not all views of family are healthy, however, and some are downright idolatrous. Christians are eager to support and promote family values, but often they do so myopically. Churches frequently are guilty of emphasizing family inappropriately while at the same time neglecting real family needs, singles, and others who do not fit traditional family patterns.

Families and family language are obviously important in both OT and NT. At the same time other and higher priorities than family are emphasized. So much is this the case that Christians were seen as a threat to the family, which is not hard to understand given the "difficult" sayings of Jesus and some teachings of the early church. Jesus and the NT writers created an alternative family of disciples that was more important than one's earthly family. Still, given the importance of the family unit in the ancient world, if one were to live the Christian faith, it would have to be lived in families, and instruction on families and life in families was therefore important. The same is true throughout the history of the church and especially in our own time. What should Christians believe and practice regarding family? The articles in this volume invite consideration of the issues involved.

At the symposium twice as much time is given to discussion of the papers as to their delivery, and the journal cannot reproduce the character of those discussions, which are always stimulating and enriching. People in attendance at the symposium include an interesting mix of faculty types, pastors, church leaders, students, and lay people. We are grateful to all who participated.

Appreciation is especially expressed once again to all the presenters and respondents who made a significant investment in the life of North Park. The friendship of these people is a gift we value. The authors of papers were given a chance to edit their contributions after the symposium, but the responses are essentially as they were presented. As is obvious, the views expressed are those of the authors and not necessarily those of the journal or of North Park. Special gratitude is expressed to Jenna Brand and Markus Nikkanen, students at North Park, for their work on the bibliography, and especially to Guylla Brown from North Park's staff, without

Introduction

whom the symposium would be impossible. Anyone who has been to the symposium knows that is true.

The Editor

FINDING HAPPINESS IN FAMILY LIFE: BIBLICAL REFLECTIONS

Stephen C. Barton

In thinking about the family as Christians today we do not start from nowhere. We have to start from where we are, somewhere "in the middle"—or perhaps we should say, "in the *muddle*." At the level of ideology, politics, and society we are engaged in what sociologist James Davidson Hunter has called "culture wars."[1] According to Hunter the culture wars are fought between (broadly-speaking) fundamentalists and relativists, a set of paired opposites reinforced powerfully by other matching pairs. In the domain of psychology we have authoritarianism versus libertarianism, in matters of lifestyle rigidity versus permissivism, in aesthetics traditionalism versus (post-)modernism, in worldview religion versus the secular, in politics conservative versus liberal, in cultural politics orthodox versus progressive, in foreign affairs Islam versus the West, and with regard to globalization we have jihad versus McWorld.[2]

One of the main fault-lines running through all these pairs of opposites has to do with "family values." Characteristically there is a polarization of views on such issues as abortion, artificial reproductive technologies, the nurture and discipline of children, sex rules, gender roles and relations, and, most recently, gay marriage—all, of course, inflected along diverse lines of ethnicity, socio-economic status, and religion.[3] This spills over into popular culture. At this level there is intense interest in exploring the "shadow side" of family life, along with issues at the boundaries. How is it, we ask ourselves, that what is thought of as "a haven in a heartless world" can become the womb of monstrous evil, such as that embodied in the juvenile mass-murderer or the home-grown terrorist? I am thinking of intimations along

---

1. James Davidson Hunter, *Culture Wars: The Struggle to Define America* (New York: Basic Books, 1991).

2. I am drawing here on James Davidson Hunter, "Fundamentalism and Relativism Together: Reflections on Genealogy," in *Between Relativism and Fundamentalism* (ed. Peter L. Berger; Grand Rapids: Eerdmans, 2010) 17–34, 19.

3. See further Don Browning et al., *From Culture Wars to Common Ground* (Louisville: Westminster John Knox, 1997) especially Part 1.

these lines in fictional works such as Lionel Shriver's novel *We Need To Talk About Kevin*[4] and before that Philip Roth's *American Pastoral*.[5] As well as explorations of the shadow side, there is the immense popularity of cultural forms that key into our deeply embedded nostalgia for a "golden age" when people knew their place. In Britain this is a national industry, the latest manifestation of which is the long-running, "upstairs, downstairs" series *Downton Abbey*. The "nostalgia industry" appears harmless enough. In fact, it may be a symptom of considerable cultural anxiety over our contemporary loss of innocence.

At the same time, understandably in light of such anxieties, we have become interested in "happiness" and what makes for human "flourishing." Charles Taylor has written about this in his major work of cultural analysis, *A Secular Age*.[6] In the social sciences a new school of psychology has developed in the past decade or so called the "Positive Psychology Movement," represented by works such as Jonathan Haidt's *The Happiness Hypothesis*.[7] The same period has also seen the birth of the *Journal of Happiness Studies*.[8] In classical studies there has been major work on Greek and Roman approaches to the attainment of *eudaimonia*.[9] In theology Ellen Charry has given us *God and the Art of Happiness*.[10] In biblical studies there is now a comprehensive collection of essays edited by Brent Strawn on *The Bible and the Pursuit of Happiness*.[11] At a more popular (though no less serious) level we have in the novels of Marilynne Robinson explorations of family life across several generations that offer a wisdom about family dynamics of a fundamentally hopeful kind—of nature and nurture transformed by grace.[12]

Somehow our reflection on the family has to speak *from and to* this complex cultural and social reality. Furthermore, I believe that the impact of such reflection on our ongoing conversion and transformation—which should be the goal of all Christian discourse—will only be possible if it touches us at an existential level. For I am sure that "family issues" affect us all. It may be the impact in late-modernity of

---

4. New York, Counterpoint, 2003.

5. Boston: Houghton Mifflin, 1997.

6. Cambridge, MA: Belknap, 2007.

7. London: Arrow, 2006.

8. The journal is published by Springer. Its first issue appeared in 2000.

9. E.g., Martha Nussbaum, *The Therapy of Desire: Theory and Practice in Hellenistic Ethics* (Princeton: Princeton University Press, 1994).

10. Grand Rapids: Eerdmans, 2010.

11. New York: Oxford University Press, 2012.

12. See Marilynne Robinson, *Gilead* (London: Virago, 2004); and *Home* (London: Virago, 2008).

confusion over gender roles in marriage. It may be the impact of divorce and single-parenthood, now running at a historically unprecedented rate. It may be the phenomenon of the absent father. It may be domestic violence or child abuse. It may be issues around sexual identity and what happens when a family member "comes out." It may be the effects of poverty, including the poverty of affluence.[13] It may be about how to cope with children or elderly parents with special needs. It may be obstacles to communication between the generations or in families that cross boundaries of religion or ethnicity. It may be the challenges peculiar to life in blended families of various kinds. We fool ourselves if we think we begin with a "clean slate" or belong to a community of "the pure." To quote from Robinson's recent collection of essays: "Wisdom, which is almost always another name for humility, lies in accepting one's own inevitable share in human fallibility."[14]

Reading wisely

My particular responsibility in this paper is to contribute to Christian discourse about the family from such wisdom as I have received as a student of the NT. Before proceeding further, therefore, I offer some comments on reading wisely.[15] I do so in the conviction that quite significant levels of conflict and anguish in Christian, Bible-reading families are a legacy of poor interpretation, often in concert with an impoverished understanding of the nature of life in Christ and failings in Christian maturity.[16]

First, there is the need for *patient discernment*—that is, for a certain quality of attention over time, a quality of attention that flows from that supreme Christian virtue which is love. As I have said in another context:

> The wrong question to ask initially when reflecting on how to live as families in the light of the New Testament is, What does the New Testament say about the family? This is the wrong question, not because there are no texts that talk about the family in general and families in particular, but because it *forecloses prematurely* on the kind of wisdom to which the New Testament testifies, and passes over the vital issue of the kinds of readers we need to be in order to understand God truly. Putting it in more general

---

13. See on this, David Sims, *The Child in American Evangelicalism and the Problem of Affluence* (Eugene, OR: Pickwick, 2009).

14. Marilynne Robinson, *When I Was A Child I Read Books* (London: Virago, 2012) 27.

15. See further, Stephen C. Barton, *Invitation to the Bible* (London: SPCK, 1997).

16. For a recent exploration of related issues see Adrian Thatcher, *The Savage Text: The Use and Abuse of the Bible* (Oxford: Wiley-Blackwell, 2008).

terms, in the rush to find out "what the Bible says," there is a failure to consider how the Bible speaks and how we as readers may hear what God through the Spirit is saying to the church.[17]

Second, and following from this, we need to resist two opposing but related approaches to the text characteristic of a modernity caught in that tension between fundamentalists and relativists mentioned already. On the one hand, there is the tendency to *stretch the text* so that the significant gap—historical, linguistic, cultural, and so on—between text and reader is reduced, almost to vanishing point, and the reader is able to declare, "The Bible says . . .," as if to ask a follow-up question would be bad manners. On the other hand, there is the tendency to *stretch the gap* between text and reader so far that any connection between the two is broken, and the reader is left wondering, "Why bother?" The former fails to do justice to the power of the text to speak precisely out of its "otherness" in relation to ourselves, an otherness of times and peoples past that may surprise us and help us to see things differently. The latter fails to do justice to the power of the text to speak precisely out of its kinship with us—that we today are who we are because we stand in a genealogy and participate in a narrative and belong to a community, all of which are in part scripturally constituted.[18]

The mention of community leads to my final point. A wise reading of the Bible is one that takes with full seriousness the kind of text the Bible is: that it is *the canon of a community*—that is to say, "sacred Scripture," constituted as such by that particular, historic community we call the church.[19] It is the church's (always fallible) reading, interpretation, and performance of the Scripture that mediates the (often opaque) witness of the text to the divine life and invites participation in that life by faith in Jesus Christ.[20]

---

17. Stephen C. Barton, "Living as Families in the Light of the New Testament," *Interpretation* 52.2 (1998) 130–44, 130; italics original.

18. Cf. Rowan Williams, *Why Study the Past? The Quest for the Historical Church* (London: Darton, Longman and Todd, 2005) 3: "[T]raditionalists sometimes miss the point because they don't expect to be surprised by the past; progressives miss the point because they don't expect to be interested or questioned by it."

19. Cf. Jaroslav Pelikan, *Interpreting the Bible and the Constitution* (New Haven and London: Yale University Press, 2004) for an illuminating exploration of the analogies between the Bible as the "constitution" of the church and the role of the American Constitution for the people of the United States of America.

20. Important here is the essay of Nicholas Lash, "Performing the Scriptures," in his collection of essays, *Theology on the Way to Emmaus* (London: SCM, 1986) 37–46.

A number of implications for family-related matters follow from this latter point. One is that the Bible is not a manual for family life. Whatever wisdom about the family we draw from the wellsprings of Scripture have to be measured against our understanding of the God to whom Scripture, rightly interpreted, bears witness. Another implication is that to understand scripturally what it means to live in and as families, we need the life, liturgy, and tradition of the church. It is the life, liturgy, and tradition of the church, shaped by its reading of Scripture, that form us in the patterns of sociality that make life possible, including life in families.[21] A third implication takes its cue from Scripture's witness to resurrection life, an inaugurated reality in time present awaiting a longed-for fulfillment in time future. What we say about families ought to be a matter, not so much of archaeology, as of eschatology. Recovering lost treasures (including lost wisdom) from the past is important, but only in so far as it offers clues to, and inspiration for, living as families towards a future whose end is God. Such life—resurrection life in families—will be dynamic not static, ever open to judgment, conversion, and transformation as the Spirit leads.

Understanding Happiness

It is time now to say something about ways of conceiving happiness. That it is a "slippery" word needs to be acknowledged. That it is a "polluted" word needs to be acknowledged also.[22] But several disciplinary perspectives offer helpful bearings. First, in anthropological perspective, happiness is inflected culturally. As anthropologist Marshall Sahlins says:

> Each people knows their own kind of happiness: the culture that is the legacy of their ancestral tradition, transmitted in the distinctive concepts of their ancestral language, and adapted to their specific life conditions. It is by means of this tradition, endowed also with the morality of the community and the notions of the family, that experience is organized, since people do not simply discover the world, they are taught it. They come to it not simply as cognitions but as values.[23]

---

21. Cf. Rodney Clapp, *Families at the Crossroads. Beyond Traditional and Modern Options* (Downers Grove, IL: InterVarsity, 1993) 67–88, on the idea of church as "first family."

22. See further Brent Strawn, "The Bible and . . . Happiness?" in *The Bible and the Pursuit of Happiness* (ed. Brent Strawn; New York: Oxford University Press, 2012) 5–7.

23. Marshall Sahlins, *How "Natives" Think: About Captain Cook, for Example* (Chicago: University of Chicago Press, 1995) 12; cited in J. B. Green, "'We Had to Celebrate and Rejoice!' Happiness in the Topsy-Turvy World of Luke-Acts," in *The Bible and the Pursuit of Happiness*, 240–61, 241.

Significant here—and challenging, perhaps, to the individualistic and affective assumptions of modernity—happiness is understood as a particular kind of human response to the way things are which, however apparently spontaneous in expression, is learned within a context of community, tradition, moral norms, and family life. Happiness, we may say, arises out of a deep, culturally-mediated sense of alignment with reality, with life in families playing a key role.

Second, in philosophical perspective, from the philosophers of Ancient Greece on and given classic articulation in Aristotle's *Nichomachean Ethics*, happiness has been understood as having two main aspects, the hedonic and the eudaimonic—happiness as a subjective feeling, on the one hand, and happiness as a kind of life, on the other. The hedonic aspect (Greek *hēdonē*) has to do with the experience of pleasure and the avoidance of pain; it is oriented to the present; and it is dependent on externalities, such as health, wealth, friends, or good fortune. The eudaimonic (Greek *eudaimonia*) has to do with the life well-lived and is oriented to long-term flourishing based on the practice of the virtues informed by reason: it is about living well and doing well. Significant here—and challenging to modernity's emphasis on subjective feeling and the present moment—is the recognition that the hedonic alone is insufficient. True happiness requires a teleology of what it means to be human, worked out over time in a certain kind of life, including, not least, life in households understood as the building-blocks of society and politics.

A third perspective, the psychological, focuses mainly on the engagement between a person's interior and exterior worlds. Here happiness may be thought of as having three dimensions: growth, integrity, and well-being. Growth has to do with "intrinsic motivation and progress on the path toward realizing one's life purpose," integrity has to do with "the internalization and assimilation of one's cultural conventions and practices," and well-being has to do with "flourishing and contentment."[24] So defined, the formative influence of the practices of family life on the pursuit of happiness is not difficult to discern and will be illustrated in what follows.

A fourth perspective on happiness is the theological. Historically the theological perspective is indebted to Aristotle and the philosophers of antiquity on *eudaimonia* but recontextualizes what they say in relation to Christian soteriology. This is well explored in the work by Ellen Charry, already cited. Evincing a concern that Christian theology has emphasized future eschatology at the expense of present happiness, Charry defines happiness as follows: "Happiness is a realizing eschatology with salvation centered in sanctification. Salvation is growing into the wisdom

---

24. Green, "'We Had to Celebrate and Rejoice!'" 242.

of divine love and enjoying oneself in the process."²⁵ Coining the term "asherism," from the Hebrew *asher* ("happy" or "blessed"), Charry continues, "Salvation is the healing of love that one may rest in God. Asherism works out that healing process in a life of reverent obedience to divine commands that shape character and bring moral-psychological flourishing and enhance societal well-being. Salvation is an excellent pattern of living that is personally rewarding because it advances God's intention for creation. It is a realizing eschatology."²⁶

For present purposes, I am not concerned to play one perspective on happiness off against another. What strikes me, rather, is the degree of potential overlap and interconnection between them. Together, they offer significant resources for a deeper understanding of ways to find happiness in family life, inspired by scriptural reasoning.

Finding Happiness in Family Life: Biblical Reflections

Having spoken of our current location in the culture wars of (post-) modernity, of the existential pressures we face in family life, and of the critical importance for Christians of wise readings of Scripture, I turn now to offer several readings of my own. Here I hope to illustrate kinds of reading that are historically and textually sensitive as well as being responsible in contemporary appropriation. My goal is to offer scripturally-informed, constructive hints about ways towards happiness in our common life in families today.

> "For the people of those regions report about us what kind of welcome we had among you, and how you turned to God from idols, to serve a living and true God" (1 Thess 1:9b).

As Paul's words of commendation of the Thessalonian believers bear witness, the Christian way involves a process of ongoing conversion and transformation—and, given the phenomenon of conversion by household (cf. Acts 10:48; 11:14; 16:15, 33; 18:8), this process will have been ongoing in the domestic sphere, as in every other sphere of life. Central to this process is a turning *from* and a turning *to*—a turning from idols and a turning to God.²⁷ It involves a turning from one orientation of the heart and pattern of life to another, from one vision of *eudaimonia* to another. This

---

25. Charry, *God and the Art of Happiness*, x.
26. Ibid., xi.
27. Valuable on idolatry in general is the collection of essays on this theme in *Ex Auditu* 15 (1999).

turning is also a crossing. The abandonment of idols and idol worship involves the crossing of a boundary. That boundary marks out a new people, a people called to lives of holiness as members of the kingdom of God.

In the faith of the Jews the avoidance of idolatry and the whole-hearted worship of God was what constituted the symbolic, ritual, and practical center of their common life, both in households and as a nation (cf. Deut 5:8–10; Isa 44:9–20; Jer 10:1–16). It was also what guarded the periphery, distinguishing the Jews from "the nations," even while of necessity they lived among them (cf. Dan 1:8). This system of values, symbols, and practices carried over into early Christianity, but with significant modifications. With the inclusion of Gentiles in the people of God the boundary lines had to be redrawn. On occasion the lines also had to be blurred. An interesting family-related case has to do with believers in a "mixed marriage," where the line is drawn around the couple (and their children), not between them (cf. 1 Cor 7:14). But the prohibition of idolatry remains constant, even as the practical inevitabilities of living with idols had routinely to be addressed.[28]

This profound tradition is relevant for how we live as families in the modern world. For one of the main impediments to happiness in family life is idolatry. If one characteristic of idolatry is misplaced devotion, setting one's heart's desire towards what is other than God, then our scriptural tradition offers a serious warning against family idolatry and idolizing the family. Note the two senses of "the idolatry of the family." There is the idolatry that we practice as families, and there is the idolatry that has as its object of devotion the family itself.

As regards the idolatry we practice as families, what appears most critical is our complicity in modernity's liberal-capitalist culture of commodification, excess, and possessive individualism.[29] Against this in the biblical tradition stands the last and climactic commandment of the Decalogue, with its strong orientation on what is destructive of household-based society: "You shall not covet your neighbour's house; you shall not covet your neighbour's wife, or male or female slave, or ox, or donkey, or anything that belongs to your neighbour" (Exod 20:17). Also in the tradition we have the witness of the Gospels to Jesus' practice of evangelical poverty, along with his call to lives of self-dispossession for the sake of the kingdom of God (cf. Mark

---

28. Cf. Christopher Rowland, "Living with Idols: An Exercise in Biblical Theology," in *Idolatry: False Worship in the Bible, Early Judaism and Christianity* (ed. Stephen C. Barton; London: T. & T. Clark, 2007) 163–76.

29. See further, David Matzko McCarthy, *Sex and Love in the Home: A Theology of the Household* (London: SCM, 2001); also Brent Waters, *The Family in Christian Social and Political Thought* (Oxford: Oxford University Press, 2007).

8:34–37). We have the witness of the Acts of the Apostles to what Joan Lockwood O'Donovan memorably calls "non-proprietary community": "All who believed were together and had all things in common; they would sell their possessions and goods and distribute the proceeds to all, as any had need" (Acts 2:44–45).[30]

As regards the idolatry that has as its object of devotion the family itself, what appears most critical is our all-consuming investment in values, habits, and practices that make the good of the family—usually the privatized, nuclear family underpinned by romantic love and the romanticization of childhood—the sum total of the good. In this context, two elements of the scriptural tradition offer grounds for critical self-examination.

The first is the tradition of eschatological singleness practiced by Jesus and Paul. For most of us today identity is constituted by a carefully-managed passage through life-stages, which normally include finding a partner, marrying, and having children. It comes as a surprise then, that contrary to what we are led to believe in *The Da Vinci Code*, Jesus was celibate and had no children. He is among those who "made themselves eunuchs for the sake of the kingdom of heaven" (Matt 19:12).[31] It comes as a surprise likewise that Paul practiced and advocated remaining single (cf. 1 Cor 7:7) on the grounds that "the present form of this world is passing away" (1 Cor 7:31)—even recommending that husbands relate to their wives, no longer as wives, but as "sisters" (1 Cor 7:29b).

The second check on idolizing the family is the clear evidence from the Gospels that discipleship of Jesus was disruptive of family ties and obligations, including his own:

> Do not think that I have come to bring peace to the earth; I have not come to bring peace, but a sword. For I have come to set a man against his father, and a daughter against her mother, and a daughter-in-law against her mother-in-law; and one's foes will be members of one's own household. Whoever loves father or mother more than me is not worthy of me; and whoever loves son or daughter more than me is not worthy of me; and whoever does not take up the cross and follow me is not worthy of me. (Matt 10:34–38; cf. Luke 14:26–27)

---

30. See Joan Lockwood O'Donovan, "The Poverty of Christ and Non-Proprietary Community," in *The Doctrine of God and Theological Ethics* (ed. Alan J. Torrance and Michael Banner; London: T. & T. Clark, 2006) 191–200.

31. On Jesus as "millenarian ascetic," see Dale C. Allison, *Jesus of Nazareth: Millenarian Prophet* (Augsburg Fortress, 1998) 172–216; also important is P. W. Van Der Horst, "Celibacy in Early Judaism," *Revue Biblique* 109.3 (2002) 390–402.

This is not an isolated teaching. It is one of a number of sayings and stories in the Gospels that provide a warning against that manifestation of idolatry that allows family ties and loves to take the place of the love of God and discipleship of Jesus.[32] Clearly, from a scriptural point of view, finding happiness in family life, especially happiness of the eudaimonic kind, does not begin and end with the family. In the time of Christian origins this qualification of "family happiness" had a certain counter-cultural aspect, as still also today. It allows for self-transcendence *within* family life, as well as the transcendence *of* family life.

> "I am reminded of your sincere faith, a faith that lived first in your grandmother Lois and your mother Eunice and now, I am sure, lives in you" (2 Tim 1:5).

If we have spoken of the most serious impediment to finding happiness in family life, it is equally important to speak of what, in Christian terms, are some of the main *contributors* to happiness—to conversion and transformation—in family life. A significant clue is offered by what the Paul of 2 Timothy says to Timothy about his spiritual formation, both in the opening of the letter and subsequently. For present purposes, the main point has to do with the family as a dynamic, intergenerational community of memory, practiced in the transmission of the faith. The following observations are pertinent.

First, Timothy's identity is grounded in *a community of kinship*. What is striking is that this community is made up of overlapping families. There is not only his natal family, but also his family of faith, with the latter overlaid on the former. Thus, Paul identifies himself as Timothy's spiritual father when he refers to Timothy as his "beloved child" (1:2a; cf. 2 Tim 1:2). Then there is the acknowledgement of Timothy's natural lineage in the persons of his grandmother and mother who are each named—first Lois, then Eunice. This is very suggestive. It speaks about the potential for ties of (what the anthropologists call) fictive kinship to strengthen, enrich, and expand ties of biological kinship. The natal family becomes embedded in a wider network of persons, values, and practices, within a whole cosmic realm, and that is life-giving. We have here intimations of a Christian wisdom that locates family sociality in the wider and deeper sociality of the family of the church.

Second, the household community to which Timothy belongs is *grounded in time and narrative*. It is constituted by multiple generations. This is so of Paul first

---

32. See further, Stephen C. Barton, *Discipleship and Family Ties in Mark and Matthew* (Cambridge: Cambridge University Press, 1994).

of all, as is implied by his reference to his "ancestors" (*progonoi*) with whom he participates in the worship of God "with a clear conscience" (1:3a). It is also true of Timothy. Who he is as a person of faith and the authority he has as a Christian teacher are rooted in two previous generations, represented by his grandmother Lois and his mother Eunice (1:5).[33] Once again, this is suggestive. Time across the generations implies identity and practice tried and tested—the patient getting of wisdom rather than a passion for transient folly. It also implies entry into, and engagement with, a shared narrative. Paul is inscribing Timothy in an intergenerational lineage of faith, and he does so by telling Timothy his (i.e., Timothy's) story: hence, the fourfold occurrence of language of remembering and remembrance (1:4-6). Remembering and remembrance are key practices in helping us know where we come from and where we are going. It also puts us and keeps us in good company, including the good company of the community of faith.[34]

Third, and related to remembering, the household to which Timothy belongs is constituted by a set of practices, important among which is *the handing on of tradition*. This is implied in 1:5, but made explicit later in 3:14-15: "But as for you, continue in what you have learned and firmly believed, knowing from whom you learned it, and how from childhood [*apo brephous*] you have known the sacred writings that are able to instruct you for salvation through faith in Christ Jesus." We have here an intimation of the importance of the role of the family—along with the church, represented by Paul himself—as both a place and process of education in the faith and how to live it out. Noteworthy also is the implication that this process of formation is lifelong. For Timothy it began "from childhood."

That the family in antiquity played a significant role in the education and formation of children is well known. Jewish tradition gave this role special emphasis.[35] In the biblical tradition this is expressed very clearly in the *Shema'*: "Keep these words that I am commanding you today in your heart. Recite them to your children and talk about them when you are at home and when you are away, when you lie down and when you rise. ... [W]rite them on the doorposts of your house and on your gates" (Deut 6:6-9). Fascinating also is the witness of Josephus to how the

---

33. It is not unlikely that the three generations belonged to the one household and were coresident: see further, Tim Parkin, "The Roman Life Course and the Family," in *A Companion to Families in the Greek and Roman Worlds* (ed. Beryl Rawson; Oxford: Blackwell, 2011) 276-290, 285.

34. Cf. Stephen C. Barton, "Memory and Remembrance in Paul," in *Memory in the Bible and Antiquity* (ed. Stephen C. Barton, Loren T. Stuckenbruck, and Benjamin G. Wold; Tübingen: Mohr Siebeck, 2007) 321-339.

35. Cf. Patrick D. Miller, "That the Children May Know: Children in Deuteronomy," in *The Child in the Bible* (ed. Marcia J. Bunge; Grand Rapids: Eerdmans, 2008) 45-63.

law of Moses—effectively, the "constitution" of the Jews—is inculcated and put into practice in the home:

> Starting from the very beginning of our upbringing and from the mode of life practiced by each individual in the home, he [Moses] did not leave anything, even the minutest detail, free to be determined by the wishes of those involved. Even in relation to food, what we should refrain from and what we should eat, in relation to the company we should keep in our daily lives, in relation to alternate periods of strenuous work and rest, our legislator set the law as the rule and boundary, so that we might live under it as our father and master and not commit any sin either wilfully or from ignorance. (*Contra Apionem* 2:173–174)[36]

Against this background, it is not surprising that Timothy is portrayed as participating in a process of tradition transmission in a household context, with the women as well as the men playing a significant role. In the chain of transmission, Paul plays a role as a fictive father;[37] likewise Lois the grandmother and Eunice the mother each play their part. Timothy, in turn, is being authorized to take his place in passing the tradition on, not just in the house, but even more in the "household of God" (cf. 1 Tim 3:15).

What all this suggests for happiness (of the mainly eudaimonic kind) in family life is the importance of the participation of the family in a dynamic process of formation in the faith, sustained across the generations, and nurtured through shared narrative and practices of remembrance, all within the wider embrace of the family of God. Such a process of formation, if it is to be effective, has to be *intentional*; and to be intentional it has to be embedded in the *habitus* of daily practice.[38] It is not without reason that Josephus in the quotation above draws attention to matters of daily life in three crucial areas of domestic polity: meal-related practices, keeping good company (a matter including, no doubt, the decision about whether and whom to marry), and Sabbath observance. Analogies for Christian practice are not difficult to name. Whatever form they take, they will reflect our calling, as people baptized into Christ, to witness as families to the divine life in the world.

---

36. The citation and translation come from John M. G. Barclay, "The Family as Bearer of Religion," in *Constructing Early Christian Families* (ed. Halvor Moxnes; New York: Routledge, 1997) 66–80, 70.

37. No mention is made here of Timothy's biological father. According to Acts 16:1 Timothy was the product of a "mixed marriage:" his mother a Jew who had become a believer; his father (unnamed) a Greek (*Hellēnos*). No mention is made of the latter's conversion. So Paul's role as a fictive father in relation to Timothy's coming to faith will have been particularly important.

38. On the notion of *habitus* see Pierre Bourdieu, *Outline of a Theory of Practice* (Cambridge: Cambridge University Press, 1977) 72–95.

> "But the father said to his slaves, 'Quickly, bring out a robe—the best one—and put it on him; put a ring on his finger and sandals on his feet. And get the fatted calf and kill it, and let us eat and celebrate; for this son of mine was dead and is alive again; he was lost and is found!' And they began to celebrate" (Luke 15:22–24).

Our previous text drew particular attention to *the family in time* and the contribution to a certain kind of life constituted by practices of remembrance and the transmission of sacred tradition across the generations, practices enriched by their location in a wider network of fictive kinship ties. The text from the famous parable of the Lost Son in Luke 15 allows us to draw attention to *the family as place and performance*, to the importance of home, homecoming, hospitality, and festivity. Here we have both *eudaimonia* and *hēdonē*. Indeed, one could say that we have in this story an exploration of *hēdonē* redeemed, of the importance in human sociality of finding and practising the right blend of *hēdonē* and *eudaimonia*.

In the younger son's request for his share of his father's inheritance, the story begins with an act of family disloyalty.[39] The request is premature and suggests a certain callousness towards the father, as if he were dead already. It also weakens the economic viability of the household estate as a whole by the division of property, and it is a willful exercise of the ego displaying no consideration for other members of the household (including, as we learn later, the older brother). Youthful folly is taken further when the young man strikes out on his own. Leaving behind the social and economic protection of his family and native land, he becomes a stranger, a disconnected figure in a distant land, and in the process loses his moral bearings: "he squandered his property in dissolute living" (15:11b). The term "dissolute living" (*zōn asōtōs*) is telling. This is *hēdonē* unbridled. Its end is a kind of death, death by shame. His resources become depleted, he loses his autonomy, his status is reduced to that of a hired hand, he is starving, his company is that of pigs (a traditional symbol of impurity), and he is without friends and the reciprocity that friendship in antiquity implies since "no one gave him anything" (15:16b).

Then comes a point of turning: "he came to himself" (15:17a). In the light of larger themes in Luke's Gospel we might want to call it a point of repentance and conversion.[40] Certainly there is placed on the man's lips a twofold confession of sin

---

39. For insightful treatments, see Joel B. Green, *The Gospel of Luke* (Grand Rapids: Eerdmans, 1997) 577–86; also, Klyne R. Snodgrass, *Stories with Intent: A Comprehensive Guide to the Parables of Jesus* (Grand Rapids: Eerdmans, 2008) 117–43.

40. Cf. Fernando Mendez-Moratalla, *The Paradigm of Conversion in Luke* (London: T. & T. Clark, 2004) 138–43.

expressed as an offence against God as well as against the man's father (15:18, 21). But we have to acknowledge as well the role of prudential considerations in the young man's "coming to himself." Be that as it may—and why should prudential considerations not play a role in conversion?—the story's downward trajectory is put into reverse. It is put into reverse, not only by the action of the son in returning, but even more by the more-than-hospitable, demonstrative actions of the father: "But while he was still far off, his father saw him and was filled with compassion [*esplanchnisthē*]; he ran and put his arms around him and kissed him" (15:20). Indeed, the upward trajectory becomes even more pronounced as the son's well-rehearsed words of confession are cut short. Instead of receiving discipline and having his status in the household reduced to that of a slave, his honorable status as son is fully restored by the giving of gifts in the form of the material signs of robe, ring, and sandals, topped off with a lavish party.

What we have here is one of the most powerful dramatizations of the importance of home, homecoming, hospitality, and festivity in the whole of the Bible. My suggestion is that, at least to a significant degree, the drama revolves around the tension between hedonic and eudaimonic happiness in human sociality, not least in the context of the family. What the story expresses is hedonic happiness *redeemed*. It is not denied, for the son's hedonism in the form of folly in a far country is replaced by the pleasures—noting the fourfold repetition of "celebrate" (*euphrainein*) in vv. 23, 24, 29, 32—of reunion with his father, the receipt of gifts, and the enjoyment of food, drink, music, and dancing at the party. Rather, hedonic happiness is redeemed by being embraced and stabilized in the wider context of a certain kind of *eudaimonia*, a certain kind of life, integral to which is the practice of the virtues of compassion, forgiveness, liberality, and joy embodied in the behaviour of the father.

Interestingly, however, the story does not end there. Unlike the two stories that precede it (15:3-7, 8-10), this one has a striking sequel (15:25-32). The exploration of the relationship of father and younger son is now complicated narratively by the introduction of the older brother (15:25). Thus, father and elder son relations come to the fore, with the rights of the first-born in the context of sibling relations among the underlying issues.[41] We cannot go into detail here. Let it suffice to observe the contrast between father and son. In a moral world where imitation of the father's example would be expected, we find the opposite. Instead of waiting and watching with his father for the prodigal's return, the son is "in the field"; instead of direct

---

41. On the rich biblical background in stories of first-born and later sons, see Jon D. Levenson, *The Death and Resurrection of the Beloved Son* (New Haven and London: Yale University Press, 1993) especially Part II.

engagement, he inquires as to what is going on via a third party; instead of responding with joy to the news of his brother's return, he responds with anger; instead of joining in the party, he acts inhospitably by refusing to go in; instead of heeding his father's pleas, he expresses resentment in the manner of righteous indignation and self-justification, and in the process shames both his brother (by slander) and his father (by refusing to acquiesce). In terms of the two types of happiness, it could be said that, for want of a mature grasp of *eudaimonia*—a sense of family life made good and sustained by ongoing practices of compassion and forgiveness—the elder brother lacks the capacity for true *hēdonē*, as well as seeking to incapacitate others. In a way, the two brothers are mirror-images of each other. Instead, it is the father who has the blend right. He has the blend right because the virtues he embodies are the virtues that have at their heart the nurturing, sustaining, and celebration of life: "This brother of yours was dead and has come to life; he was lost and has been found" (15:32).

Conclusion

Finding happiness in family life requires wisdom. The quest for wisdom is a profoundly ecumenical undertaking. It was so in antiquity, and it remains so today. Given that our scriptural heritage is one we share, in part, with Judaism, I draw attention in conclusion to some fine words of Chicago Professor of Jewish Studies, Michael Fishbane, in his recent work *Sacred Attunement: A Jewish Theology*.[42] Writing about what he calls the "central places"—home, synagogue, and homeland—which make fulfillment in life possible, his words help to explain the pull of home and family to the Prodigal Son. Home and family are the place, the people, and the practices that offer protection, nurture, identity, belonging, a past opening onto a future—and happiness. He says this:

> *Home* is fundamental. It is the womb space of daily rebirth, the special place of gestation and growth. Home is also a realm of familiarity and shelter. Here generations are ordered and cared for; here they are instructed in the past and prepared for the future; and here too they are sheltered against the dangers or disruptions of the outside world. Home is a sphere of intimacy, threaded by family bonds. It has its own character. The narrative of the family is of a particular kind: it is shaped by distinct memories and hopes; the hierarchy of the family is also particular in nature: it is ordered

---

42. Michael Fishbane, *Sacred Attunement: A Jewish Theology* (Chicago: University of Chicago Press, 2008).

> by specific parents with specific names and histories; and the culture of the family is of a particular character, guided by specific forms of honor and respect, nurture and regard.... The family shares food and words, it opens the door to the neighbour, and it teaches paternity and maternity—and child care. None of this is natural, for all our naturalness. Home is thus the primary ground of self-transcendence. When family members so live with God in mind, the mere house, or *bayit*, becomes a *bayit ne'eman*, a home of faithfulness, firmly and faithfully grounded in the mystery of things. The home is first community.[43]

Yet, for all the wisdom, not to mention poetry, of these words, the gospel and the Gospels give reason to pause. The Gospels present us with a divine Son of Man who is *homeless*: "Foxes have holes, and birds of the air have their nests, but the Son of Man has nowhere to lay his head" (Matt 8:20). They present us with one who summons a seriously-pious prospective disciple with the shocking command, "Follow me, and let the dead bury their own dead" (Matt 8:22). They present us with one who, when sought by his mother and brothers, says to the people sitting around him, "Who are my mother and my brothers? . . . Here are my mother and my brothers! Whoever does the will of God is my mother and sister and brother" (Mark 3:33–35).

So the Christian may wish to qualify Fishbane's sentiments, while also recognizing their wisdom. Recalling Charry's claim that happiness is a "*realizing*" eschatology, it may be that Fishbane's affirmation of home as "first community" represents an eschatology that is "*over*-realized." For the Christian it is not home (and family) that is "first community." The Christian's "first community" is the kingdom of God, opened up by Jesus' death and resurrection, and made present as gift through the Spirit in the church and in the world—even in families.

---

43. Fishbane, *Sacred Attunement*, 176–77, 178; emphasis original.

RESPONSE TO BARTON

Luke A. Powery

"Sometimes I feel like a motherless child": What is happiness when I do not have a family? A person's reflections are not acontextual; thus as I begin, let me set the table of my own personal and professional context. Two parents raised me in a loving, supportive, traditional Christian home with four siblings. I am the fifth child of five children. My parents have been married for over fifty years. All of my siblings are married and have children of their own, and we support one another from afar still to this day. We love to get together to have the Powery Olympics to compete in various sports in a very friendly manner without any signs of sibling rivalries! My own current situation is traditional as well. I have one wife and two children, a boy and a girl; some call this the million-dollar family but I have yet to see a million dollars show up at our front door.

I am an ordained minister, a preacher, pastor, and dean of a university chapel, but I am also a teacher and scholar of preaching, a homiletician, who is a professor of homiletics at a divinity school. This professional vocation is one in which I read biblical texts and take them seriously, but I also read contexts and worlds and take them seriously too, discerning the intersection of text and context in order to proclaim a gospel message for our present day with the hope that hearers may realize that the gospel is *pro nobis*. In a play on the words of Sojourner Truth, "I don't [only] read such small stuff as letters, I read men and nations."[1]

In reading the world in which we live, and even the city of Durham, North Carolina, in which I now live, I recognize the fact that the family situation or background which is true for me is not the reality for many, especially for those who are the least of these, the marginalized, dispossessed, or who Howard Thurman calls, "the disinherited."[2] Rather, those who are marginalized or on the underside of society inhabit a space on the borderlands of human existence. Because they are on the margins, they are not usually central to an academic conversation, including this one about family. Thus I want briefly in this response to Barton's paper to explore

---

1. See http://www.poemhunter.com/sojourner-truth/quotations/.
2. Howard Thurman, *Jesus and the Disinherited* (Boston: Beacon, 1996).

what it might mean to "find happiness in family life" through the lens of marginal members of the human family in order to bring some underprivileged voices into this conversation. What I will say has more to do with context and human experience in relation to the presented ideas, rather than specific detailed responses about the nuances of textual interpretation.

I want to thank Stephen Barton for a clear, well-structured, interesting, insightful, constructive, and thought-provoking approach to the topic of finding happiness in family life through a biblical perspective. In particular, I affirm how he begins his paper with our current "muddled" cultural milieu and acknowledges that there is not a "clean slate" or "pure" community when it comes to the subject of family. There is a diversity of perspectives and experiences in society and in various fields about what entails happiness in the family; thus it is important in approaching Scripture to read wisely, including the confession that the Bible is a "canon of a community." Barton lays a foundation for the conversation before jumping into the Bible, and this is indeed wise so that we do not veer towards bibliolatry in relation to this topic. When discussing each portion of Scripture, there is an attempt to appropriate it for the contemporary scene, which I highly appreciate as a homiletician. All three NT texts offer some insight into the intersection of happiness and family, but at the same time there is an attempt to complicate certain paradigms about family happiness via his remarks about Jesus as single and celibate, disrupting family ties (Matt 10:34–38; Luke 14:26–27), his own homelessness (Matt 8:20), and questioning who his mother and brothers and sisters really are (Mark 3:33–35). These marginal, passing comments about Jesus, which are not the heart of Barton's expositions, are in fact possible creative biblical avenues for those thinking from the social margins about family issues.

Jesus's existential reality and spiritual pedagogy raises questions that are critical for those who are dispossessed and marginalized: 1) Who or what is family? 2) Where is home? and 3) What is happiness?

Who or what is family? Barton's title "finding happiness in family life" suggests that everyone has an active, living family. The raw realities in our world suggest that this is not the case, and we perhaps need to (re)define the meaning of "family." There are orphans, widows, and persons on death row or imprisoned, who have been cut off from family resources and relationships. They do not have the benefit of the intergenerational nature of faith that Barton mentions with a grandmother Lois and mother Eunice or what he calls the "community of kinship" as drawn from 2 Tim 1:5. The least of these are basically, to use the words of James Weldon Johnson's poem, "gone, forgot, unfamed . . . untaught, unknown, unnamed."[3] Perhaps nothing has been passed on to the marginalized except a memory of being unloved. Their past memory of any relationship perhaps does not contribute to their happiness as Barton suggests is the case in 2 Timothy. For a motherless child in an orphanage, who is its family? It could be that a family sociality is not located in the "deeper sociality of the family of the church," as Barton writes, but could be rooted in a larger notion of the family of God, a broader sense of the human community, churched and unchurched.

Where is home? Where is home for someone disconnected from a family home or homeless? How does one appropriate the prodigal son story when there might not be a father or home to welcome one, when there are no parties, just lots of pain and an agonistic existential reality? What do you do when from the perspective of the elder son, home is viewed as a place of injustice? Home may not be a healing place on earth, yet we hear in the cultural musical sermon of the African American spiritual, "Sometimes I feel like a motherless child, sometimes I feel like a motherless child, sometimes I feel like a motherless child, a long ways from home, a long ways from home." Perhaps "home" is not a traditional family setting, but home is ultimately being in communion with God from the womb to the tomb. As the preacher of Hebrews declares, we are strangers and foreigners on earth, on a pilgrimage, seeking a homeland, a heavenly country, a city God has prepared as architect and builder (Heb 11:10, 13–16). Or, as another spiritual declares, "soon-a will be done with the troubles of the world, goin' home to live with God."

What is happiness? In light of the problematization of the notions of family and home for those dispossessed and marginalized, what is happiness for the marginalized and those suffering on the fringes? How can one be happy when one's back is up against the wall? How do the least of these fit into this discussion about happiness in family life? To use Ellen Charry's notion, is their "realizing eschatology" happiness or might it be "hope" instead?

Let me conclude by raising two more inquiries. A response from the underside of society that questions the scope of family, the nature of home, and the presence of happiness for the marginalized or least of these may shape the meaning of reading wisely today. Are there other guidelines for reading wisely that may not suffer from socio-theological amnesia and forget the least, the lost, and left out? May one attempt to read Scripture from the possible perspective of the margins and that be

---

3. James Weldon Johnson and J. Rosamond Johnson, *The Books of American Negro Spirituals, Two Volumes in One* (Reprint, New York: Da Capo, 1977 [1969]) 11–12.

deemed a wise reading? I am wondering why Barton chose these three particular parts of Scripture to explore this topic as opposed to others and whether their order in his paper has specific meaning for him.

Attempting to bring a marginal lens to this topic also causes me to wonder if idolatry is, as Barton writes, "the most serious impediment" to happiness in family life. Whatever happiness is, it is true that God is the ultimate source of it, and turning from God to another object of devotion is idolatry. But what about those who idolize God or worship the Bible but despise God's creation? They worship God but abuse their family or the vulnerable in the world? Is idolatry necessarily the problem, or is it a lack of love, an issue of sanctification in which the "rule of love" that includes love of neighbor, especially the least of these, is disobeyed? Perhaps "finding happiness in family life" is not a "pure" or "clean" pursuit because our world has been soiled by the problem of systemic and personal sin and that bad s-word, sin, is really the culprit that has infiltrated human life to hinder divine happiness on the human plane.

IMPOSTER HAPPINESS OR THE REAL THING? MARRIAGE, SINGLENESS, AND THE BEATITUDES IN THE TWENTY-FIRST CENTURY

Jana Marguerite Bennett

When I, as a single woman, first began thinking about singleness,[1] I was thinking largely about the fact that marriage is so much the focus at many churches that singleness hardly ever enters the conversation. Churches direct so much energy and time and attention to helping form and foster good marriages and families. This is important work, but our focus on marriage and family has been to the detriment of good thinking about what it means to be single, to the point that singleness becomes maligned and that the church's ability to witness to Jesus suffers as a result. This view among Christians mirrors what we think in culture at large. According to research done at the Pew Research Forum in 2010 and confirmed in the latest study in 2011, the rates of marriage are declining. Just over half (51 percent) of all adult Americans are married compared with 72 percent in 1960; rates among the youngest adult generation (age 20–34) are declining even more rapidly, down from 59 percent in 1960 to 20 percent today. Many scholars give several reasons for the decline: economic factors, education (people with more degrees wait longer to get married), an increasing societal norm to wait to marry, and caution due to high divorce rates in previous generations. At the time the study was published, news outlets loudly vaunted the statistics about decline, as they should. These are important indicators of how Americans understand marriage and family, and they are important statistics to grapple with in thinking about Christian marriage and family, for Christians often (depending somewhat on denomination) have divorce rates that are equal to those of the general population.

What does such a view of marriage mean for the variety of single adults?[2] There are strong indications that it means marginalization of singleness in all its forms.

---

1. I first discussed marriage and singleness in my book *Water is Thicker than Blood: An Augustinian Theology of Marriage and Singleness* (New York: Oxford, 2008).

2. I am using "singleness" here to mean a variety of what my Catholic tradition calls "states of life": monasticism, holy widowhood, vowed celibacy (which is distinct from monasticism because one is not necessarily living as a monk), never-married, divorced, and so on. When I presented this paper,

Marriage is presumed clearly better. One author writes: "The truth is celebrating singleness—i.e., celebrating 'not doing something'—makes no sense. Loving is better than not loving."[3] Single parents get an added dose of guilt with their marginalization when they read headlines such as: "Children of Single Parents More at Risk, UVA Study Finds."[4] In yet another study several psychologists discuss the fact that their patients do not want to be single because it is perceived as very childish. *Adults make choices for marriage.*[5] A University of Missouri and Texas Tech joint study that asked women in their thirties to discuss being married found similarly that they felt marginalized or rather like "losers." One study author notes, "These were very successful women in their careers and their lives, yet almost all of them felt bad about not being married, like they were letting someone down."[6]

Christians are as good at promoting such marginalization, which I think runs counter to the witness Scripture offers. While Christians rightly understand marriage as good, Scripture (e.g., Matt 19:10–12) also says clearly that singleness is good. For the past two thousand years we have been accustomed to separating these two forms of life and debating which one is superior. Monasticism reigned for a while; I would say that marriage reigns today. One piece of evidence for this might be in the sheer number of Christian dating sites available online or the fact that many church singles' events are focused on fixing up single Christians. Singleness in all its varieties has been made to seem odd and strange. Celibate priests and nuns become suspicious characters in news media, and single pastors are often likely to be marginalized in the sense that something seems off if they are unmarried.

Given all this, in my earlier work I focused on this dichotomy and tried to find ways to think well about the importance of marriage and singleness in order to have a good understanding of what it means to be the church.

---

one of the questions was why I did not use the word "chastity," but chastity, for Catholics, is what all Christians are called to: chaste marriages, chaste singleness. Chastity takes on different forms though. For some it is lifelong vowed celibacy, for some it is monogamous marriages that do not use artificial contraception where couples abstain for a period of time, for others it might be sexual abstinence that is more temporary than lifelong vowed celibacy would be.

3. Maggie Gallagher, "The New Singleness," The Witherspoon Institute blog online (October 20, 2011) http://www.thepublicdiscourse.com/2011/10/4164 (accessed Sept 2, 2012).

4. Samantha Koon, *Daily Progress* (August 11, 2012) http://www2.dailyprogress.com/news/2012/aug/11/children-single-parents-more-risk-uva-study-finds-ar-2124656/ (accessed Sept 2, 2012).

5. Natalie Schwartzberg, et. al., *Single in a Married World: A Lifestyle Framework for Working With The Unmarried Adult* (New York: Norton, 1995).

6. Quoted in Tara Parker-Pope, "In a Married World, Singles Struggle for Attention," *New York Times Online* (Sept 19, 2011) http://well.blogs.nytimes.com/2011/09/19/the-plight-of-american-singles/ (accessed Sept 2, 2012).

The Pew Study mentioned above from 2010, however, suggests that there is another, perhaps more overlooked, point that needs addressing. While most news articles covered the decline in marriage rates, what they often omitted was that sixty-one percent of those who said they were *not* married *hoped* to be married someday.[7] That point struck me as more interesting than the rest—that our desire for marriage remains quite strong even as we have all kinds of reasons for delaying marriage. A still-strong wedding industry perhaps reflects this intense desire. While wedding-related business fell during the economic downturn, it has picked up again in the past two years, so that it is growing at a rate of ten percent.[8] Wedding industry experts are starting to argue that the people their businesses should attract are Millennials because that is where the data say the growth is, despite the Pew Forum statistics noting a decline in marriage in this age group.[9] What we seem to have, then, is a situation where the number of adults living lives of singleness is on the rise, while at the same time a desire for marriage remains strong. In this contemporary situation where marriage is desired but about half the population remains single, it is imperative for people to think about marriage and singleness and what we expect from both these states of life. Studies from the National Marriage Project, for example, note that people expect marriage to be part of the reason for greater happiness,[10] and they further rank marriage as highly important to having a successful life.

In this paper, therefore, I wish to focus particularly on questions of desire, choice, and whether and how we *choose* marriage or singleness. My ultimate aim is to offer some thoughts on how churches might best teach lay people about choice and desire in marriage and singleness. My focus on choice in relation to states of life is related to what I name as imposter happiness in the title (which I describe further below). I will suggest that we Christians tend to overemphasize the idea of choice in these states of life, but this emphasis on choice ultimately marginalizes both mar-

---

7. D'Vera Cohn, et. al., "Barely Half of US Adults are Married—A Record Low," Pew Research Center (December 14, 2011) http://www.pewsocialtrends.org/2011/12/14/barely-half-of-u-s-adults-are-married-a-record-low/ (accessed Aug 29, 2012).

8. http://www.ibisworld.com/Common/MediaCenter/Wedding%20Industry.pdf.

9. Part of the reason industry experts advocate focusing on this age group is that the 20–34 age group is comparatively a much larger proportion of the overall population than it was in the 1990s and early 2000s. They are beginning to see the effect of the second "baby boom" that happened in the late 1980s and 1990s.

10. Lois M. Collins, "Poor Value Marriage, are more Traditional in Some Ways than Wealthier Counterparts," *Deseret News* (July 13, 2012) http://www.deseretnews.com/article/765589735/Poor-value-marriage-are-more-traditional-in-some-ways-than-wealthier-counterparts.html?pg=all (accessed September 2, 2012).

riage and singleness. While we make choices, choice is much less significant to either state of life that we often think. I will therefore offer a conclusion that suggests how we can understand singleness and marriage morally, even when choice is not the main focus. This is especially important in our contemporary society when so few singles actively choose to be single. (That is, we usually do not choose to remain never-married, or to get divorced, or become widowed. Vowed celibacy is a distinct rarity in Christianity these days.)

In order to do this, I will first treat briefly one prominent passage (1 Cor 7:1–11) that explicitly discusses the state of being unmarried in comparison with being married. While there are assuredly other passages that lend likewise to this kind of comparison (e.g., Matt 19:3–12), it is the 1 Corinthians passage that has shown up again and again in theological discussions about marriage and singleness, and so it is that passage that lends itself to further clarification and discussion.

What I will claim is that the focus we have had on this passage in both ancient and contemporary translation and theological discussion has been detrimental because of the way it has fed our view of choice about states of life. It is that dis-ease with scriptural focus on 1 Cor 7 that leads me to the passages mentioned in this essay's title, the Beatitudes (especially the Matthean version). My decision to use the Beatitudes as a focal point may seem unusual, but as I hope to show by the paper's conclusion, the Beatitudes provide a better entry into theological thought about choice, marriage, and singleness in the twenty-first century. In my brief conclusion I will suggest a few concrete responses Christians might make in relation to the contemporary scene on marriage and singleness with the hope that this provides a starting point toward some fruitful discussion.

"By Way of Concession": Paul's Discussion of Marriage and Singleness

When I read 1 Cor 7, it seems that Paul treads carefully between marriage and celibacy (which is one of the single states of life). He wants to highlight the particular single state of life of celibacy. But in what direction does he tend? Is he aiming more toward advocacy of singleness as the state Christians ought to embrace, or does he care *whether* people are married or single at all? Serious scholars have suggested both these answers: those who answer with the first option I name as taking an "ascetic view" while those who answer with the second option have a "moderate view."

In v. 1 he writes, "Now concerning the matters about which you wrote it is well for a man not to touch a woman." Immediately we are drawn into a theological argument driven by exegesis, and especially where to place colons, commas, and quotation marks which were not in the Greek text. This is one of those prominent places in Scripture where the task of placing punctuation marks can drastically change the text's interpretation. Ascetic translators might see "It is well for a man not to touch a woman" as Paul's own directive to be celibate. On that reading Paul's words in the subsequent verses make it clear that marriage is a "concession" (v. 6) and being celibate as Paul is (v. 7) is clearly the best for Christians.

Moderate translators (probably a majority, these days),[11] however, read Paul's statement in v. 1 as quoting the Corinthians' own question back to them. The statement "It is well for a man not to touch a woman" should be in quotation marks in the text itself, following a colon or dash after "Now, concerning the matters about which you wrote:" On this view, the Corinthians themselves believe that celibacy is better than marriage, and sex and marriage are to be avoided at all costs. Paul's words to them admonish the Corinthians to take a much more moderate view. Marriage enables people to avoid sexual immorality and enables people with weak self-wills to live righteously before God. "Because of sexual immorality, each man should have his own wife and each woman her own husband. The husband should give to his wife her conjugal rights, and likewise the wife to her husband" (vv. 2–3). On this view too Paul's repeated statement, "Remain as you are," stands as a directive not to be overly concerned about whether one is married or single but to focus instead on how faithfully one is living a life in Christ.

In the text we do not necessarily know what Paul thinks about choice in relation to states of life. Does he think that we ought to be able to control ourselves enough that we should not have to burn with desire for other people? Or does he suspect that our emotions can and do get the better of our will, such that choice is impossible, and "concession" is necessary? Either the moderate or the ascetic view could hold here.

Later in ch. 7 Paul discusses the advantages of a life of celibacy or virginity. Unmarried men and women can be dedicated to the Lord and remain free of the kinds of worries that having a spouse and children bring (vv. 32–34). In v. 35 Paul emphasizes: "I say this for your own benefit, not to put any restraint upon you, but to promote good order and unhindered devotion to the Lord." An ascetic view of these verses focuses on "devotion to the Lord" and the assumption that this makes a person's state of life much better. A moderate view, however, notes v. 36 where

---

11. See, for example, Will Deming's *Paul on Marriage and Celibacy* (New York: Cambridge University Press, 1995). Some of the major Bible commentaries, like *The New Interpreter's Bible* (Nashville: Abingdon, 2002) also take this tack.

Paul writes that someone who marries commits no sin; indeed, "let him marry as he wishes."

In both ways of reading the passage it is essential to remember Paul's earlier discussion about sexual immorality in this letter. In ch. 5 he chastises the Corinthians because they have allowed one of their members to marry his father's wife. He sees this as even worse than whatever immorality pagan people might dream up. In ch. 6 he commands, "Shun fornication!" (v. 18). These passages are understood by those who think Paul really promotes celibacy/asceticism as confirming that Paul is very concerned about the Corinthians' lack of sexual propriety. Those who think Paul really promotes a moderate stance understand them as confirming that Paul makes a clear distinction between proper marriage and sex between people (Christian or not) and a variety of other, unchaste sex acts. In context with surrounding chapters it becomes a bit more evident that Paul thinks we do have a choice when it comes to sex and sexuality. We are able to avoid giving into sexual impulses (in order to shun fornication, for example) because we have a greater hope and call.

That greater hope and call becomes most evident at the end of the letter. In ch. 15 Paul deals with the resurrection of the dead and puts the letter into a clearly eschatological light. He describes the time when we will inherit the kingdom of God, when death has no victory over us. He concludes this chapter by saying, "Therefore, my dear brothers and sisters, stand firm. Let nothing move you. Always give yourselves fully to the work of the Lord, because you know that your labor in the Lord is not in vain" (v. 58). On an ascetic reading this eschatological focus enables interpreters to think about singleness as better precisely because it leads us directly toward God, our final happiness. We can and should choose singleness because it is better; anything else is okay but not the fullness of what we can be. Yet, on a moderate reading this eschatological focus enables us to put our marriages or lives of singleness in context: we will be raised, and nothing else much matters (and especially *not* marriage or singleness) in light of that kind of happiness that we will have in God.

Thus, it seems that the main scriptural debate regarding Paul's instructions in 1 Cor 7 is whether Paul pushes Christianity toward celibacy (and asceticism) or whether Paul advocates a moderate stance toward both marriage and singleness. The mainstream consensus these days seems to be that Paul is more moderate. As one commenter writes after exegesis of the passage, "The only thing of truly spiritual significance in life is whether a person is in Christ or not. Whether one is married, or single, Jewish or Gentile, or male or female is utterly inconsequential in the kingdom of God."[12]

Initially I rather liked this moderate reading of Paul because I thought that perhaps it could "solve" the concerns I raised earlier about marriage and singleness in our culture. Here was a way that single people could both faithfully desire marriage but yet be content with a life of singleness. Here was a way that perhaps marriage and singleness both could be intertwined in the church, and neither state of life would have to take precedence over the other. For example, Christians could use this kind of theological interpretation to suggest doing more "whole congregation" programming and to find ways of decreasing an emphasis on marriage.

On second thought though, I am not convinced. My concern is that a moderate view de-emphasizes marriage but also de-emphasizes singleness, and I am not quite willing to go quite so far as the moderates in saying that a life of singleness does not matter. Paul uses words like "concession" and "it is better to be as I am," which should at least make us think twice about overly homogenizing states of life as though they were the same thing. Verse 38 solidifies this sense: "So then, he who marries his fiancée does well; and he who refrains from marriage will do better." It is troubling indeed that the moderate view seems to ignore Paul's words here. Taking singleness seriously (and especially taking seriously the plight of those singles who feel marginalized) requires not simply glossing over Paul's words. At the same time, taking Paul's words seriously need not mean denigrating marriage. I think that to date no group of Christians has been able to avoid one or the other of these pitfalls, and no group has consequently been able to use the word "choice" rightly in relation to these states of life.

To see this, it is important to note how this debate has played out historically in theological discussion. In the history of Christianity these kinds of dichotomies also persist, though in relation to how to interpret 1 Cor 7. This Scripture passage in particular has proved difficult for theologians seeking to figure out whether and how Christians ought to be married or whether and how Christians ought to remain single. In the fourth-century church Jerome (the person who translated Greek Scriptures into Latin) very nearly maintained that marriage was an evil, that Christians could not truly follow God unless they were single. His contemporary Jovinian, by contrast, discussed that marriage was a complete good, equivalent to singleness in terms of married peoples' abilities to follow Christ. Those who sided

---

12. Nick Nowalk, "Rethinking Paul on Marriage and Singleness," *The Strange Triumph of the Lamb* (April 12, 2012) http://strangetriumph.wordpress.com/2012/04/09/rethinking-paul-on-marriage-and-singleness (accessed Jan 30, 2013).

with Jerome on the matter wondered though why Jovinian would so freely reject or ignore Paul's words to us in 1 Corinthians.[13]

These two positions have been alternately embraced or caricatured in much of Christian history. One of Martin Luther's great concerns was that Catholics focused on monasticism at the expense of others' faith. Luther accordingly promoted marriage as a civil, earthly function that did not relate to one's status with God.[14] Even centuries later Catholics seemed to validate Luther's concern. One vocation pamphlet from the 1930s depicted nuns as people who were choosing to follow Christ, as contrasted with married women, who were following their own desires and therefore seemed not to want to follow Christ.[15] Married women had made a poor "choice" because they were not following Jesus.

I think the recent emphasis for both Protestants and Catholics has been on affirming *marriage* as almost the sole means and choice toward following Christ, precisely because it makes us happiest and leads us most closely to God. As I suggested in the introduction, marriage is often touted by Christians as the happiest state of life, the best way to follow Jesus. The Quiverfull Movement in some Protestant circles is likely the most energetic and vocal in espousing the view that marriage leads to fulfillment in God.[16] However, Christians from a range of denominational backgrounds also tend to support this view,[17] and it therefore seems almost to be a sin *not* to be married, even when circumstances do not allow for that kind of choice.

To be fair, this kind of one-sided focus on marriage is changing; there are more single Christians (across the range of Christian communities) writing books about single vocations. Nonetheless, it is striking that many of these books will begin with some kind of statement about how theirs now breaks ground, because singleness has been so long ignored in Christian life.[18] Still, many books on singleness, such

13. For a more thorough discussion of early Christians and their readings of 1 Cor 7, see David G. Hunter, "The Reception and Interpretation of Paul in Late Antiquity: 1 Corinthians 7 and the Ascetic Debates," http://uky.academia.edu/DavidHunter/Papers/1484980/1_Corinthians_7_and_Asceticism (accessed Sept 2, 2012).

14. For Luther's writing on this, see his treatise titled "On Monastic Vows."

15. Florence Caffrey Bourg, *Where Two or Three Are Gathered: Christian Families as Domestic Church* (Notre Dame: University of Notre Dame Press, 2004) 6.

16. See Nancy Campbell, *Be Fruitful and Multiply: What the Bible Says About Having Children* (San Antonio: Vision Forum, 2003).

17. For example, Don Browning, *Equality and the Family: A Fundamental, Practical Theology of Children, Mothers and Fathers in Modern Societies* (Grand Rapids, Eerdmans, 2007).

18. Barry Danylak has written a book tellingly titled *Redeeming Singleness: How the Storyline of Singleness Affirms the Single Life* (Wheaton, IL: Crossway, 2010). That singleness needs to be redeemed already suggests the ways in which we Christians marginalize singleness.

as Carolyn Culley's book *Did I Kiss Marriage Goodbye? Trusting God with a Hope Deferred*, speak about the need for Christians to hope continually for marriage because it is so integral to many Christians' sense about being able to follow Christ.[19]

The first part of my essay's title, "Imposter Happiness," is a nod to the ways we Christians speak about happiness in relation to marriage. What I mean in part by imposter happiness is the way we believe our happiness seems integrally connected to our state of life and particularly to being married. This focus on marriage does raise the same discrepancy that Jovinian's detractors noted: what about Paul's words in v. 38 that it is better to be single? How would we form churches that would acknowledge singleness as important, even as we acknowledge the good of marriage? I argue that Christians through the centuries have wrestled with this conundrum and have yet to find the kind of balance that I think is espoused in Paul's letter. Marriage as the sole, good choice is imposter happiness because it ignores key witnesses in Scripture and particularly makes marriage out to be our good eschatological aim, when, of course, God is our only eschatological aim.

On the flip side, we might say that the vacuum created by the church's nondiscussion of singleness has led to some very unhealthy but widely held views about singleness in the culture at large. "Hook up" culture, found on many college campuses, as well as the myth of the single woman as being more free, sexy, and interesting than married women, comes to the fore in popular culture.[20] This meme begins with *Sex and the City* in the late 1990s and early 2000s; it continues these days in MTV's *Jersey Shore* and HBO's *Girls*, which promote the idea of casual sex with no strings among twenty-something women.

While I think there are multiple reasons why singleness has been so marginalized and why a vacuum has been created, I think the almost continuous debate over the meaning of 1 Cor 7 has been present in the background, for this passage is listed in almost every book about singleness and in many books about marriage. The marriage and singleness debate is a difficult debate to have, exactly because there is a need for a kind of balance in thinking about choice, that is, not to overlook that making a choice for one or the other state of life can be important. But there is also a need not to overemphasize that choice, because of course, the moderates are right. Neither marriage nor virginity equals our eschatological happiness in God.

---

19. Carolyn McCully, *Did I Kiss Marriage Goodbye? Trusting God with a Hope Deferred* (Wheaton, IL: Crossway, 2004).

20. For some scary, yet important, reading on "hook up" cultures, read Donna Freitas, *Sex and the Soul: Juggling Sex, Spirituality, Romance and Religion on America's College Campuses* (New York: Oxford University Press, 2008).

The recent scholarly emphasis in Scripture studies on asceticism as bad (because it rejects the body), and on trying to make Paul not look like a curmudgeon who hates sex, has been harmful. Despite the fact that 1 Cor 7 seems promising on account of its subject matter, the predominant moderate view, which advocates making no choice at all because the choice does not matter, does not enable us to address peoples' desires for marriage or singles' sense of marginalization within the culture at large. The broader, centuries-old debate about the place of 1 Cor 7 also does not address these concerns. This is not to say that 1 Cor 7 is not important reading nor that we might have better ways of reading it than has been done. It is mainly to suggest that 1 Cor 7 has not served us well as a starting point for discussion about marriage and singleness.

The rest of this paper serves then to shift focus from 1 Cor 7 and from this dichotomous context in which we find ourselves, where marriage (especially for Christians) and singleness (especially in secular culture) are both pushed as happy, but imposter, endings that we get to choose.

Why the Beatitudes?

My focus on the Beatitudes may seem odd, but it is not arbitrary. I will suggest below that the Beatitudes, focused as they are on "happiness" or "blessedness," may provide a way forward in thinking beyond the kind of imposter happiness I note above. This is not my only reason for wanting to reflect further on the Beatitudes however.

At some point in the early stages of preparing for this paper, I was looking up some entries on singleness in the Catholic *Catechism*, so that I could get more of a sense of what my own tradition suggests. Curiously, the entry on singleness mentions the Beatitudes:

> We must also remember the great number of *single persons* who, because of the particular circumstances in which they have to live—often not of their choosing—are especially close to Jesus' heart and therefore deserve the special affection and active solicitude of the Church, especially of pastors. Many remain *without a human family* often due to conditions of poverty. *Some live their situation in the spirit of the Beatitudes, serving God and neighbor in exemplary fashion.* The doors of homes, the "domestic churches," and of the great family which is the Church must be open to all of them. "No one is without a family in this world: the Church is a home

and family for everyone, especially those who 'labor and are heavy laden'" (emphasis added).[21]

I found the mention of the Beatitudes to be curious especially because I happen to know that the Beatitudes are also one of the recommended Gospel passages for Roman rite Catholic weddings. The text of the Beatitudes from Matthew's Gospel was, in fact, the passage that my husband and I chose for our wedding. "Unusual," remarked the priest who presided at our wedding. "Most couples don't choose this one. They choose the wedding at Cana or some other more explicitly wedding-related Gospel." Thus, across these states of life contemporary Catholicism connects marriage and singleness in a small way via the Beatitudes.

Accordingly, the Beatitudes became the text I wanted to reflect on theologically for this paper. In what follows I propose to think about the Beatitudes as a whole in order to see whether and how we might rethink the states of marriage and singleness. (I focus on the whole passage, particularly that in Matthew, rather than focusing on each of the Beatitudes. While I think it would be fruitful to reflect on individual Beatitudes, this is a task that could and should easily turn into a book.) My first reflection will be on the meaning of happiness as found in the Beatitudes, and my second reflection will be on the various ways theologians have understood the Beatitudes in relation to choosing Christian life. I claim that the Beatitudes offer a more balanced way to begin understanding choice in Christian life and therefore provide a good place for thinking about choice in terms of marriage and singleness.

Happiness

A first point about the Beatitudes is that they are recognized as a unique literary form, distinct from blessings. That is, there is a difference between the kind of blessing that God bestows on Abraham in Gen 12:3–4, where Abraham receives something directly from God, and the Beatitudes, which are statements of praise or congratulation—e.g., Ps 1:1: "Blessed is the one who walks not in the counsel of the wicked." These statements, called *macarisms*, are present in both OT and NT, as well as in other ancient literature. It appears that the translators for the Septuagint were quite aware of this literary distinction because the verb they used for blessing was

---

21. *Catechism of the Catholic Church*, section 1658. http://www.vatican.va/archive/ENG0015/_P56.HTM (accessed Sept 2, 2012). The final lines of this Catechism entry are from John Paul II, *Familiaris Consortio* 85, http://www.vatican.va/holy_father/john_paul_ii/apost_exhortations/documents/hf_jp-ii_exh_19811122_familiaris-consortio_en.html.

eulogemenos, but the word for a beatitude was *makarios*.²² Sometimes *macarisms* are written in contrary voice, called "woes," as we see in Luke's version of the Beatitudes. He begins with four blessings but contrasts them with four woes.

What purpose *macarisms* provide is a bit of a thornier question. Commenter Warren Carter suggests that *macarisms* may be liturgical in origin, for they often occur in connection with Israel's worship of God. They are frequently found in the Psalms, for example, but Carter also suggests that they "provide a brief summary of essential doctrine. Often it assured and instructed about destiny in the afterlife or about divine justice, but in a way that has clear implications for present ethics and morality."²³

The main point is that the "blessedness" of the Beatitudes relates in some way to fullness of life in God, an acknowledgement that we cannot be truly happy without finding and seeking the One who is the source and Savior of our being. Jesus' words are quite clear on this point. Five of the eight Beatitudes in Matthew refer directly either to relationship with God or life in God's kingdom: "theirs is the kingdom of heaven" (vv. 3 and 10); "they will see God" (v. 8); "they will be called children of God" (v. 9); "Rejoice and be glad, for your reward is great in heaven" (v. 12). A common reading of the other three Beatitudes is to see those too in terms of relationship with God. For example, receiving mercy (v. 7) or being filled with righteousness and justice (v. 6) are seen as only properly bestowed by God. We humans could not really practice true mercy, justice, and righteousness.

This account of blessedness (or happiness, as another way in which *macarios* is translated) is distinct from the kind of imposter happiness associated with marriage and singleness in the discussion of 1 Cor 7. The happiness of fullness of life in God is noted, of course, by numerous theologians, in my tradition especially by Thomas Aquinas. In his most famous writing, the *Summa Theologica*, Thomas says, "Final and perfect happiness can consist in nothing else than the vision of the Divine Essence."²⁴ Any other kind of happiness that we seek is necessarily a secondary desire that cannot possibly measure up to life with God. These secondary desires are imperfect compared to God; imperfect happiness might be obtained through the "stuff" of this world, but it will only be imperfect. Still, these imperfect secondary desires relate very much to how we think through our *choices* in our daily lives. Thus,

---

22. Raymond Collins, "Beatitudes," in *The Anchor Bible Dictionary* (New York: Doubleday, 1992) 1:629.

23. Warren Carter, "Beatitudes," in *Eerdmans Dictionary of the Bible* (ed. David Noel Freedman, Allen C. Myers, and Astrid B. Beck; Grand Rapids: Eerdmans, 2000) 158.

24. *Summa Theologica*, II–I. q. 3. 8.

we will still be aware of a restlessness, to use the word that Saint Augustine mentions. We will want to find our completeness in God because our secondary desires and choices do not satisfy.

What is less clear in Jesus' words is how the activities or dispositions that appear in the first part of the Beatitudes (e.g., "Blessed are the peacemakers" in v. 9) relate to the happiness we find in God. Are these properly actions we can *choose* to do in order to see God's rewards? Are they primarily words of comfort for those who mourn or who find themselves persecuted through no choice of their own?

Part of the difficulty in making this determination is in the fact that the Beatitudes are not uniform in their relationship to human activity. Peacemaking might be considered something that we do partly by our own wills; persecution for Jesus' name's sake, however, is something that only results from others finding your life to be strange—whether it is strange because of belief in Jesus' name, or strange because of how you live, or some combination of the two is not clear. It is likewise unclear how we could will ourselves to become "poor in spirit" though there are ways we might be able to be "meek." Hungering for justice and righteousness might not necessarily entail anything other than praying for justice and righteousness, though I think "hungering" could be read in such a way as to require actively seeking justice and righteousness.

So, while the Beatitudes clearly denote our happiness in God as opposed to imposter happiness, they also plunge us directly into another age-old debate among Christians: the question of good works or faith and the related discussion of the degree to which we have free will and ability to choose to work toward good. While I will fully claim my Catholic background here, which, on my view, notes the necessity of faith and free will both and which professes the need for humans to submit their wills to God (and in doing so, make a "choice" for God), I do not think that such an answer still fully addresses the difficulty since so many of the Beatitudes would appear to have little to do with human action or will. Yet, some of them do. Furthermore, only a few verses later, we find Jesus saying: "Let your light shine before others that they may see your good works and glorify the Father" (v. 16).

I will hope to address this point further in the next section. Here I note that the simple connection I made earlier about "real happiness" and "imposter happiness" goes much deeper precisely because of the presence and role of choice. Perhaps the Beatitudes stand not only to press us on our too-easy visions of human happiness but also stand to make a theological connection between our understanding of choices and how those choices link to "imposter happiness." So it would seem that in addition to understanding happiness as complete fullness in God, the Beatitudes may also offer some wisdom on the state of marriage and singleness exactly because of questions they raise about will and choice.

Ways to Read the Beatitudes

In this section I discuss two of the ways that theologians have thought about the Beatitudes in relation to fostering Christian life. This section serves as a way to discuss vocation and Christian discipleship in relation to the Beatitudes but also to deepen reflection on the question of choice I raised above.

In the twentieth and twenty-first centuries, one of the most prominent ways of reflecting on the Beatitudes has been by relating the verses to social justice for the poor, especially as a wake-up call for Western Christians. As one commenter writes in a book tellingly titled *Spirituality of the Beatitudes: Matthew's Challenge for First World Christians*, "Whoever follows these instructions for correct behavior, by good-doing, will be personally constituted with a further share in the goodness of God's blessed presence."[25] More than that, following the Beatitudes "may bring down society's yoke of oppression and rejection."[26] The Beatitudes offer a chance for disciples—from all walks of life, married and single—actively to follow Jesus.

Surely this is one of the reasons the Catholic Church includes direct mention of the Beatitudes in the *Catechism* entry on singleness and includes the Beatitudes as a Gospel reading for weddings. Discipleship and witness, in this case directed explicitly to the poor, come about via actions of people striving to be so like Christ in their lives that they become "like the master." Such a view emphasizes the vocation of all baptized Christians, regardless of whether they are married or not, to live as constant witnesses to Christ's good news. This view seems to undergird too the idea mentioned earlier that "the only thing of truly spiritual significance in life is whether a person is in Christ or not." Being in Christ necessarily involves participation in social justice in all the ways that has come to mean: working against unjust societal structures through protests, mission work, and creating new structures, questioning political ideologies, advocating non-violence, and so on.

This kind of reading necessitates a sense of willed, chosen action on the part of disciples, people who recognize that God himself makes a preferential choice for the

---

25. Michael H. Crosby, *Spirituality of the Beatitudes: Matthew's Challenge to First World Christians* (New York: Orbis, 1981) 23. See also Jim Langford, *Happy Are They: Living the Beatitudes in America* (Ligouri, MO: Triumph, 1997).

26. Ibid., 217.

poor, and God's disciples are therefore asked to follow suit. A focus on making the right choices, choices directed toward God, are essential on this view. Thus, Mary E. Jensen examines the possible words Jesus might have used in his native tongue, rather than being content with the Greek of the NT authors: "When I look further back to Jesus' Aramaic, I find that the original word [*makarios*] was *ashray*, from the verb *yashar*. *Ashray* does not have this passive quality to it at all. Instead it means 'to set yourself on the right way for the right goal; to turn around, repent; to become straight or righteous.'"[27] The Greek is deficient because it is passive and suggests a lack of will for people. Megan McKenna uses this basis as a beginning for thinking through Luke's first Beatitude: "Blessed are you poor, the kingdom of God is yours." She argues that rightly seeing the four Beatitudes in Luke, and the eight Beatitudes in Matthew (which for her provide further development and reflection on Luke's four) requires reading all of the Beatitudes through this first Beatitude. On her view they all come back to blessing the poor and recognizing all the ways in which poverty affects hunger, weeping and mourning (a consequence of hunger), and persecution (since poverty involves persecution). Rightly living the Beatitudes requires making direct, concrete choices toward poverty at every possible turn.

Without denigrating or totally rejecting this view—for I think a social justice/discipleship view is an important one for Christians to wrestle with—I worry that such an emphasis is overly positive about human ability to enact justice in this world. I worry, moreover, that it is too positive about the kinds of choices that humans are able to make, especially in those organizations that we deem most social-justice oriented. Too often, the choices we have are poor ones; too often we can see that the action we do will be a mere trifle in relation to the very large problems that exist. I think of the sheer difficulty of dealing with mental illness. A friend of mine has a brother with schizophrenia; he has lived on the streets off and on and has no ability to hold down a job or take care of himself full time. He would be counted among "the poor" many times, having no regular access to food, shelter, or clothing. When he is on his own, he forgets to take his medications regularly, which induces schizophrenic episodes that land him in the emergency room. When he is at his sister's house, he might take his meds or he might not; his sheer size compared to hers means that she cannot compel him to do so. If he remains unmedicated for long, the possibility for serious injury to her or him or to property is high. While he is often admitted to a psychiatric hospital following such incidences, he is a high enough function-

---

27. Mary E. Jensen, *We Belong to the Land* (San Francisco: Harper 1990), cited in Megan McKenna, *Blessings and Woes: The Beatitudes and the Sermon on the Plain in the Gospel of Luke* (New York: Orbis, 2001) 23.

ing schizophrenic that once he is stabilized on medications enough, he is deemed "healthy" enough to be sent home, and the cycle repeats. In this situation—repeated all too often throughout the United States and elsewhere—the "good" choices or "actions" are not highly apparent. A reading of the Beatitudes that focuses so heavily on "right choice" as a means to obtain heaven is itself an injustice to those who face scenarios where there are few or no right choices.

Martin Luther provides an interesting contrast to the views suggested above, for as we might expect, Luther consistently highlights the need for grace over against whatever supposedly righteous works Christians think they can do. Luther's account of the Beatitudes suggests that it is not "about how we become Christians, but only about the works and fruit that no one can do unless he is already a Christian and in a state of grace."[28] Following the Beatitudes will not make a person righteous; rather, the Beatitudes can only be lived if one already has faith in God.

Particularly relevant to this essay on marriage and singleness is the fact that Luther thought that the Beatitudes had been co-opted by monks in previous centuries. According to Susan Schreiner, a popular view in Luther's time was that living the Beatitudes was work that only the "spiritual elite" (monks and nuns) could do, but Luther insists that "the humble ordinary life in the world was not at all easy, and in fact was much more difficult than the strictest monastic rule."[29] Luther was not confident in the goodness of the world but saw that evil lies at every turn. In this situation as we have it on earth, a life of perfection such as the blasphemous "holiness" of monks is impossible. What Jesus means when he preaches that we should be perfect as our Father in heaven is perfect, and what Jesus means when he says we should be pure of heart is instead "that one is watching and pondering what God says and replacing its own ideas with the Word of God. This alone is pure before God."[30] Luther contrasts the false purity of heart of monks with the image of a dirty shoemaker, married with children, who places the Word of God in his heart. The choice and action this married shoemaker has comes only because of his faith in God.

By the same token, it would not really matter whether that shoemaker was married or single; what matters is the shoemaker's single-hearted faith in God. Marriage

---

28. Martin Luther, "Sermon on the Mount," in *Luther's Works*, vol. 21 (ed. Jaroslav Pelikan; St. Louis: Concordia, 1956), cited in Susan E. Schreiner, "Martin Luther," *The Sermon on the Mount Through the Centuries: From the Early Church to John Paul II* (ed. Jeffery P. Greenman et al.; Grand Rapids: Brazos, 2007) 109–27, 110.

29. Schreiner, "Martin Luther," 113.

30. *Luther's Works* 21.34, cited in Schreiner, "Martin Luther," 126.

is merely a means toward ordering secular society, but it is only in that secular society that we attempt to live the Beatitudes by faith. Thus, while Luther's approach to the Beatitudes is quite different from the twentieth century views described above, he supports a similar view of marriage and singleness. State of life does not matter at all, but this is a serious deficiency (as discussed earlier) if we are to take seriously both Paul's words about singleness as better and also the sheer difficulty of being single in contemporary Christian communities that remain overly focused on marriage.

Another approach, and one that I find most fruitful when it comes to specific questions about choice comes to us from the fourth century. John Chrysostom, a famous preacher in his own day (and influential still in ours), preached a series of sermons in which he focused on the political nature of the Sermon on the Mount. This political nature was not an earthly politics but a heavenly politics revealed on earth. In this context the Beatitudes become a description of the way a heavenly citizen sees the world and self:

> For the one who is humble also will mourn over his own sins; and the one who mourns will also be meek and just and merciful; the one who is merciful and just and contrite is also pure of heart; and such a person is also a peacemaker; and the one who has succeeded in all these things will be well-positioned in the face of danger and will not be perturbed when they hear badly of themselves or suffer countless terrible things.[31]

The difference between Chrysostom's reading and some of the twentieth-century readings mentioned earlier is in its focus on humility rather than poverty. Being "poor in spirit" is not primarily about money, class, ability to work, and the other aspects that go into considering poverty; rather, it is a virtue. A virtue is a habit that aims us toward being good as opposed to a vice that aims us toward acting in evil ways. Humility is a curious virtue, however, because it involves putting God's will and desire or some relevant person's will and desire (like that of a spouse or children) ahead of your own. Once this step has been taken, the Christian is then able to mourn, be meek, and so on, but all of this comes only following the giving up of choice and will. In this way God's kingdom truly becomes present here and now for Chrysostom, but only because the heavenly citizens on earth have submitted themselves to God. These heavenly citizens will find themselves doing some of the

---

31. John Chrysostom, Homily 15.193 B–C, cited in Margaret Mitchell, "John Chrysostom," *The Sermon on the Mount Through the Centuries: From the Early Church to John Paul II* (ed. Jeffery P. Greenman, et al.; Grand Rapids: Brazos, 2007) 19–42, 35.

kinds of things McKenna would hope for (such as giving up all their possessions to aid the poor), but this comes first from being humble.

Chrysostom's view strikes me as being much more like a spiritual journey than the twentieth-century emphasis on exhorting acts of justice by which the kingdom comes. The kingdom is still partially present for Chrysostom, but it is not due to any choice of ours save the choice of submitting our will to God.

If Chrysostom is correct in his reading, then if we were to read the Beatitudes in the broader context of the Sermon on the Mount, we would find that Jesus calls us to citizenship in the heavenly city, but this means that we become more and more concerned for the welfare of our brothers and sisters on earth. The Beatitudes are followed directly by discussions of being salt and light for the earth (vv. 13–16). These in turn are followed by several of Jesus' statements about how to act in relation to other human beings.

In this broader context of the Sermon on the Mount, Jesus refers at least obliquely to issues relating to marriage several times. He advocates not committing adultery but not looking at a person with lust either (vv. 27–28). He admonishes the people not to be overly loving toward family, for Christ asks for even more: "If you greet only your own people, what are you doing more than others?" (v. 47). Jesus does not negate the importance of marriage or family, but he puts it in the context of the Beatitudes, and especially of being humble before God.

Thus, while I am sure there are more theological accounts than this one that could adequately address the questions I have posed in this paper, I suggest that Chrysostom's kind of reading stands as one account that is able to address Paul's concern for making good choices in marriage and singleness but also his simultaneous concern that whichever choice we make for marriage and singleness is not the "ultimate" choice. Our choice for marriage and singleness matter, but only in proper relationship to the main choice we have. This main choice is the choice for humility that enables life in God and that hopefully yields the kinds of fruits that Jesus mentions in the Beatitudes.

Thoughts for Christian Practice

I offer these readings of the Beatitudes (and secondarily of 1 Cor 7) as correctives to the plight, as I described in the introduction, of choice and desire in relation to marriage and singleness. Both marriage and singleness lure us to the thought that we are making an adult choice, upon which all (or most) of our future happiness in God relies. Indeed, for some groups of Christians a choice for marriage is the only way to follow Christ, while singleness often ends up being a default state of life.

In what follows I suggest some practical ways this impacts how we might preach and teach about both marriage and singleness. First, be very careful about the language of choice and in that context speak much more about marriage and singleness as part of Christian vocation. Vocation (in all senses of the word) is not always or usually a choice as in a "willed decision" we make. For example, most pastors I know describe their call to ministry as one where God kept dogging them until they finally said "Yes." Marriage and singleness might be seen similarly. A couple's decision to marry is never an individual choice but relies on the consent and mutual choice of the spouse.

De-emphasizing our spoken discussions of choice must go hand-in-hand with de-emphasizing dating programs or online dating websites that a church might use. Classes that specifically address the goodness of marriage might discuss marriage and singleness in the context of the whole church. In addition, emphasis might be made on serious adult formation that discusses vocations without reference to marriage and family.

I think it can be appropriate to mention choice in the proper context. When someone is about to make a lifelong vow to marry someone else (or in the Roman Catholic or Orthodox traditions makes a lifelong vow to singleness in community), it might be worth noting that this choice is possible only because God has first made an eternal choice for us. God always chooses us, and this is the key difference between our choices and God's. What we do when we make a lifelong vow is hope to "become perfect, therefore, as your heavenly Father is perfect" (Matt 5:48). We attempt to be heavenly citizens through those vows, but if John Chrysostom is right in his reading of the Beatitudes, those vows are themselves subordinated to the humility and submission to God that we seek in the Beatitudes.

Second, in backing away from the language of choice, we clear some space to think more deeply about singleness, especially for those who find themselves in the sixty-one percent of currently single adults who hope to be married someday. One possible way forward, especially for Protestants, might be to create prayers or blessing services for those who suspect they might have a call for lifelong celibacy. Single Protestants who find themselves with that kind of vocation should not have to feel caught between joining a tradition that offers that form of life or staying single in a congregation that privileges marriage. Like those who are married, the main choice must be emphasized as the one in which we choose humility. This should then enable those who are single to consider and reflect on the ways in which their lives might mirror what Paul suggests in 1 Cor 7. *Are* they freer than their married friends? If so, how? If not, how might they embrace singleness (whether it is temporary or not) so as to follow Christ more freely?

Even more than this, reflection on unwanted or unchosen singleness as a *vocation* might prove fruitful. Roger Mehl writes in *Society and Love*, "The most reliable callings are born from reflecting on a situation that is more or less imposed on us. A vocation is nearly always a way of accepting a situation that was first of all considered a limitation."[32] We can consider all the people called in the Scriptures whose vocations sprung from limitations and imposed statuses in life (e.g., Moses, Mary, Jeremiah). Giving truthful accounts of limitations and impositions, but yet showing how grace and vocation can flow from those, provides a more positive witness.

In closing I recall a quote from my doctoral advisor, Stanley Hauerwas: "... we necessarily live out a story we have not chosen. To come to terms with our beginning requires a truthful story to acquire the skills to live in gratitude rather than resentment for the gift of life."[33] In short, I think the task before us is to tell a more truthful story, one that reminds us again and again of our true happiness, our beginning and end in God, even as we choose (or fall into) vocations for marriage and singleness.

---

32. Roger Mehl, *Society and Love: Ethical Problems of Family Life* (Philadelphia: Westminster Press), cited in Rodney Clapp, *Families at the Crossroads: Beyond Traditional and Modern Options* (Downers Grove, IL: InterVarsity, 1993) 89.

33. Stanley Hauerwas, unpublished notes with his reflections on book reviews for *Hannah's Child: A Theologian's Memoir* (Grand Rapids: Eerdmans, 2010).

RESPONSE TO BENNETT

Jo Ann Deasy

Jana Marguerite Bennett begins her paper with a series of statistics and observations that highlight the "perplexing" nature of the current discourses surrounding marriage and singleness in our society. While more people are waiting to get married, getting divorced, or choosing to remain single, there remains a dominant discourse within our society that values marriage and sees it as linked to living a happier life. Bennett highlights the strength of this discourse by observing the current strength of the wedding industry. Despite all evidence that suggests a large number of marriages will end in divorce, people still believe in marriage and pour thousands of dollars into creating a public spectacle of the event.

In his writing on leadership Ronald Heifetz, founder of the Center for Public Leadership at Harvard University, argues that such a gap between espoused values and behavior is one of the key indicators that society is facing an adaptive challenge, a challenge that cannot be solved "through the application of authoritative expertise" or "through the organization's current structures, procedures, and ways of doing things." Rather, "adaptive challenges can only be addressed through changes in people's priorities, beliefs, habits, and loyalties."[1] Adaptive challenges require communities to learn together new ways of thinking and acting. I am very appreciative of Bennett's paper which begins to look at these deeper issues behind the discourses surrounding marriage and singleness.

Bennett's paper focuses on two aspects of singleness and marriage—choice and happiness—and how they seem to be linked in today's culture. Marriage is considered a choice for happiness. Singleness is a bit more complicated. In some instances, such as the illustration Bennett gives from *Sex and the City*, singleness is seen, at least in the short-term, as a choice for freedom and happiness. As Bennett highlights, however, singleness often is not chosen by people in our culture. Rather, it becomes a byproduct of other choices or of a particular cultural situation that makes the choice of marriage less possible or probable. Bennett suggests that this focus on

---

1. Ronald Heifetz, Alexander Grashow, and Marty Linksy. *The Practice of Adaptive Leadership: Tools and Tactics for Changing Your Organization and the World* (Boston: Harvard Business Press, 2009) 19. For a list of the four archetypes that signal an adaptive challenge, see pp. 77–87.

choice in relation to our marital state is not a helpful dialogue and tends to lead to a marginalization of both marriage and singleness in church and society. Bennett goes on to craft an argument in which choice is central but has a different focus, that of first choosing "humility that enables life in God and . . . yields the kinds of fruits that Jesus mentions in the Beatitudes." She views this as a choice for happiness, though a happiness that is now defined in terms of being blessed, living into the kingdom of God, and choosing humility.

While I think the discussion of ultimate choice is helpful, I also think that such a focus can be problematic in our society, especially for women. Bennett encourages singles to embrace their singleness and the freedom that it has given them to devote their lives more fully to God. They are encouraged to focus on the ultimate choice rather than the secondary choice of marriage or singleness. Unfortunately, in our culture a decision to focus on the ultimate choice is often interpreted differently for men and women. Men who focus on this ultimate choice, who devote their lives more fully to God, are seen as making choices that enhance their desirability in the church as a husband and father. A choice for God can be a choice for family as well. Those two choices are perceived as overlapping in men's lives. However, when women focus on the ultimate choice to follow God, they are often seen as making an intentional choice against marriage. In women's lives a choice for God and a choice for marriage are seen as pulling women in two different directions. This is often resolved in more conservative Evangelical circles by equating a woman's Christian vocation with that of being a wife and mother. Then the ultimate choice for a woman is marriage. If, however, we argue that the ultimate choice is something other than marriage, we must remember that for women the consequences of seeking first the kingdom of God may be greater or at least different from those for men.

I also found myself dissatisfied with how Bennett applied her thesis to issues of Christian practice. I am still trying to sort through my dissatisfaction. Perhaps as a single woman in her forties, I am just tired of being told to embrace my vocation of singleness and rejoice in all the extra time I have to follow God. I found myself frustrated with what seemed to be a suggestion that, if we just humble ourselves before God, our choices regarding marriage and singleness are just not that important. Bennett seems to focus on what we do after we are either married or find ourselves in a prolonged state of singleness, but is there something in these texts that can actually address the decisions we make to get married or stay single?

While Bennett chooses to deemphasize 1 Cor 7 and its focus on choice, I wonder if perhaps moving more deeply into the choices that are highlighted in this passage and connecting them to the broader context of the Sermon on the Mount, rather than just focusing on the Beatitudes, might be a way to help us have a more robust discussion and make deeper connections between marriage, singleness, and the issue of ultimate choice that Bennett desires. Let me provide two examples.

Early in her paper Bennett highlights how singles are often marginalized by quoting someone who considers singleness a choice "not to do something," a choice not to love another person. In 1 Cor 7, however, the discussion about marriage is not linked to love but to lust and self-control: "But since sexual immorality is occurring, each man should have sexual relations with his own wife"; "Do not deprive each other . . . so that Satan will not tempt you because of your lack of self-control"; "But if they cannot control themselves, they should marry, for it is better to marry than to burn with passion" (1 Cor 7:2, 5, and 9). In the Sermon on the Mount Jesus connected lust to issues of the kingdom by saying, "Anyone who looks at a woman lustfully has already committed adultery with her in his heart" (Matt 5:28). Jesus' discussion of lust comes in the context of his promise that those who practice and teach the commands of the law will be called great in the kingdom of heaven. There is a connection between our ultimate choice for the kingdom and choices we make about sex, lust, and self-control.

Rather than debating whether or not Paul is arguing for a more ascetic or moderate stance towards marriage and singleness, perhaps we should be having a more honest conversation about sex and lust within the church and its relationship to our ultimate choices for the kingdom. What would it mean for married couples to discuss how they balance sexual intimacy with spiritual practices as a way of making an ultimate choice for God? What would it mean if premarital counseling challenged people to consider staying single so that they could spend more time serving God? What would it mean if we truly acknowledged how difficult it is for single people to live a life of celibacy within church communities that are so afraid of intimacy? What if our discussions about all of our sexual choices, including those of singleness and marriage, were seen not as secondary choices related to the ultimate choice but instead as practical choices that are made in an attempt to live out that ultimate choice to follow Christ and live as a disciple? In a culture that often equates sex and intimacy with happiness, how might this discussion help us reflect more deeply on how often we choose the happiness we believe is promised by sex, either through or outside of marriage, rather than the happiness God promises to those who seek and follow after Jesus?[2]

---

2. As was pointed out in our discussion at the symposium, Paul writes 1 Corinthians with the belief

While choices regarding our response to lust and sex are explicit in 1 Cor 7, there is another choice that Paul is asking people, especially women, to make in this passage that is much more implicit, but I believe just as significant and perhaps just as helpful for our discussion of marriage and singleness today. We often read back into Scripture the romantic nature of marriage that has dominated our cultural discourses in the United States and Europe since the industrial revolution. Paul, however, was writing in a time when marriage was much more of a practical and economic arrangement. It had to do with the merging of families and creation of sustainable households. In that context, what were the implications of Paul's suggestion that widows, virgins, and those who were divorced remain single? Rather than a choice for or against love or romance, Paul seems to be asking people to make economic choices, to risk living in the economic insecurity of singleness. While singleness does not present quite the same economic insecurity today that it did two thousand years ago, or even one hundred years ago for that matter, it still can have economic implications. Nowhere is this more apparent than in the battle over same-sex marriage and its implications for shared benefits and joint property and finances.

How much of our desire to get married and its connection to our desire to be happy is actually a desire for safety and security both economically and relationally in an ever more disconnected culture. The Sermon on the Mount makes explicit the connection between our choices for economic security and an ultimate choice for God. We are called to store up treasures in heaven rather than here on earth. We are told that we cannot serve both God and money. We are told not to worry about what we will eat or drink or what we will wear, for the pagans run after these things, but seek first the kingdom of God. How might we help churches reflect on the ways marriage or singleness have become substitutions for the security, happiness, and blessing promised by God? Such substitutions are choices for an imposter happiness and fail to acknowledge that "we cannot be truly happy without finding and seeking the One who is the source and savior of our being."

I conclude by saying that I very much appreciated Bennett's bringing these two passages into dialogue and pushing toward a more robust discussion of singleness in the church. I think it is desperately needed. Her focus on the connection between happiness and marital status is significant and worth further exploration.

---

that Christ will return at any moment. Such an imminent eschatology has a significant impact on the suggestions that Paul is making in this passage. They cannot be applied simplistically to our current context without discussion of how such realities might, or whether such realities should, be lived out over decades and centuries rather than weeks and months.

JESUS, PAUL, AND FAMILY VALUES

Julie Hanlon Rubio

Families and Discipleship

Traditional Catholic theological treatments of family and Scripture often centered on a few standard texts. The Genesis creation narratives were used to establish God's plan for human beings to marry, gender relations within marriage, and the call to fertility. Often the story of Hosea and Gomer was referenced to give evidence of God's enduring love in the face of obstacles and provided a model for Christian marriage. Jesus' affirmation of lifelong marriage (Matt 19:3–9) was a central text. Along with the story of the wedding at Cana (John 2:1–11), Eph 5:21–33 was drawn upon to establish the sacramentality of marriage, which was viewed as a contract. The household codes also underlined the need for Christ-like sacrifice on the part of the husband and holy submission on the part of the wife.[1] Contemporary theologians found greater equality in Genesis and Ephesians and emphasized the idea that marriage is the primary metaphor for God's relationship with human beings and should be lived as covenant rather than contract, but they were often similarly selective and positive.[2]

More recently, scholars have begun to look at NT texts that were rarely considered in earlier theological treatments of marriage—the radical words of Jesus and Paul. Turning to these "hard sayings" is difficult given the contemporary valuing of family, but recognizing the diversity in Scripture can help theologians make sense of a Christian tradition that seems not at all of one mind when it comes to family. In the Catholic tradition in particular, celibacy is upheld as a privileged way of life with God, even as images of the holy family dominate parish life and much of popular theological writing. Contemporary theology on the family is marked by a desire to reconcile the hard sayings that have been central to the argument for celibacy with the affirmation of marriage that lies behind the tradition of the holy family.

---

1. Pius XI's *Casti connubii*, published in 1930 (New York: Paulist, 1939) is a good example, no. 5. See also Theodore Mackin, *The Marital Sacrament* (New York: Paulist, 1989) 24–36, 59–78.

2. See Michael G. Lawler, "Marriage in the Bible," *Perspectives on Marriage: A Reader* (2nd ed.; ed. Kieran Scott and Michael Warren; New York: Oxford University Press, 2001) 7–16.

What sort of reconciliation is possible? In my earlier work, I tried to argue that a contemporary Christian family ought to avoid the idolatry of family that Jesus warns of and the distractions of family that Paul worries about by adopting intentional practices oriented toward discipleship. It was an idealistic plan but one, I hoped, could inspire ordinary Christian families. Today, in view of increasing interreligiosity in families, I am less sure radical reprioritization is possible. In this essay I revisit the tension that first intrigued me, examine some key biblical texts on interreligious marriage, and argue for a commitment to accompany the family one is given, finding grace in the unexpected.

The Original Tension: Leave Your Family Behind or Be a Holy Family

The "Hard" Sayings of Jesus

Taking Jesus seriously seems to necessitate a radical rethinking of family. Despite traditional theological claims to the contrary, family values are hardly prevalent in the Gospels. Jesus himself locates his vocation outside of his family. This can clearly be seen in the Gospel of Mark when, in response to his family's attempt to interfere with his preaching, he identifies those who do God's will as his true family (Mark 3:31–35). This passage can easily be misread as complete denial of the moral value of family life or too easily explained away as a lesson about priorities for families of faith. One example of the latter, in my view, is Andreas Köstenberger's claim that Jesus is simply situating family in its proper context:

> Jesus' teaching on natural family ties relativizes their significance and places them within the larger context of God's kingdom . . . . Marriage, while remaining the foundational divine institution for humanity, is therefore to be viewed not as an end in itself but as properly subordinated to God's larger salvific purposes. . . . Many of the implications of Jesus' teachings on marriage and the family are further developed in the writings of Paul.[3]

This interpretation does not seem to get at the tension in the story. Surely any good Jew would have seen marriage within the context of God's creation, so the significance of Jesus' teaching must be something more. Moreover, it is not clear that marriage is as "foundational" for Jesus or Paul as it is for the writers of the Genesis creation stories. If it were, why would we so often find in their teachings instances of family ties conflicting with duties to God?

3. Andreas Köstenberger, "Marriage and Family in the New Testament," *Marriage and Family in the Biblical World* (ed. Ken M. Campbell; Downers Grove, IL: InterVarsity, 2003) 247.

Mark 3:31–35 is a story of just this kind of conflict. Halvor Moxnes claims that in this passage, while Mary has come to protect the family honor by taking Jesus home, Jesus rejects it in order to fulfill his mission.[4] Jesus names the community of believers as his true family and finds his vocation in and through this community.[5] Here and in other "hard sayings" Jesus poses troubling questions about the compatibility of discipleship with commitment to family.

Some posit that these teachings are directed only to a small group or refer to extraordinary situations rather than ordinary life.[6] Susan Calef convincingly argues on the contrary that the hard sayings were meant to "compel a radical reprioritization on the part of his contemporaries, with Jesus and his cause, the reign of God, displacing blood kin as the ultimate and defining priority of one's identity and way of life."[7] Therefore, Calef says, though Jesus does not want his followers to reject or negate family, he does ask them to become part of a new, demanding family of disciples (Luke 8:21).[8]

This shift in primary loyalty is key. The naming of the community of disciples as first family and the example of Jesus inspired some women and men in the early church to embrace vowed celibacy or contract marriages without the unnecessary distraction of sex.[9] Stephen Barton has written about how this new source of identity, the flipside of the negative judgment on family, is radical, even if it does not and should not lead most Christians to abandon family altogether:

> What it *does* say to us, however, is that the family is *not an end in itself,* and that modernity's "idolatry of the family" stands under judgment. It says to us that belonging to Jesus and the "new" family of Jesus—theologically speaking, the church—is the prior, more profound (because eschatologi-

---

4. Halvor Moxnes, "Introduction," in *Constructing Early Christian Families: Family as Social Reality and Metaphor* (ed. Halvor Moxnes; New York: Routledge, 1997) 28.

5. See Julie Hanlon Rubio, *A Christian Theology of Marriage* (New York: Paulist, 2003) 46–60. Recently, Moxnes named Jesus' challenge to the household as his primary challenge, noting that he relocates people from family to the body of believers. See Halvor Moxnes, *Putting Jesus in His Place: A Radical Vision of Household and Kingdom* (Louisville: Westminster, 2003) 15, 53.

6. See Peter Balla, *The Child-Parent Relationship in the New Testament and Its Environment* (WUNT 155; Tübingen: Mohr-Siebeck, 2003) 155–56, who holds that the hard sayings refer to exceptional situations and are not meant to be general guidelines.

7. Susan A. Calef, "The Radicalism of Jesus the Prophet: Implications for Christian Family," in *Marriage in the Catholic Tradition: Scripture, Tradition, and Experience* (ed. Todd A. Salzman, Thomas M. Kelly, and John J. O'Keefe; New York: Crossroad, 2004) 53–65, 57.

8. Ibid.

9. Peter Brown, *Body and Society: Men, Women, and Sexual Renunciation in Early Christianity* (New York: Columbia University Press, 1988).

cal) reality to which human beings are called and in terms of which human relationships, including familial relationships, are to be judged.[10]

Barton's synthesis cuts between overly negative judgments of the text and problematic attempts to explain away its hard edges. In a review of Barton's earlier work, *Discipleship and Family Ties in Mark and Matthew*, John Barclay pushes for an even more serious reckoning with the "revolutionary potential" of the Gospels, which display, in his view, "no concern" for the family as a site of traditioning and discipling.[11] While Barton, along with Calef, hopes for transformation of family life in light of the claims of discipleship, Barclay is not sure this is what Jesus had in mind.

Yet, the same Jesus who challenges his followers with hard sayings also looks back to the Genesis creation narrative in order to uphold the sanctity of the marriage covenant (Mark 10:6–9, Matt 19:6). Jesus also shows concern for families by healing sick family members, affirming teachings against divorce and adultery, and entrusting his widowed mother to his beloved disciple at the cross.[12] His worry, one could argue, is not about marriage itself but rather about idolatry of family that can stand in the way of the broader mission that is integral to discipleship. Thus, he affirms the goodness of marriage and yet challenges his hearers by calling them to "hate" their families (Luke 14:26) and by asking them to leave their families behind for his sake and their own (Mark 10:29–30).

While it is easy to see how the money and power that show up as roadblocks in the stories of Jesus could present difficulties for the person seeking discipleship, it is much more difficult for many Christians to see just what family interferes with or how people could love their families too much. However, when Jesus' public ministry to the marginalized is taken seriously, according to moral theologian Lisa Sowle Cahill, it becomes clear that "loyalty to one's own group and dedication to the status of that group over all others and at the expense of whoever stands in the way are incompatible with a life of mercy, service, and compassion for the neighbor in need or for the social outcast and the poor."[13] In her view Jesus preaches that devotion to family can be dangerous to the person who wants to live a life marked by compassion for others, which implies that his disciples who marry and become

---

10. Stephen Barton, *Life Together: Family, Sexuality and Community in the New Testament and Today* (Edinburgh: T. & T. Clark, 2001) 48.

11. John Barclay, "Review of Stephen Barton, *Discipleship and Family Ties*," *Studies in Christian Ethics* 9 (1996) 49–50.

12. Calef, "Radicalism of Jesus the Prophet," 57.

13. Lisa Sowle Cahill, *Family: A Christian Social Perspective* (Minneapolis: Fortress, 2000) 29.

parents must resist the temptation to make care for kin their only mission in life. Cahill envisions "a Christian family [that] defines *family values* as care for others, especially the poor."[14]

Development in the Teachings of Paul

However, this sort of radical Christian family ethic, this way out of the hard sayings, does not seem prevalent in the Pauline epistles.[15] Instead, we find Paul in 1 Corinthians to be very suspicious of marriage because of its potential to distract the person who wants to devote everything to Christ (1 Cor 7:32–35). This rigor seems in keeping with Jesus' sayings about the cost of discipleship, though not necessarily in line with his affirmation of marriage. For Paul something seems to have changed so that the ideal is no longer marriage but celibacy, though it is "better to marry than to burn" (1 Cor 7:9). Marriage "in the Lord" is good, but not ideal (1 Cor 7:38–40).

In other epistles stable, ordered families are endowed with theological, social, and ecclesial significance, but this does not mean Paul's serious reservations about family have been left behind. When family language is used metaphorically to speak about church and about relations among church members, the value of family is upheld even as it is challenged. Calef makes a similar claim about the Gospels, saying that Jesus challenges family values because he, "abandoned his household and its work and called others to do the same," "pits discipleship against family loyalty," and "dismisses the priority of the duty to kin."[16] Yet, she argues, his use of family language should be understood as affirming the values associated with families, such as love, fidelity, and care.[17] In addition, Moxnes claims that Jesus' use of the language and imagery of the household in his parables is meant to challenge the reality of exploitation in Palestinian society, which indicates that compassion in families is not problematic but worthy of imitation.[18] Even as Jesus' followers are encouraged to see fellow disciples as their first family, core aspects of family life are upheld.

14. Ibid., 135.

15. Though I tend to side with those who see the letter to the Ephesians, as well as Colossians, 2 Thessalonians, and the pastoral epistles (1 and 2 Timothy and Titus,) as written in Paul's name rather than by Paul, I will not address issues of authorship in this essay but will treat the Pauline corpus as a whole.

16. Calef, "The Radicalism of Jesus the Prophet," 56–57.

17. Ibid., 57.

18. See Moxnes's claims Jesus revives "household sharing and village solidarity" that had been lost with the rise of large estates and wage labor, *Constructing Early Christian Families*, 25.

It is similar in the letters of Paul. Thus, when in Eph 5:21–33 husbands and wives are compared to Christ and the Church, familial love becomes the most important biblical analogy for God's love for humanity. The contemporary Catholic interpretation from Pope John Paul II is that in marriage "spouses are bound to one another in the most profoundly indissoluble manner. Their belonging to each other is the very real representation, by means of the sacramental sign, of the very relationship of Christ with the church."[19] Their marital relationship is a participation in the cross and a sign to others of Christ's self-giving love.[20]

This interpretation is perhaps attractive to contemporary believers who want to reconcile discipleship with married love. On the one hand, family ties seem to be of great importance because they can suggest something of God's passionate love for human beings. On the other hand, marriage in this passage is not the sort of marriage that is highly regarded in contemporary American culture. Here, spousal love is not romantic and spontaneous but enduring and sacrificing. It is not simply the private concern of two people. Rather, the love of two particular people is a crucial sign to others of something far more important: God's love for all. Sacrament, in contemporary Catholic thought, is both a gift and a task. Marriage thus conceived is a way of living out one's commitment to Christ in the home and for the world.

However, the strong statements on the social import of well-ordered marriage here and elsewhere in the Epistles are troubling for those looking for a counter-cultural message about family.[21] Interestingly enough, very conservative and very liberal scholars tend to agree in their interpretation of these passages. Köstenberger argues that because the assumption of the ancient Hellenistic household codes was that order in the household would promote larger societal order, Christians' conformance to the ethical standards of a code would show Christianity to be respectable and aid in the spread of the Christian message.[22] In the Pastoral Epistles the household codes (particularly those concerning the role of the husband/father in overseeing the household) are connected to potential church leaders' abilities to oversee the church. "If anyone does not know how to manage his own family, how can he take care of God's church?" (1 Tim 3:5), for the church is "the household of God" (1 Tim 3:15). "There is thus a close relationship between church and family," Köstenberger

---

19. John Paul II, *Familiaris consortio* (Washington, DC: United States Conference of Catholic Bishops, 1981), no. 13.

20. Ibid., no. 14.

21. David E. Aune, "Household Rules," in *The Westminster Dictionary of New Testament and Early Christian Literature and Rhetoric* (Louisville: Westminster John Knox, 2003) 221–22.

22. See Köstenberger, "Marriage and Family in the New Testament."

claims, "and Christian maturity in the fulfillment of one's duties as husband and father becomes one of the most essential requirements for those aspiring to the office of pastor or elder."²³

The different roles of men and women in marriage emphasized in the household codes is likewise affirmed as significant and of enduring value by some conservative scholars. Köstenberger argues that "proper submission" is not outdated, for the husband is to rule over his wife as Christ rules over marriage.²⁴ This distinction in ruling cannot be explained away by the initial command, "Be submissive to one another." Rather, the order, social respectability, and submission of both spouses to Christ, as well as of women to men, are interpreted as central and positive.²⁵ On this interpretation, the household codes reinforce social norms rather than challenge them.

Feminist biblical scholar Elisabeth Schüssler Fiorenza essentially agrees with this understanding of what the households codes represent, but her negative evaluation of the model being promoted leads her to a different conclusion about its enduring value. She, too, reads the codes as an attempt by the early Christians to show their social respectability, but she views this movement negatively, as a betrayal of the radical egalitarian ethos of the Jesus movement.²⁶ She concludes that because the codes contradict an essential aspect of Jesus' ministry (i.e., the radical discipleship of equals), they simply cannot be relevant for contemporary Christian communities.²⁷ Instead, we should recover and return to the radical beginnings reflected in Gal 3:28, which Schüssler Fiorenza believes to be a baptismal formula indicating that becoming a Christian meant throwing off the limits of gender and social roles.²⁸ While Schüssler Fiorenza acknowledges some intent of the author of Ephesians to soften the patriarchal code by exhorting husbands to love their wives, because the wife's role remains submissive, and because this role is cemented through theologizing, she claims that the text "participates in the trajectory of the patriarchal household-

---

23. Ibid., 277

24. Ibid., 249, 253.

25. On the need of passing on faith as the context for the household codes, see John Barclay, "Review of Stephen Barton," 49–50.

26. Elisabeth Schüssler Fiorenza, *In Memory of Her: A Feminist Theological Reconstruction of Christian Origins* (New York: Crossroad, 1989) 279. See also, Margaret Y. MacDonald, "The Role of Women in the Expansion of Early Christianity," *Early Christian Families in Context: An Interdisciplinary Dialogue* (ed. David L. Balch and Carolyn Osiek; Grand Rapids: Eerdmans, 2003) 175–76.

27. See Sue Walrond-Skinner, *The Fulcrum and the Fire: Wrestling with Family Life* (London: Darton, Longman & Todd, 1993), among others.

28. Schüssler Fiorenza, *In Memory of Her*, 205–18.

code tradition insofar as it takes over the household-code pattern and reasserts the submission of the wife to the husband as a religious Christian duty . . . the author was not able to 'Christianize' the code."[29] Thus if codes are far more socially conformist than the radical teaching of Jesus and his earliest followers, perhaps they weaken the case for a family ethos centered in discipleship.

Is Schüssler Fiorenza's view of radical egalitarianism in early Christianity overly idealized? Barton criticizes Schüssler Fiorenza for claiming to know too much about Jesus' discipleship of equals and for using this liberative strain of the gospel as a hermeneutical key to marginalize the Pauline household codes.[30] Even more strongly, Amy-Jill Levine argues, "positing an ideal early tradition of radical egalitarianism now lost . . . is bad history and inevitably leads to anti-Judaism and anti-Catholicism."[31] Barton offers a way to affirm the household codes in their historical context while still finding them meaningful for modern family life, saying, "Neither the 'conservative' (proclaim them as observance of the household codes is the only hope for modern families) or 'liberal' (ignore them or reject them) responses to the household rules are sufficient." Rather, the household rules should be interpreted with sensitivity to what "the Spirit of Christ might be saying to the church about human sociality," and Christians should respond with their own attempts to live "in ways that witness with full integrity to our true, eschatological identity as members together in a *new* household, the 'household of God.'"[32]

This is a helpful way to resolve some of the tension between the egalitarian, family-relativizing message of Jesus and the praise of stable, obedient, hierarchical-ordered families so prominent in the later Epistles. Levine's point that even the most conscientious Christian theologians and ethicists tend to oversimplify the NT message and overemphasize the disjunctions between Christianity and contemporaneous cultures is crucial. Yet, since many excellent scholars still speak of a radically egalitarian ethos of Jesus that was later watered down, it is important not to explain away all of the tension.[33] Peter Lampe lends support to Schüssler Fiorenza's claims

29. Ibid., 270.

30. Barton, *Life Together*, 141.

31. Amy-Jill Levine, "Theological Education, the Bible, and History: Détente in the Culture Wars" in *Early Christian Families in Context* (ed. David L. Balch and Carolyn Osiek; Grand Rapids: Eerdmans, 2003) 327–36, 334.

32. Stephen Barton, "The Epistles and Christian Ethics" in *Cambridge Companion to Christian Ethics* (2nd ed.; Cambridge: Cambridge University Press, 2012) 54–64, 62–63.

33. See Margaret Y. MacDonald, *Early Christian Women and Pagan Opinion* (Cambridge: Cambridge University Press, 1996) for a thorough discussion of women's roles in early Christian communities and how they changed as Christianity grew.

about Gal 3:28, even though he concludes that few took it seriously, while the majority attempted to "ton[e] down the new Christian context of meaning a little instead of being radicalized by it . . . . The new Christian context became accommodated to the Hellenistic Roman context. Thus, over time, hierarchical structures also developed in the church in spite of the doctrine of equality."[34] It does seem as though some of the earlier message was lost as Christianity grew and adapted to surrounding cultures.

Cultural adaptation and change are not always negative, and one can see a need for some way to affirm family more strongly than Jesus did. Strong families can certainly play a role in creating a stable social order. However, much of the accommodation that occurred in the early church appears now to be problematic. This is a strong argument for leaving behind the sexism, the worry about social respectability, and the undue concern for order that permeates the household codes while bringing forward the egalitarian ethos and outward focus suggested by both the household codes and the hard sayings of Jesus. The New Testament's radical wisdom should be the core of Christian family ethics.

Radical Prioritization and the Domestic Church

The language of the domestic church, which links household to discipleship, seems especially promising. For models one can turn to the early church where at least some Christians evidently tried to re-center their lives around mission rather than kin. As a result, they were sometimes called "homewreckers" by critics who questioned their willingness to let faith conflict with duty to family.[35] Scholars of early Christianity tell us that both in Roman and Jewish contexts some Christians seem to have stunned others with their refusal to honor cultural norms prioritizing the family.[36] New Testament affirmations of marriage such as the household codes indicate that most Christians ultimately tried to reconcile their faith with their highest estimations of ordinary family life. Still, the dominant strain of early Christian

---

34. Peter Lampe, "The Language of Equality in Early Christian House Churches: A Constructivist Approach," in *Early Christian Families in Context* (ed. David L. Balch and Carolyn Osiek; Grand Rapids: Eerdmans, 2003) 73–83, 83.

35. Andrew Jacobs, "A Family Affair: Marriage, Class, and Ethics in the Apocryphal Acts of the Apostles," *Journal of Early Christian Studies* 7:1 (1999) 106.

36. Brown, *Body and Society*, 1–17.

thinking appears to have been suspicion of the value of family life when compared with the value of single-hearted discipleship.[37]

When trying to understand how early Christians thought about family, it is important not to overlook scriptural passages which seem to recommend avoiding marriage altogether, including Matt 22:30 ("For in the resurrection they neither marry nor are given in marriage, but are like angels in heaven") and 1 Cor 7:38 ("So that he who married his betrothed does well; and he who refrains from marriage will do better").[38] Patristics scholar John O'Keefe explains that believers in Paul's time expected Jesus to return any day and cared little about the maintenance of social institutions like marriage, while Jesus envisioned a kingdom of God that similarly lacked the structures of life taken for granted today.[39] Some early Christians turned to ascetic practices in imitation of Christ and because they "believed that through their practices of physical renunciation they could begin to live now in anticipation of the way we will live after the resurrection."[40] Embracing a lifestyle of renunciation was seen by these Christians as key to discipleship, regardless of one's state in life. Celibacy may have been the most obvious way of doing this, but many came to see that married life also offered abundant opportunities for renunciation for the sake of others.[41]

Modern Christians seeking to make sense of the radical edge of the NT tradition on family should, according to many contemporary scholars, acknowledge that radical reprioritization is required. Being a Christian family means becoming part of the larger family of the church, embracing prayer, charity and justice, and critical reflection on use of possessions, the works of mercy, and hospitality. All of these difficult practices are made possible by the knowledge that because of Jesus, families are not limited by the options chosen by the many. Rather, they know "it could be otherwise."[42] Contemporary Christians can do all of this in families rather than by leaving their families behind. For if Jesus redefines family, linking it primarily to

---

37. Ibid., 36.

38. John O'Keefe, "Marriage Is Good, Celibacy Is Better," in *Marriage in the Catholic Tradition: Scripture, Tradition, and Experience* (ed. Todd A. Salzman, Thomas M. Kelly, and John J. O'Keefe; New York: Crossroad, 2004) 76–85, at 78.

39. Ibid., 79.

40. Ibid., 82.

41. See also, William C. Mattison III, "'When they rise from the dead, they neither marry nor are given to marriage;' Marriage and Sexuality, Eschatology, and the Nuptial Meaning of the Body in Pope John Paul II's Theology of the Body," in *Sexuality and the U.S. Catholic Church: Crisis and Renewal* (ed. Lisa Sowle Cahill; New York: Herder & Herder, 2006) 32–51.

42. Calef, "Radicalism of Jesus the Prophet," 63–64.

obedience to God rather than to blood ties, he and his followers also use family language to describe themselves and depend on families in their itinerant ministry. "It is through the houses of his supporters that Jesus extends his mission and in them that he meets with his disciples, his family."[43] Like Paul he questions the centrality of family while laying claim to some of its central values. Reconciling the fullness of the early Christian tradition then may mean placing a strong valuing of marriage, rooted not primarily in kinship but in faith, alongside a challenge to bring families outside of their own concerns to embrace a larger mission and use their unique strengths.

To sum up, earlier generations of Catholic theologians limited their scriptural analysis of marriage to a few positive texts in order to mount a strong defense of the holy family and support its private obligations. Negative texts were used primarily to support celibacy for the most devoted of the faithful. Recent scholarship relies on a broader reading of a range of scriptural texts and supports a view of the family as a counter-cultural domestic church made up of committed disciples. The holy family of Gen 1:26–28 and Eph 5:21–35, the radical discipleship of the hard sayings of Jesus, and Pauline warnings about marriage all confront Christian believers. Contemporary theologians favoring a synthesis that privileges radical reprioritization seem to have the best grasp of the fullness of the early Christian tradition.

The Complication: Religious Diversity in the Family

The domestic church model is not without its problems because Christian families are not always fully unified in belief and commitment. Spouses choose each other for many reasons and promise to be together for life regardless of how one or the other might change in belief or practice. Children do not choose their parents, and they certainly do not sign up for membership in a domestic church. Interfaith families (in which spouses who practice different religions or different Christian faiths are united) are the most obvious example of diversity in faith, and they are becoming more and more numerous. Before Vatican II intermarriage between Catholics and Protestant spouses was all but impossible inside the Catholic Church, and most Catholics avoided it. Today, however, forty percent of Catholics are in interchurch

---

43. John Painter, "When Is a House not Home? Mark 3.13–35," *New Testament Studies* 45 (October 1999) 513.

or interreligious marriages,[44] and the Catholic Church, like most other Christian churches, recognizes the validity of interfaith unions.[45]

There is a need to address this issue and examine its relevance to all couples, for interfaith couples are not so different from same-faith couples. No doubt, interfaith marriages have greater challenges, and the differences between same-church and interfaith marriages should not be overlooked, but often the gap between the two groups is overstated. For instance, in a large Creighton University study researchers found that seventy-eight percent of same-church couples reported no differences in ideas about how much emphasis to place on the religious aspect of child rearing, while sixty-three percent of interchurch couples reported a similar like-mindedness.[46] The gap of fifteen percent is not overly wide, and the majority in both groups attests to a great deal of like-mindedness. However, it seems likely that both groups could be over-reporting conformity in the context of a general question. There are many kinds of religious differences that can affect married couples, as no one's faith is just like another's. To cite just one example, a recent worldwide comparative study found that "in most families the mother is the primary figure in the children's religiosity."[47] The pervasiveness of this gap shows that there are real differences between many spouses about how much to emphasize religion in child rearing. Some plurality of belief and practice exists even in same-church families, and this situation complicates the argument that Christian families should act as domestic churches and engage in shared practices.

Religious differences such as those delineated above limit opportunities for joint religious activities that nurture shared identity and purpose. This is most obvious for interfaith couples. They are the ones who are "most at risk for drift from church belonging and practice."[48] They are also less likely to emphasize religion in

44. Lee M. Williams and Michael G. Lawler attest to the growing numbers of intermarried Christians, "Marital Satisfaction and Religious Heterogamy: A Comparison of Interchurch and Same-Church Individuals," *Journal of Family Issues* 24 (2003) 465. I will use the term "interfaith" to describe marriages between a Christian and a person of another religion and between two Christians of different denominations.

45. John Paul II, *Familiaris consortio*, no. 68 and no. 77, respectively.

46. Williams and Lawler, "Marital Satisfaction and Religious Heterogamy," 474.

47. Chris J. Boyatzis, "The Family as a Context for Religious and Spiritual Development in Children and Youth" in *The Handbook of Spiritual Development in Childhood and Adolescence* (ed. Eugene C. Roehlkepartain, et al.; Thousand Oaks, CA: Sage, 2006) 302. This is so for interreligious families as well, in which children most often are reared in the mother's faith tradition. Women are more religious, attend services more often, pray more, and have more conversations about religion with their children.

48. Center for Marriage and Family Creighton University, *Marriage Preparation in the Catholic Church: Getting It Right* (November 1995) 35. Still, much depends on the couple's religiosity at engage-

childrearing. Their children are less likely to remain faithful in adulthood. Key predictors of religious inheritance include parental religiosity, quality of family relationships, and family structure.[49] The lower religiosity in interfaith families contributes to the diminished possibilities for religious inheritance.[50] Williams and Lawler think it "likely that developing a joint religious life requires a greater effort for interchurch couples."[51] Serious obstacles exist for faith formation in interfaith families, and these ought not be overlooked. All of these factors make sustaining a common faith life, let alone radical choices, more difficult for couples of different faiths.

R. R. Reno offers a rare glimpse of the pain of interfaith marriage through an analysis of his own experience in an Episcopal-Jewish marriage. Reno clearly knows the joys of intermarriage, but he also knows the pain and darkness, or what he calls the "blows" of intermarriage. He acknowledges that choosing and practicing different faiths means separation. Reflecting on his daughter's bat mitzvah, he provocatively writes, "My daughter loves me very much, but she is very conscious that this day of her bat mitzvah is also a hating of her father."[52] Choosing to be a Jew, like her mother, means leaving her father outside and renouncing the faith that is everything to him. He can deeply respect and admire her commitment, but he cannot follow her, nor can he deny the sadness her choice brings both to him and her. The pain will not simply dissolve with time.

This is not to say that there is nothing to be gained from interfaith marriage. Reno eloquently describes the way seeing those he loves embrace another faith forces him to question his own.[53] Reno's unrelentingly honest portrait of the joy and pain of unity in difference illustrates how difficult achieving unity in practice can be. John Paul II's words to interchurch couples in 1982, "You live in your marriages the hopes and difficulties of the path to Christian unity," are instructive, for though we can now better see that these couples prophetically "mark out the path by which divided churches can reach their goal,"[54] it is crucial not to overlook the painful and difficult nature of the path itself.

---

ment, see Williams and Lawler, "Marital Satisfaction and Religious Heterogamy," 476.

49. Williams and Lawler, "Marital Satisfaction and Religious Heterogamy," 466.

50. Ibid. 475. The authors report that this is consistent with other studies.

51. Ibid., 476.

52. R. R. Reno, "Interreligious Marriage: A Personal Reflection," in *Marriage in the Catholic Tradition* (ed. Todd Salzman et al.; New York: Crossroad, 2004) 239–46, 248.

53. Ibid., 244.

54. Ibid.

Interfaith couples, I contend, are not so different from the majority of Christian families who seek shared religious or spiritual practice in spite of differences that could pull them apart. Few couples are totally unified in belief and commitment. One spouse might be more religious while the other struggles with faith. One might be drawn to traditional faith practices while the other finds God more easily outside organized religion. One might be very comfortable as a lifelong adherent of the faith of his or her childhood, while the other practices more cautiously, having converted before marriage. The convert's zeal is not matched by the faith of the cradle Catholic. Spouses—even same-church spouses—do not always agree on matters of faith and may find faith to be a source of tension as often as a source of unity.

Children are also diverse in their religious needs, beliefs, and doubts. In contemporary Christian homes children are more likely to question the faith of their parents because they encounter on their streets, in their classrooms, among their friends and relatives, and in their own parents, people of different faiths and no faith at all. Early on, they realize that some people do not go to church every Sunday or engage in daily family prayer. Parents themselves are less likely to be strongly affiliated with their faith traditions.[55] They are less likely to encourage children to practice their faith in the home. When one's parents and neighbors are praying at meals or going to church on Sunday, sustaining similar practices for oneself is easier, but without that reinforcement different practices look increasingly unattractive, and this explains why researchers are seeing such strong declines in faith among young adults.

Although the United States remains unique among developing countries in its relatively high levels of belief, even here religion becomes a question much earlier, and doubt and resistance are more likely to surface.[56] A recent study by the Pew Forum on Religion and Public Life found that forty-four percent of Americans have changed their faith affiliation.[57] Twenty percent of Americans (and thirty-two per-

---

55. The Pew Research Center's Forum on Religion and Public Life reported in February 2009 that while 85 percent of women and 79 percent of men are affiliated with a religion, only 63 percent of women and 49 percent of men say that religion is very important in their lives, only 66 percent of women and 49 percent of men pray daily, and only 44 percent of women and 34 percent of men attend a worship service weekly. The data is drawn from the "U. S. Religious Landscape Survey," http://religions.pewforum.org.

56. See Laura H. Lippman and Julie Dombrowski Keith, "The Demographics of Spirituality Among Youth: International Perspectives" in *Handbook of Spiritual Development* (ed. Roehlkepartain et al.; Thousand Oaks, CA: Sage, 2006) 109–23,118. Eighty-four percent of American youths age 13–17 believe in God, and about half report that religion is very important to them,

57. "Changes in Religious Affiliation in the U.S.," http://www.pewforum.org/faith-in-flux.aspx.

cent of young adults) now count themselves as "unaffiliated," more than double the percentage who were raised that way.[58] Moreover, Catholics have suffered the biggest losses in recent years, as thirty-one percent of Americans were raised Catholic, but only twenty-four percent now consider themselves Catholic.[59] Millenial Catholics (those born after 1983) are the least likely of all Catholics to claim strong Catholic identity and practice.[60]

The high numbers of interfaith marriages, the recognition of diversity even in same-church couples, and the decline in religious affiliation all render problematic both the overly idealized "holy family" of the past and the radical domestic church centered on hearing the word and doing it.[61] The reality of varying degrees of commitment among men, women, and children can no longer be denied. Plurality, doubt, and lives unmarked by faith exist not only "out there" in the world, but also "in here"—in the church and in Christian families.[62] Even those families that begin with the same faith may not always be united in belief and practice because many people change their minds over the course of their lives. Thus the ways theologians have found to reconcile the hard sayings with the household codes and other positive family imagery in the NT may have to be adapted. While the domestic church model may work for the most committed families, many more will find themselves lacking sufficient faith and will.

Staying with Unbelievers

Turning back to the NT may provide some guidance. We know from Pauline letters that Christian-pagan marriages existed. In 1 Cor 7:12–16 Paul advises a believing woman to let her unbelieving husband go if he wishes, but to stay married if he will, "for the unbelieving husband is consecrated through his wife, and the unbelieving wife is consecrated through her husband. Otherwise, your children would be

---

58. "Nones on the Rise," http://www.pewforum.org/Unaffiliated/nones-on-the-rise.aspx

59. "U.S. Religious Landscape Survey," http://religions.pewforum.org.

60. In "Generations of American Catholics," *Proceedings of the Catholic Theological Society of America* 53 (2008) 1–17, James Davidson reports that only thirty-five percent of Millenials say they would never leave the church (versus sixty-nine percent of the pre-Vatican II generation), and even lower percentages attend Mass weekly or worry about disagreeing with the Magisterium on moral issues. The generational effect is much more significant than age.

61. Calef, "The Radicalism of Jesus the Prophet," 63.

62. Paul Elie argues for a shift in how we read Flannery O'Connor ("What Flannery Knew: Catholic Writing for a Critical Age," *Commonweal* [November 21, 2008] 12–17). Whereas she pitted the church against the world, we must see the blurring of the two, acknowledge doubt among Christians, and understand her stories as addressed not only to "them" but to us. This is my approach here.

unclean, but as it is, they are holy." This hope for the conversion of an unbelieving spouses in repeated in 1 Peter 3:1, where wives are asked to "be submissive to your husbands, so that some, though they do not obey the word, may be won without a word by the behavior of their wives." John Barclay notes that in both cases the couples "are not required to separate themselves in order to create a new 'Christian family.'"[63] Paul and the writer of 1 Peter hope for the conversion of the unbelieving spouse rather than worrying, as other early Christians did, about the pollution of the believing spouse.[64] Instead of fearing the contagiousness of unbelief, they leave open the possibility that belief will spread. According to Hodge, "a contagious *holiness* seems to be at work."[65] Even more remarkably, "Paul has granted—or perhaps acknowledged—the sanctifying power of the bodies of believing wives. This subverts traditional household ideologies and the expectation that women and other subordinates will follow the loyalties of the male head of household."[66]

It is not clear if many believing wives were able to convert their unbelieving spouses, but at least some early church fathers and some non-Christian authors worried about that possibility. For a woman to hold a faith different from that of her husband threatened the authority of the head of the household and the social order. Celsus, a second century pagan author, criticized Christianity for allowing women and other subordinate members of households to seek the conversion of others, saying, "They alone, they say, know the right way to live, and if the children would believe them, they would become happy and make their home happy as well."[67] Plutarch advises new wives that they must participate in the household practices of their husband's religion.[68] Even if Celsus and other critics of Christianity were engaged in an "attempt to denigrate early Christianity by appealing to the gender and status of its main proponents," there is significant evidence for the participation

---

63. John M. G. Barclay, "The Family as Bearer of Religion," in *Constructing Early Christian Families: Family as Social Reality and Metaphor* (ed. Halvor Moxnes; New York: Routledge, 1997) 66–80, 73.

64. Margaret Y. MacDonald, "Was Celsus Right? Role of Women in the Expansion of Early Christianity," in *Early Christian Families in Context* (ed. David L. Balch and Carolyn Osiek; Grand Rapids: Eerdmans, 2003) 157–84, 179. Her comparison of 2 Cor 6:14 ("Do not be mismatched with unbelievers. For what partnership have righteousness and iniquity?") and patristic writers such as Tertullian and Justin Martyr, who speak of the revulsion of believers who have to share bed and board with pagans, is instructive.

65. Carolyn Johnson Hodge, "Married to an Unbeliever: Households, Hierarchies, and Holiness in 1 Corinthian 7:12–16," *Harvard Theological Review* 103 (2010) 1–25, 17.

66. Ibid., 19.

67. Celsus is quoted in Origen, *Contra Celsum*, cited in MacDonald, "Was Celsus Right?" 157.

68. Plutarch, *Advice to the Bride and Groom*, quoted in Hodge, "Married to an Unbeliever," 1.

of women in early Christianity.[69] Women were engaged in missionary activities, patronage and leadership of household churches, as well as efforts to convert others in their household, even though they may not have been very successful at the latter.[70] Paul was allowing for something new. He "seems to imagine that this sort of 'mixed marriage' could work, at least for the short term."[71] Some historians of Christianity believe that mixed marriages were a way for early Christians to keep connections with the outside world open and perhaps influence children and slaves.[72]

By the second and third centuries socialization of children and their obedience to believing parents was being encouraged in Christian texts.[73] Yet this concern seems absent from the Gospels.[74] We also know that, while some Christian children were part of converted households, others may have converted on their own and remained with unbelieving parents. The potential for conflict within households when children were recruited into Christianity was real.[75] These children must have had to work out their Christian practice on their own, without a family context.

All of this means that when we read about seemingly ideal Christian families in the writings of the early church fathers, we should view these accounts with healthy suspicion, for:

> The idealized image of the public ruler of the house (rarely at home) with a modest and docile wife and children to support him, though sometimes evoked by patristic writers (cf. Syriac *Didascalia*) and advocated as a divinely appointed scheme to heal the "more natural proclivity of females" to frivolous enterprises (Clement of Alexandria, *Pedagogue* 2.33.2; *Letter of Aristeas* 250) was always more a rhetorical trope than any serious analysis, let alone description of, social realities in the early Christian world.[76]

If early Christian writings sometimes present idealized images rather than real descriptions, can we imagine that households from the beginning of Christian

69. MacDonald, "Was Celsus Right?" 159.

70. Ibid.,162–72, 180.

71. Hodge, "Married to an Unbeliever," 3.

72. Cited in MacDonald, "Was Celsus Right?" 178. The fact that mixed marriages were condemned is evidence that they were common.

73. Margaret Y. MacDonald, "Kinship and Family in the New Testament World," in *Understanding the Social World of the New Testament* (ed. Dietmar Neufeld and Richard E. DeMaris; New York: Routledge, 2010) 29–43, 41.

74. Ibid.

75. Ibid., 42.

76. John A. McGuckin. "Family," in *The Westminster Handbook to Patristic Theology* (Louisville: Westminster John Knox, 2003) 141–42.

history would have included as much variation in belief, doubt, and consistency of practice as households do today?[77] Even though we can read from every major Christian thinker exhortations to parents to raise their children "in the Lord," is it not wise to assume that some parents were more up to this task than others? That not all children (or adults) loved family prayer or looked forward to community liturgy? That not all wives were submissive, not all children were obedient, and not all husbands cared to be the religious authorities in their homes? That there were always some whose faith burned stronger, whose practice was more rigorous, whose connection to the church as first family was more intense? If so, perhaps we need to think more about how the more ordinary families (in which most Christians have always resided) appropriate the New Testament's vision. To do that I will briefly turn in my conclusion to a more contemporary figure who knew well the pervasiveness of sin, doubt, and diversity in faith.

Flannery O'Connor and Salvation of the Clean and Unclean

Catholic fiction writer Flannery O'Connor wrote honestly about the struggle of keeping faith and taking it seriously. This nuanced understanding of faith, though sometimes hard to discern in the midst of casts of grotesque characters, is central to her work. As she put it:

> I don't think you should write something as long as a novel around anything that is not of the gravest concern to you and everybody else, and for me this is always the conflict between an attraction for the Holy and disbelief in it that we breath with the air of our times. It's hard to believe always but more so in the world we live in now. There are some of us who have to pay for our faith every step of the way and who have to work out dramatically what it would be like without it and if being without it would be ultimately possible or not.[78]

In families the difficulty of belief and life without faith are perhaps even harder to see than in individuals because families are likelier to engage in traditional faith practices. Yet, even for them larger questions of what faith really means and how

---

77. Hodge explores this possibility by reconstructing life in Corinth, where "domestic religion was multifarious, adaptable, and a part of daily life. Thus Christian practices may have mixed and mingled with traditional worship practices without much conflict. Or, a wife may have been able to conduct her practices in secret" ("Married to an Unbeliever," 24).

78. Flannery O'Connor, "To John Hawkes," in *The Habit of Being: Letters of Flannery O'Connor* (ed. Sally Fitzgerald; New York: Noonday, 1979) 349-50.

it shapes life from the center out—or does not—remain unasked and unanswered. O'Connor's narratives beg readers to ask those questions.

Her best known protagonist, Hazel Motes, hero of the novel *Wise Blood*, struggles with faith.[79] Tempted by atheism, he tries to run from the faith of his ancestors. He mocks his grandfather's life as a preacher by going from town to town, standing on top of his big Cadillac, and preaching the "Church without Christ." Many of O'Connor's intellectual readers believe Hazel to be a hero because he rejects and mocks the simplistic faith of Southern fundamentalism. However, O'Connor writes that in Hazel's character there are "a number of conflicting wills in one person."[80] His struggle is difficult because as much as he wants to, he simply cannot leave faith alone. This, O'Connor says, is why she admires him.[81]

Many of the characters in O'Connor's stories are baptized members of a church who nonetheless find it hard to live up to the ethical implications of their faith. In "The Displaced Person," Mrs. McKinley, a land owner, attempts to be a good Christian woman by inviting a family of immigrants, the Guizacs, to work on her property and by trying to treat all of her workers as well as she can.[82] Yet she cannot see that her black workers deserve more than her tolerance of their supposed moral weakness and lax work ethic, or that her view of her own largess depends on a false picture of her independence. She, like the rest of her household, does not want to recognize Mr. Guizac's goodness and in the end she and the others watch as he is plowed under by a tractor.[83] Yet these characters are not so evil that they can be dismissed. Readers can sympathize with those who, so like themselves, stand by in the face of moral atrocity because they cannot see.[84]

Despite O'Connor's pessimism about human nature, she offers hope in her portrayals of people who are not perfect but searching. Though they might go through most of their daily lives unperturbed by questions of faith, in the end, most of her characters reveal themselves to be spiritually hungry.[85] Most people, O'Connor

---

79. Flannery O'Connor, *Wise Blood* in *3 by Flannery O'Connor* (New York: Signet, 1983).

80. Ross Labrie [*The Catholic Imagination in American Literature* (Columbia: University of Missouri Press, 1997) 220–21] describes O'Connor's conception of free will as it applies to Hazel, who struggles to reconcile divine will with his will and the wills of others.

81. O'Connor, *Wise Blood*, 2.

82. Flannery O'Connor, "The Displaced Person," in *Flannery O'Connor, The Complete Stories* (New York: Noonday, 1971) 194–235.

83. Ibid., 234.

84. Labrie, *The Catholic Imagination*, 16.

85. O'Connor, "The Displaced Person," 231.

maintains, want to see, even if they struggle to do so. With honesty she acknowledges the struggles many people have in trying to believe and practice their faith.

O'Connor not only treated the complexity of faith, she painted striking portraits of evil. Professing to adhere to Christian teaching about the dual nature of human persons marked by grace and sin, she writes, "I believe that the basic experience of everyone is the experience of human limitation."[86] Her characters are stark symbols of limitation. Characters that reminded readers of their limits were important to O'Connor, for she believed it is because "we are afflicted with the doctrine of the perfectibility of human nature by its own efforts that the vision of the freak in fiction is so disturbing. The freak in modern fiction keeps us from forgetting that we share in his state."[87] O'Connor's use of the grotesque helps readers see what might be lacking in their lives and opens them to the possibility of grace.[88]

In contrast, Christian theology centering on family can often fall into the language of perfectibility. In John Paul II's discussion of the family as domestic church, for instance, he writes, "the Christian family has a special vocation to witness to the paschal covenant of Christ by constantly radiating the joy of love and the certainty of the hope for which it must give account."[89] The language of calling, vocation, and mission animates theological writings about families and seems to ask of them unanimity, certainty, and constancy that are often in short supply in the real world.

O'Connor's fiction does not deny the high vocation of families, but it recalls another piece of Christian understanding of human beings—their failures in joy, hope, and love, their experience of being insufficient in themselves. In "The Displaced Person," Mrs. McKinley misunderstands herself as financially rather than spiritually poor and fails to recognize her true needs.[90] In contrast, a priest and Mr. Guizac are both humble and content to do what they can in imperfect situations. Reading O'Connor's stories helps us recognize human limitation, including the limits of any one family or community.

---

86. Flannery O'Connor, "The Teaching of Literature," in *Mystery and Manners: Occasional Prose* (ed. Sally and Robert Fitzgerald; New York: Noonday, 1969) 131.

87. Ibid., 133.

88. Granville Hicks wrote that O'Connor used extreme characters to portray reality: "In these times the most reliable path to reality, to the kind of reality that seems to her important, is by way of the grotesque." Quoted in Rosemary M. Magee, *Conversations with Flannery O'Connor* (Jackson: University Press of Mississippi, 1987) 84.

89. John Paul II, *Familiaris consortio*, no. 2.

90. O'Connor, "The Displaced Person," 217, 221.

The recognition of finitude, so evident in O'Connor's fiction, should affect the way Christians think about families. O'Connor offers a reminder of how hard it is for human beings to see their own weakness. Much of contemporary Christian theology on marriage suffers from a failure to take the reality of human imperfection as seriously as O'Connor did. Its optimistic portrayal of married life seems alien to the reality of most. This optimism stems from good intentions. Contrary to earlier theologies of marriage, contemporary theology confidently attests that the married state of life is an excellent way to live out a Christian vocation. Thankfully, we have moved beyond earlier suspicions that sexual passion and family care must be distractions from the spiritual life. The aim has been to explore the spiritual and moral meaning of sacramental marriage, to describe how grace is present not only in the juridical bond of marriage but in the lives of married people and their children, and to call Christians to live into their vocation. However, though recognition of the grace and calling is important, overly idealistic visions of spousal love and family mission can inadvertently obscure the reality of human finitude.

Theologians in the post-Vatican II generation tend to be more conscious of the difficulties of achieving perfect union.[91] Richard Gaillardetz's consciousness of human finitude pushes him to put less emphasis on the actions of married men and women and more emphasis on God's abiding presence. He reminds Christian spouses that, "their communion with each other is, at the same time, communion with God . . . the ground and source of our existence who sustains us and abides in us."[92] Gaillardetz does not revert to an earlier view of marriage that fails to recognize the need for the work of love, but he does recognize that husbands and wives do not make grace present on their own, and he knows that God is not only present when they love each other well. Rather, "God is [also] found in the 'between' of the relationship of husband and wife," in the solitude and pain, in the waiting through the wintry seasons of a marriage, in the "sense of absence, longing, and the embrace of the limits of the relationship."[93] Christians who have passed through these seasons

---

91. In his recent survey of contemporary Catholic theology on marriage, Charles E. Curran notes that post-Vatican II moral theology was rooted in the theological contributions of the Council (the importance of conscience and an optimism about the goodness of life in the modern world and marriage in particular), while the newest theology draws more from the experience of married life, which is more mixed. See Curran, *Catholic Moral Theology in the United States: A History* (Washington, DC: Georgetown University Press, 2008) 214–16.

92. Richard R. Gaillardetz, *A Daring Promise: A Spirituality of Christian Marriage* (New York: Crossroad, 2002) 43.

93. Ibid., 44 and 69, respectively.

can know that God is present, even when they fail to live up to the potential of their marriage vows.

The key point here is that not by their efforts alone but in "faithful endurance . . . [spouses] will discover their marriage as grace."[94] This is hard to recognize, but in the best of contemporary theology, there is an insistence that despite our flawed efforts, God remains steadfast, pouring out love. As David Matzko McCarthy puts it, "If marriage in the church is a grace, then marriage and family life will be sustained despite our ambiguous choices and our lack of interpersonal expertise."[95] During the down times of marriage, spouses may make a conscious choice to rely on the covenant they have made. Even if they know they will not leave their spouse, working on their problems is not always possible. So they keep going, trusting that the marriage will pull them through, and very often, it does.[96] According to McCarthy marriage is "structured to accommodate dysfunction."[97] It is allows for grace and redemption, despite sin and suffering, despite imperfect faith and practice.

The best of Christian theology of marriage does not assume perfect love or faith. Rather, this theology sees God working in and through limited human beings. Although the tradition can be justly criticized for minimizing the role of sin and finitude, most lay theologians do give some attention to the reality of married life that includes light and darkness, steadfast love and failure to love. Far less attention is given to the 40 percent of couples with mixed faith marriages or to the many more who struggle with faith or its expression. A theology that hopes to speak to a broad audience will have to reckon more closely with O'Connor, who took the messy reality of grace and sin, faith and unbelief, as her starting point and still managed to find grace and point the way—however bleakly—toward something better.

Most of O'Connor's stories concern the seemingly mundane issue of how family members treat one another. Mrs. Turpin of "Revelation" fails to appreciate her daughter, Sheppard of "The Lame Shall Enter First" ignores his own son's grief over the loss of his mother, and the parents in "A Good Man Is Hard to Find" seem blissfully unconnected to their children (which is why the grandmother is left to instruct them in manners and morals). Often O'Connor's stories give us parents shocked into recognition of their misunderstanding and neglect through the intervention of

---

94. David Matzko McCarthy, *Sex and Love in the Home* (London: SCM, 2004) 204.

95. Ibid., 206.

96. Linda Waite's research shows that even couples that are most dissatisfied tend to get through difficult times and emerge satisfied, if they are willing to maintain their commitments. See Linda J. Waite and Maggie Gallagher, *The Case for Marriage* (New York: Broadway, 2000) 148–49.

97. McCarthy, *Sex and Love in the Home*, 274.

a stranger. Sometimes there are heartbreaking moments of self-knowledge that lead to change. Sally Fitzgerald once said that O'Connor was concerned with original sin, and "if she stuck with family relationships and situations as a ground, it was because she wrote of obscure, 'unimportant,' people, and some kind of family community is where most of us live, and where even our cosmic dramas are enacted and our souls won or lost."[98] Families, Fitzgerald suggests, are the loci of most people's significant spiritual struggles, even when, perhaps especially when, their members are not of one mind or practice.

What ought Christians take from O'Connor? One of O'Connor's last and best stories provides a helpful compass. In "Parker's Back," an interracial married couple remain faithful to each other but share little warmth or understanding. Parker is distinguished mainly by the tattoos that cover most of his body, except for his back. His wife is notable for her violently strong faith, which Parker does not share. A near-fatal tractor accident shakes Parker up and sends him back to a tattoo artist to ask for a large portrait of Christ on his back. When he arrives home, he expects his wife to understand the change that has come over him, but she does not recognize the face on his back. "Don't you know who it is?' he cries. "It ain't anybody I know," she says.[99] And failing to recognize the image of Christ in her husband, she beats him, leaving red welts on his back, hardening her heart as he cries.[100] Grace goes unrecognized in her partner and the unity that marriage is supposed to embody is destroyed in their estrangement. Violence flows directly out of misperception, revealing distance between husband and wife, black and white, faith and practice.

The fiction of Flannery O'Connor offers much wisdom for a contemporary theology of the family. In her vivid, strange stories, O'Connor portrays the struggle of faith, the depth of human finitude, and the moral significance of everyday life in families where habits of being are cultivated over time. Theology often offers a vision of how things ought to be and speaks with compassion about exceptions to the rules. O'Connor pushes us to go further. Her stories draw us to limitation and call out, like Parker does, "Look at it! Don't just say that! *Look* at it!" Instead of responding, like Parker's wife, "I done looked," we may need to spend more time with imperfect

---

98. Sally Fitzgerald, "Introduction," *3 by Flannery O'Connor*, xxiii.

99. O'Connor, "Parker's Back," in *O'Connor, The Complete Stories*, 529.

100. Farrell O'Gorman, *Peculiar Crossroads: Flannery O'Connor, Walker Percy, and Catholic Vision in Postwar Southern Fiction* (Baton Rouge: Louisiana State University Press, 2004). O'Gorman notes that the woman "cannot see the presence of God in the flesh of her own husband," 104.

families, pondering how they can expand our understanding of what it means to be Christian and help us focus not on purity but on possibility.[101]

Conclusion: Families as Schools of Discipleship

The high theology of the Genesis creation narratives and the household codes has led Christian theologians throughout the history of the tradition to speak eloquently about holy families headed by like-minded parents with obedient children and about the radical discipleship embodied by missionary couples who give up the distractions of ordinary family life to spread the gospel. Much of contemporary Christian theology builds upon one of these models, which may be very appropriate for families with like-minded people of faith. However, in view of the diversity that exists within families where most Christians reside, it is no longer clear that these models are adequate.

It may be necessary to think more about Paul's question, "How do you know, wife, if you will save your husband; or how do you know husband, whether you will save your wife?" (1 Cor 7:16). Unlike Paul, I am not at all sure that all the saving will be done by believers, since they too struggle and are sometimes graced by the loving compassion of their unbelieving partners, but I think Paul's question is important—and not just for adults. Children, too, deserve more from us. Parents are obligated to pass on their faith, yet children have wills and ideas of their own. There are no guarantees of parental holiness or obedient children, as the history of Christianity attests.

Perhaps Christians who find themselves in interfaith families of some sort can think about their church as their first family in faith and cultivate a vision of their family as a school of discipleship where they work out their salvation even though—and maybe even precisely because—others are involved in struggles of a different kind. Instead of attempting shared mission, perhaps it would be more realistic to simply be with "those you are stuck with" (Stanley Hauerwas's famous definition of family), respect where each person is, ask not for total agreement or obedience but for companionship on the way, and cultivate appreciation for God's presence in everyone all the time. Some families may be capable of more explicit shared mission, but for the many who are not as capable this limited "schooling" in love may be more appropriate.

---

101. O'Connor, "Parker's Back," 529.

My hope is that both families of like-minded believers and the more mixed families in which many of us live can still find in the Christian tradition an inspiring vision of commitment, communion, and service to others. The tradition has something beautiful and distinctive to offer, especially if we can acknowledge and work through the messiness of families as they really are. However strong or weak in faith we are, we need to share each other's burdens and help each other live in the imperfection of this world, where "God has called you to peace" (1 Cor 7:15).

RESPONSE TO HANLON RUBIO

Michelle Clifton-Soderstrom

If I were to offer a second title for Julie Hanlon Rubio's paper, it would be "Reconcilable Differences: Accompaniment, Companionship, and Staying with the One You're Stuck With." Her conclusions are rooted in the hope that in spite of very fundamental differences in the religiosity of human beings, God is at work everywhere, in all things, and at all times. In my response to her fine work I take up two lines of reflection. First, I underscore the importance of the virtue ethic that is operative in her work because it offers a framework for thinking through the impasse of shared mission for the interreligious couple. Second, I urge Hanlon Rubio to develop a Trinitarian dimension to her work as it has potential to reveal the way God is at work in shared missions that transcend the boundaries of religious differences.

Hanlon Rubio begins with the question of how the hard sayings about family in Scripture function for families today, and in particular for interreligious and interfaith marriages. She argues that the kind of radical reprioritization underlying the sayings may be overly idealistic and even impossible to achieve in a climate of increasing interreligiosity in families. She notes that the call to discipleship has the potential not only to destabilize marriages but also one's faith. Such images as the Holy Family, the perfect celibacy of Paul, and the criteria marking love of Christ—hating father, mother, wife and even self—are extraordinary and need rethinking for an ethic of marriage and family.

Any marriage taken seriously requires a radical reprioritization if it is to flourish and even function. The radical reprioritization that Hanlon Rubio shies away from is constituted by a sense of shared mission that is based on discipleship as primary allegiance to Christ and supported by the couple's relative accord in doctrine, ethos, and religious practices. While rethinking this ideal may be necessary, I do believe a radical reprioritization centered on cultivating virtues, as opposed to shared doctrine or religious ethos, has potential for transcending the boundaries of particular religious contexts and hence might serve as a shared mission for the interreligious marriage.

Michelle Clifton-Soderstrom   *Response To Hanlon Rubio*

According to Hanlon Rubio the problem with marriage is "the idolatry of family that can stand in the way of the broader mission that is integral to discipleship." She explores this idolatry in more detail in her book *Family Ethics*,[1] but in short, she believes a *telos* of marriage is the cultivation of the virtues of love and faithfulness through the practice of an open home—one that chooses sustainability over consumption, hospitality over privacy, and outwardness over insularity. Woven throughout Hanlon Rubio's work is a preference for the mundane over the extraordinary. In the repetition of the daily, persons have time and space to habituate themselves toward the excellences of faith and love.

The ordinary marriage habituated in ways that cultivate excellence is no small thing when one considers the overall work of God in creation. At work in Hanlon Rubio's approach is the revelation of God in and through creation, or natural theology. Natural revelation is the idea that all of creation in some way references God. The psalmists attest to creation proclaiming the splendor of God, Augustine's theology of signs enumerates all of the ways the world refers to the Supreme Good, Bonaventure's ascent iterates vestiges of God as he shines his light, and the functional view of the *imago dei* presumes that humans refer to their maker. Christologically speaking, the *imago dei* is evoked through seeing the face of Christ in another and hence is other-oriented.

The assumption behind the ability to find or see God outside of God's revelation in Scripture is an openness to the transcendent—to recognize patterns of grace with a posture of gratitude. Bonaventure is particularly helpful in this pursuit. In "The Journey of the Mind to God"[2] he claims that humans are illuminated when they consider the potential excellence of things and the habitual course of things, for these are vestiges of the Creator. The potential excellence of marriage is love and faith. The habitual course is those daily habits that bring love and faith about by an openness not only to the marriage itself but to the greater patterns of grace that sustain it.

Hanlon Rubio's description of the "habitual course" of marriage is grounded in everyday life—habits that are cultivated slowly over time, often boring, not spectacular, ordinary, etc. However the virtues, or "potential excellence" of good habits, are anything but mundane and ordinary. In other words, the morality may be ordinary, but faith and love are extraordinary. They are cause for shared mission, for

---

1. Julie Hanlon Rubio, *Family Ethics: Practices for Christians* (Washington, DC: Georgetown University Press: 2010).

2. St. Bonaventure, *The Journey of the Mind to God* (ed. Stephen F. Brown; Cambridge: Hackett, 1993).

sustaining life together, and even a structure for the unconventional discipleship of the interfaith pair. Hanlon Rubio's work provides a needed articulation of how a loving and faithful marriage might be a witness to a loving and faithful God, in spite of the very real pain of religious differences.

Next, the flip side of what Hanlon Rubio calls the difficult sayings is the contrast, namely that familial love is an important biblical analogy for God's love for humanity. She makes a strong case for this possibility in interreligious marriages, while at the same time reminding us not to overlook the pain of "unity in difference" that emerges from the struggles that accompany the path of religious differences. Hanlon Rubio might strengthen her argument by developing an explicitly Trinitarian theology of God at work in and through struggles surrounding diversity because differentiation in unity defines the very nature of God. It also delineates grace at work in the differences, both honoring differentiation while sustaining unity.

As it stands, Hanlon Rubio wonderfully unpacks the power of grace in the imperfect through her examination of Flannery O'Connor. O'Connor's stories force readers to do two complementary things. On the one hand, readers are invited to take a step back and examine the universal phenomenon of faith itself. On the other, readers are drawn into utter creatureliness, including the muck and repetition of daily life, and it is not pretty. It involves darkness, depravity, and turpitude.

Central to O'Connor's short stories is the idea that human beings come to know themselves in and through the other. O'Connor's antiheros require other, often contemptuous, characters for transformation. Readers wrestle with how the limitations, the imperfections, and, perhaps most importantly, the stranger offer "the heartbreaking moments of self-knowledge that lead to change."

Hanlon-Rubio sides with O'Connor in the belief (or hope) that in however dissolute a manner, what it means to be human is to be searching, to be creaturely, to have capacity for faith, and for finding patterns of grace. A theology of the Trinity that draws human beings more deeply into the "unity in difference" underlies the possibility for accompaniment in Hanlon Rubio's paper. Similar to the communion of the Godhead itself, humans also come to know themselves in and through another, sometimes radically different other. This process is one that invites a deeper sense of communion if one is open to transformation. With respect to interreligious marriages, the guiding ethic is one of searching, a sense of creatureliness, and of capacity for a faith whose content is love, plain and simple.

Many references to the incorporating activity of God and its human parallels exist within Hanlon Rubio's own tradition of Catholic social teaching. For example, the United States and Mexican Bishops wrote a letter called "Strangers No Longer."[3] The pastoral challenges include the call toward conversion, toward communion, and toward solidarity. Specifically, this means to see the face of Christ in the stranger, to practice hospitality, and to work for the participation of all. While this is a letter about migration, the challenges of conversion, communion, and solidarity offer one way through the dilemma that Hanlon-Rubio's paper raises in that these three specific habits allow room *both* for shared mission and for accompaniment.

Some may question whether this trifold call is enough to ground the mission of Christian discipleship. However, if at the heart of the Christian faith is the triune God at work reconciling the world to himself, then an openness to conversation toward the ends of communion and solidarity must in some way be participating in the work of the triune God. This, it seems, is what Hanlon Rubio means by accompaniment and companionship in the face of otherness.

Hanlon Rubio's work is full of reconcilable differences and radical reprioritizations. Shared mission might be possible, assuming that the marriage patterns itself by an openness to grace and to the potential excellences of marriage and habits that support them. In the language of the Christian faith, the Holy Spirit precedes, accompanies, and follows the work of God in Christ. Maybe religiously diverse families leave the extraordinary to the work of the Triune God and instead strive for the more mundane, the creaturely work of accompaniment, companionship, and staying with those you are stuck with.

---

3. United States Conference of Catholic Bishops, Inc. and Conferencia del Episcopado Mexicano, *Strangers No Longer: Together on the Journey of Hope* (Washington, DC: USCCB Publishing, 2003).

TYRANNY, AUTHORITY, SERVICE: LEADERSHIP AND HEADSHIP IN THE NEW TESTAMENT

Lynn H. Cohick

In the popular 2002 movie *My Big Fat Greek Wedding* several women are sitting at a restaurant table planning ways to promote a daughter's educational opportunities. The fear is that the father will veto their ideas. Then the mother reminds the group that while the husband is the head (of the house), the woman is the neck, and she can turn the head any way she wants. This clever line with its ring of truth pokes fun at the dynamics of contemporary marriage. This essay hopes to explore the metaphor of "head" as it is used by the Apostle Paul in his discussion about marriage in the letter to the Ephesians.[1] I will argue that Paul's use of the metaphor "head" in Ephesians is best understood as emphasizing responsibility and a service-focused relationship rather than indicating a power or authority differential. The "head" metaphor, interpreted in its social and rhetorical context, reveals a principle of reciprocity between humans as they seek to model Christ's love to one another. I argue that in Ephesians, there is no "principle of headship," only the metaphor of head.

Custom and the Laws of Nature

Humans are cultural creatures; much as a fish does not know it is wet, so too we often assume that how we do things in our culture must be based on simple common sense, observable truths, and rightly followed traditions. We normalize custom and assume that cultural differences or social conventions are actually laws of nature. For example, in the West the possibility of miracles seems remote at best; however, in many other places in the world Christians embrace the concept of miracles. Craig Keener has recently argued that the Western philosophical default position is indebted to the Scottish philosopher David Hume (d. 1776), who postulated non-supernaturalism, rendering miracles impossible. Keener notes, "Plausibility structures—what intuitively strikes us as rational—are culturally determined."[2] And in

---

1. For a defense of Ephesians as Pauline, please see Lynn Cohick, *Ephesians: New Covenant Commentary* (Eugene, OR: Cascade, 2010). This paper will assume the traditional authorship in part to read Ephesians canonically with the church.

2. Craig Keener, *Miracles* (2 vols.; Grand Rapids: Baker Academic, 2011) 1:211.

some cases, cultural assumptions about what seems natural might instead cover over sin. As another example, Hume (and later Immanuel Kant) took as self-evident the secondary, inferior capacities of Africans.[3]

In the first century CE Aristotle's vision of social order prevailed, including his assessment of male and female. He concluded that the female was not simply opposite the male, but was the negation of the male.[4] Aristotle viewed the free person and the slave likewise as inherently and essentially distinct beings. Society was highly stratified and quite class-conscious. These values were supported by observations and were seen as natural or normal.[5] In his *Politics* (written ca. 335 BCE) he makes several points. First, he notes that when talking about the city, one must begin with marriage, the union of the natural ruler and the natural ruled/subject. Second, when a slave is added to this unit, you have a family or house. This complex set of relationships is natural in its hierarchy because man is a political animal by nature.[6] As Dan Browning notes, Aristotle spoke "about the tyrannical rule of master over slave, the aristocratic rule of husband over wife, and the monarchical rule of father over children."[7] In his *Nicomachean Ethics* 8.10, Aristotle notes that, "the association of a father with his sons bears the form of monarchy, since the father cares for his children . . . . Tyrannical too is the rule of master over slaves; for it is the advantage of the master that is brought about in it . . . . The association of man and wife seems to be aristocratic; for the man rules in accordance with his worth."[8] Alexander the Great, Aristotle's pupil, spread this teaching throughout his empire, and it lived on

---

3. Ibid., 1:225. Kant noted that, "by nature [the Black person had] no feeling that rises above the trifling" and had inferior intellect. See his *Observations on the Feeling of the Beautiful and the Sublime* (Berkeley, University of California Press, 1960) 110. See also Hume, *Works* 3:252, as cited by Keener.

4. See Prudence Allen, *The Concept of Woman: The Aristotelian Revolution, 750 B.C.–A.D. 1250* (Grand Rapids: Eerdmans, 1985) 83–126.

5. For a discussion of Aristotle's views, see Lynn Cohick, *Women in the World of the Earliest Christians: Illuminating Ancient Ways of Life* (Grand Rapids: Baker, 2009) 66–69.

6. Aristotle, *Politics* 1 1253b 1–14 writes "Now it is clear what are the component parts of the state, we have first of all to discuss household management (*oikonomia*), for every state is composed of households. Household management falls into departments corresponding to the parts of which the household in its turn is composed; and the household in its perfect form consists of slaves and freemen. The investigation of everything house begins with its smallest parts, and the primary and smallest parts of the household are *master and slave, husband and wife, father and children*. We ought therefore to examine the proper constitution and character of each of these three relationships, I mean that of mastership, that of marriage and thirdly the progenitive relationship."

7. Don Browning, "The Problem of Men," in *Does Christianity Teach Male Headship? The Equal-Regard Marriage and its Critics* (ed. David Blankenhorn, Don Browning, and Mary Steward Van Leeuwen; Grand Rapids: Eerdmans, 2004) 4. See Aristotle, *Politics* 1:12.

8. Ibid., 5. See Aristotle, *Nicomachean Ethics*, 8.10.

in Stoic thought in imperial Rome. In general, the primacy of the Greek over the barbarian, the man over the woman, and the free over the slave was the organizing principle of society.

There were dissenting voices such as Alcidamus, student of Gorgias, who believed no man was born a slave; that is, nature did not make any man servile to another man. This fit with the general Stoic assumption that slavery was an internal state, and Stoics were basically indifferent to the institution of chattel slavery.[9] Seneca argued that women and men had similar capacities for virtue and wisdom. He wrote to a grieving mother not to be overcome with grief, but to control her passions.[10] Plutarch (46–125 CE) believed that women are capable of showing courage and bravery but also are naturally the weaker partner in the marriage relationship. Plutarch enjoined the husband to lead and the wife to obey.[11]

Jewish authors such as Josephus reflect similar views. He notes that, "the woman, says the law, is in all things inferior to the man. Let her accordingly be submissive, not for her humiliation, but that she may be directed, for the authority has been given by God to the man."[12] Philo of Alexandria shared similar views, "Organized communities are of two sorts, the greater which we call cities and the smaller which we call households.... The government of the greater is assigned to men, under the name of statesmanship, that of the lesser, known as household management, to women."[13]

The question we face as biblical interpreters is how to understand the impact of the early church's social and cultural world as they sought to live out the gospel message. Paul looked beyond the confines of social stratification. His famous line to the Galatians, "there is neither Jew nor Greek, slave nor free, male and female, for you are all one in Christ" (Gal 3:28) summarizes his views nicely. The key is "in Christ." The human disadvantages and "disabilities" that naturally attach to Gentiles, slaves, and women fall away in Christ.

With the first pair, Jew and Gentile, we can see how these categories are transformed "in Christ." Having established in Ephesians the magnificent, wondrous plan of salvation instituted by the Trinity (Eph 1:3–10, 20–23), Paul articulates how that great mystery is effective in people's lives. He declares in Eph 2:14 that two peoples—

---

9. Craige B. Champion, *Cultural Politics in Polybius' Histories* (Berkeley: University of California Press, 2004) 76–77.

10. Seneca, *On Consolation to Marcia*; see Allen, *The Concept of Woman*, 167–72.

11. See Plutarch, *Bravery of Women*, and *Advice to the Bride and Groom*.

12. Josephus, *Against Apion* II.199.

13. Philo, *Special Laws* III.169–71.

Jews and Gentiles—have become one, in Christ. The darkness that had formally characterized Gentiles is in Christ made light (Eph 5:8, "Once you were darkness, but now in the Lord you are light"). And the ones who were nearer to God, the Jews, were made into a temple with Gentiles, a holy temple in the Lord (Eph 2:17–22). What did this look like? It seems that Gentile believers did not follow Sabbath and food laws, but some (at least) of the Jewish believers continued to do so. As Paul cautions in Rom 14:13–20, "Let us therefore no longer pass judgment on one another, but resolve instead never to put a stumbling block or hindrance in the way of another. . . . Do not, for the sake of food, destroy the work of God," (see also 1 Cor 9:19–23). Paul celebrates distinctions of cultures, but he squelches any hierarchy of cultures. Even more, Paul does not allow the God-given practices of Sabbath, food laws, and circumcision to form a hierarchy within the church nor bring about a Gentile ghetto within the church. Paul declares to the "strong" in Corinth, "We are no worse off if we do not eat, and no better off if we do," (1 Cor 8:8). In other words, Gentiles do not need to become Jews to be part of the church. The historical people of God, the Jews, were not privileged in the church, although they had certain natural advantages having grown up knowing the one true God.[14]

The truth of Jew/Gentile parity in terms of salvation and godly living in Christ seems self-evident to us now, two thousand years later. Today, we wrestle with the third pair noted in Gal 3:28, "male and female." In Ephesians most commentators focus on the first pair, "husband and wife," especially the call for wives to submit to their husbands, their "head." I will say more about "head" below, but briefly let me note that our English translations of Eph 5:22 do us a disservice. To best understand Paul's message to husbands and wives, we must go back to Eph 5:18 where Paul commands his readers to be filled with the Spirit. This injunction is elaborated upon in the next several verses with five participial phrases: speaking in songs and hymns, making melody, singing, giving thanks, and submitting to each other out of reverence to Christ. The direction for wives to submit to their husbands in 5:22 is grammatically tied to 5:21. The Greek sentence in 5:22 does not have a verb; it borrows the participle from the preceding sentence that states, "Be subject to (or submit to) one another out of reverence for Christ."

In Eph 5:21 Paul states that being filled with the Spirit involves submitting to one another out of reverence for Christ. The participle (*hypotassomenoi*) is from the verb *hypotassō*, a verb found also in Eph 1:22, which states that God has put all things under or submitted all things under Christ's feet (see also 1 Cor 15:27 and

---

14. See for example the Jerusalem Council's discussion in Acts 15:6–29.

Heb 2:8). The participle in Eph 5:21 might be middle, suggesting that each believer makes the choice to submit to other believers, or it could be passive. In either case the verb presupposes an honor/shame culture that demands that proper respect and honor be given to those in a higher social status. The term implies that one accept the position or place in society in which one finds oneself, be that a subordinate or superordinate. The position shifts based on one's context; for example, a wife is subordinate to her husband or father, but is superordinate to her slave or her child. Often wealth trumped social status. Thus a wealthy freedman or freedwoman might have more social clout than a poor free man or woman.

The question before readers today in interpreting Eph 5:21 is whether Paul enjoins all members of the church to forgo their social status and instead honor the other, especially in a church meeting. Would this approach leave room for leadership by some members? Or is Paul stating that among believers submission should take place in the following ways in the three main household relationships that Paul then describes?[15] If the latter, is Paul codifying the household relationships as organized in his day? I will argue below that Paul undercuts the institutions of patriarchy (male hierarchy over women) and slavery, even as he promotes a leadership style and model of authority that emphasizes slave-like submission to those whom one serves. Thus Paul calls himself a slave to all (1 Cor 9:19) and urges the Galatians through love to serve each other as a slave (Gal 5:13). He has already asked the Ephesians to bear with each other (4:2) and be kind to one another (4:32) and even to think of themselves as members of one another (4:25). When one is "in Christ," the posture must be one of service, which includes submitting one's own way to the betterment of others. Paul explains in Eph 5:1–2 that the Ephesians are to love each other as Christ loved them, without regard to their status as male or female, free or slave. Christ is described here both as loving (*agapan*) the church and as giving himself up for his church, a phrase repeated in 5:25.

Craig Keener makes a compelling case for the backdrop of Eph 5:18–21 as one of contrast to the typical banquets and celebrations of the mystery cults such as those which worshiped Isis and Dionysus.[16] In these cults of Isis and Dionysus drunkenness and debauchery were a matter of course with bawdy songs sung and music played specifically designed to arouse. Paul speaks not only against paganism

---

15. Peter T. O'Brien, *The Letter to the Ephesians* (Pillar New Testament Commentary; Grand Rapids: Eerdmans, 1999) 401–4. See also Harold Hoehner, *Ephesians: An Exegetical Commentary* (Grand Rapids: Baker Academic, 2002) 717.

16. Craig S. Keener, *Paul, Wives and Women: Marriage and Women's Ministry in the Letters of Paul* (Peabody, MA: Hendrickson, 1992) 258–66. See also the e-book by Baker Academic, 2012.

but also addresses the negative portraits of both men and women that these cults espoused. For example, the priests of the Isis cult practiced castration, a severe form of role reversal that appalled Roman sensibilities. Again, the maenads who worshiped Dionysus were associated with sexual immorality; whether such behavior actually occurred is difficult to determine, but perception is reality. David Balch argues similarly for the situation faced by the initial readers of 1 Peter.[17] He argues that Romans viewed the mystery cults and Eastern religions with suspicion in large part because of their inversion of traditional gender behavior, and Peter urges the church to avoid appearing as socially deviant or anti-social in the relationships of wives and slaves to their husbands and owners. Balch rightly notes that Romans believed wives were especially susceptible to foreign religious influence.[18] In Peter's churches pagan wives were converting to Christianity without, apparently, their husband's approval. In this the church could take on the appearance of being just another Eastern cult or mystery religion. To counter such slander, Peter urged both women and slaves, and everyone in the church to submit to those above them (the emperor [2:13], owners [2:18], and husbands [3:1, 5]).

If Balch is right, then Peter uses the social convention of submission missionally in at least three ways. First, he shows that Christianity is not anarchist; thus believers honor or submit to the emperor, and by extension his emissaries and government officials. Second, he highlights how slaves model the Lord's martyrdom, witnessing to the foundational truth of the cross and suffering within Christian faith. Third, Peter offers that wives' submission actually has the Spirit's power to convert their pagan husbands. Such submission is hardly passive; it is life changing for the husband and calls into question basic tenets of pagan religious and social beliefs.[19]

In the case of Paul, he finds himself between a rock and a hard place. He must navigate between presenting his congregation as just another mystery cult with wild women and effeminate men and responding to the Spirit's call that empowers persons irrespective of gender or social status. Paul attempts this near impossible task by taking advantage of metaphor and by using "head" and "body" in creative ways, as we will see.

The term "head" (*kephalē*) has been the source of recent, robust interpretative disagreement. In the 1980s several Evangelical scholars weighed in on its definition

---

17. David L. Balch, *Let Wives Be Submissive: The Domestic Code in 1 Peter* (Chico, CA: Scholars, 1981) 81–109.

18. Ibid., 66–73.

19. Karen H. Jobes, *1 Peter* (Baker Exegetical Commentary on the New Testament; Grand Rapids: Baker, 2005) 202–10.

and often came to vastly different conclusions. Mickelson and Mickelson cited the monumental Liddell and Scott lexicon, first published in 1843, as including over twenty-five definitional entries for *kephalē*, but none with the meaning of "leader" or "having authority." They argue for the meaning "source," as in "source of life."[20] Gordon Fee, in his commentary on 1 Corinthians, puts forward the claim that "head" is best understood as "source" as in "source of life." He holds that *kephalē* rarely meant "authority" or "chief," and that "the Greek translators of the LXX, who ordinarily used *kephalē* to translate *rō'š* when the physical 'head' was intended, almost never did so when 'ruler' was intended, thus indicating that this metaphorical sense is an exceptional usage and not part of the ordinary range of meanings for the Greek word."[21] While Thiselton in his commentary does not ultimately agree with this interpretation, primarily because it lacks sufficient lexicological basis, he suggests that 1 Cor 11:12, with its claims of woman coming from the man and man coming out of woman, is parallel to Paul's terminology about God and Christ in 1 Cor 8:6. Perhaps Paul hoped his readers would recall this earlier statement and use it as a lens for his discussion in chapter 11.[22] Moreover, Thiselton adds that the ancient world understood that the brain was the "source" of thought, emotions, and will; for example, Seneca writes to Nero that the head is the source of human well-being.[23]

Conversely, Wayne Grudem[24] has argued for the definition of "leader" or "authority over." However, what he demonstrates most clearly in his extensive examination of 2,336 examples of *kephalē* is that about eighty-seven percent of the occurrences refer to a physical head of a body. In five percent of the occurrences *kephalē* carries the metaphorical sense of referring to the whole person, while three percent convey the sense of "top" or "starting point." Only 2.1 percent of the occurrences have the sense of "authority over," and several of these passages are in LXX Judges, which might suggest a particular translation decision on the part of that text's translator.

20. Berkeley Mickelsen and Alvera Mickelsen, "What Does *kephalē* Mean in the New Testament?" in *Women, Authority and the Bible* (ed. Alvera Mickelsen; Downers Grove, IL: InterVarsity, 1986) 97–110, see esp. 98–99 and 105–10.

21. Gordon D. Fee, *The First Epistle to the Corinthians* (New International Commentary on the New Testament; Grand Rapids: Eerdmans, 1987) 502–3.

22. Anthony C. Thiselton, *The First Epistle to the Corinthians* (The New International Greek Testament Commentary; Grand Rapids: Eerdmans, 2000) 820.

23. Ibid., 816–17.

24. Wayne Grudem, "Does *kephalē* ('Head') Mean 'Source' or 'Authority Over' in Greek Literature? A Survey of 2,336 Examples," *Trinity Journal* ns 6:1 (Spring, 1985) 38–59, and "The Meaning of *kephalē* ('Head'): An Evaluation of New Evidence, Real and Alleged," *Journal of the Evangelical Theological Society* 44:1 (2001) 25–65.

A more likely figurative meaning is "honored part" or "prominent." Thiselton's lengthy excursus in his commentary on First Corinthians presents this position quite well, suggesting that "head" is used as a synecdoche. That is, "*heads* [sic] denotes persons or animals (for which the part denotes the whole . . .)."[25] He states that in terms of 1 Cor 11:3, "head" is best understood as preeminent, foremost, and also as "*synecdoche for the whole. The public face is linked with responsibility and representation in the public domain, since head is both the part of a person which is most conspicuous and that by which they are most readily distinguished or recognized.*"[26] In Corinth this means that women used prophetic speech in public worship just as did men. Yet this freedom from social norms that viewed women's speech as immoral or unseemly cannot be used to degrade one's family or one's husband. Thus conventions that signaled modesty, such as appropriate hair styles/covering for women and men, should be followed.

Parenthetically, the ancient commentators on 1 Cor 11:3 were very keen to distinguish the nuances of this "head" metaphor. Its multivalency must be taken into account to avoid a subordinationist Christology. Chrysostom noted that Paul is not using "head" here to mean rule and subjection otherwise he would have chosen master/slave as the human example. "It is a wife (or woman) as free, as equal in honor; and the Son also, though He did become obedient to the Father, it was as the Son of God; it was as God."[27]

In both First Corinthians and in Ephesians one probable reason Paul uses "head" language is that he wants to talk about "body" in both the figurative and literal senses. In 1 Cor 11:2-3 Paul wants to talk about hair, and thus "head" becomes an adroit way to speak both figuratively and literally. Paul follows a similar pattern in the second half of chapter 11 when he uses the term "body" to refer both to the figurative body of Christ, the church, as well as the literal body of Christ that died on the cross. Paul combines these figurative and literal meanings in metaphorical juxtaposition to generate new ways of imagining life in the Spirit, life in Christ.

Interestingly, although everyone at this time spoke of wives submitting to their husbands, almost no other author uses the verb *hypotassō*.[28] The verb root is

---

25. Thiselton, *The First Epistle to the Corinthians*, 812-22.
26. Ibid., 821.
27. Ibid., 819; see Chrysostom, *1 Cor. Hom.* 26:2.
28. Exceptions include Ps.-Callisthenes (ca. 100 BCE), *A Narrative, Remarkable and Really Marvelous, of the Lord of the World, Alexander the King* I.22.19-20; and Plutarch, *Advice to the Bride and Groom* 33 (Moralia 142E).

used thirty-one times in the LXX.²⁹ Most often it refers to humans submitting to God, as in Ps 8:7, which is cited twice in the NT (1 Cor 15:27–8; Heb 2:8). Perhaps the NT uses it because for Paul the marriage relationship's submission pattern was subsumed under the larger umbrella of godly submission between believers of any social status. Said another way, what the society required in terms of wives honoring their husbands was reshaped in Christ to stand as a model for all believers to honor all other believers in Christ. Rather than see the household codes as placing limits on wives or slaves, I suggest that Paul takes advantage of the assumptions of the day with regard to honor and submission to explain godly Christian behavior. In essence, Paul builds on the common understanding that wives are to submit to their husbands and that slaves must obey their masters. He creates a visual image in the minds of his congregation and then throws a curve: this posture is what every believer should have to any other believer because every believer is *in Christ*. If Christ is in each one of them, then each honors Christ when honoring one another. Paul applies this idea in the negative to the Corinthians. He admonishes them that when they dismiss another believer because of their lack of status or wealth, as was the practice at the communion meal in Corinth, then they humiliate believers and show contempt for God's church (1 Cor. 11:22). Paul tackles the hierarchical social world head on—not by denying that honor should be given, but by demanding that *all* individuals in the church be given honor. The vehicle Paul uses is the principle of reciprocity, about which I will say more below. First we will look at the slave/owner pair in the household.

Customs and the Normalizing of Prejudices

Sojourner Truth, in an address to a Women's convention, December 1851, spoke these powerful words:

> That man over there says that women need to be helped into carriages, and lifted over ditches, and to have the best place everywhere. Nobody ever helps me into carriages, or over mud-puddles, or gives me any best place! And ain't I a woman? Look at me! Look at my arm! I have ploughed and planted, and gathered into barns, and no man could head me! And ain't I a woman? I could work as much and eat as much as a man— when I could get it— and bear the lash as well! And ain't I a woman? I have borne thirteen children, and seen most all sold off to slavery, and when I cried out with my mother's grief, none but Jesus heard me! And ain't I a woman? . . . Then that little man in black there, he says women can't have

---

29. Balch, *Let Wives Be Submissive*, 98.

as much rights as men, "cause Christ wasn't a woman"! Where did your Christ come from? Where did your Christ come from? From God and a woman! Man had nothing to do with Him.[30]

I believe that our country's experience with slavery and its underlying racism can provide helpful lessons for our current struggles in the debate over women's leadership in the church and the discussion about the proper conception of marriage. Many of our current social structures are rooted in sexism, which serves to normalize unbiblical attitudes and behaviors.

In Eph 5:22–6:9, Paul presents the family as it was known in his day. This section of Scripture is often identified as the household codes. Note that spouses, parents and children, and owners and slaves make up the three pairs in the average household. Every time Paul mentions marriage, he also refers to slavery, even in 1 Cor 7. That fact highlights his social reality; slavery was part and parcel of anyone's conception of family. This does not mean that every family had slaves, even as some families were without a parent or were childless, but the guiding assumption of his day concerning the makeup of family was that it would include slaves. The structure institutionalized authority legally, such that slaves, women, and children could not represent themselves in court and had different legal rights than adult, free males. Only the latter had full authority over their person.

In Eph 6:5–9 Paul speaks about real slaves, those men and women (and children) who are owned by other men *and women*. In this chapter Paul speaks of slave owners having a Master as well, namely God who shows no partiality. Thus Paul places owners, metaphorically speaking, in the role of slaves.

Given that slavery is illegal in this country, the American church has a tendency either to romanticize the slave metaphor or to quickly redefine the reality of slavery as roughly equivalent to one's employment. Both interpretive options run aground on the shoals of self-determinism. When we sentimentalize the slave metaphor, we retain in our imagination and heart a sense of "veto power" over God's orders. When we circumscribe slavery as employment, we ignore the reality that slaves were owned twenty-four-seven, and they were owned sexually. They lacked the freedom to say "no" and the right to relocate.

There is a second, insidious problem as we struggle to understand slavery as metaphor and as social reality. We skip over the issues that made slavery acceptable in the ancient world and ignore the important lesson of our own history about slavery. In a single word the issue was racism. Although the ancient world did not have

---

30. Available at http://www.nps.gov/wori/historyculture/sojourner-truth.htm

racism of color underpinning the institution of slavery, prejudices and stereotypes rooted in ethnicity abounded—especially Roman or Greek over against everyone else. In the more recent United States context, a conversation about the institution of slavery became a way to deflect discussion of the deeper issue—racism.[31] Those who supported slavery never imagined that a black man or woman would purchase a white person. Slavery made sense because the underlying racism suggested that blacks "naturally" fit the role of slaves. Hold onto this thought—that what seems natural might instead cover over sin—because we will return to the idea.

Metaphor and Meaning

Metaphors are figures of speech or verbal constructions; they are a type of analogy. G. K. Chesterton wrote:

> The essential point is that somebody must be at work adding new symbols and new circumlocutions to a language. *All slang is metaphor, and all metaphor is poetry.* If we paused for a moment to examine the cheapest cant phrases that pass our lips every day, we should find that they were as rich and suggestive as so many sonnets. To take a single instance: we speak of a man in English social relations "breaking the ice." If this were expanded into a sonnet, we should have before us a dark and sublime picture of an ocean of everlasting ice, the sombre and baffling mirror of the Northern nature, over which men walked and danced and skated easily, but under which the living waters roared and toiled fathoms below.[32]

Metaphors have the tendency to reify and become symbols having one direct meaning. Instead, they should instead create in our minds and souls visions of distant horizons, echoes of places not yet visited, desires that cannot be captured in words. Carolyn Osiek explains, "An overly literal interpretation of any biblical text out of context can lead to an impoverishment of symbols . . . . When a symbol or metaphor becomes fixed and no longer points beyond itself, it loses its power to reveal the mystery of God."[33]

---

31. For an excellent discussion of this topic see Mark A. Noll, *The Civil War as a Theological Crisis* (Chapel Hill: University of North Carolina Press, 2006).

32. G. K. Chesterton, *The Defendant*. Available at http://www.gutenberg.org/files/12245/12245-h/12245-h.htm#A_DEFENCE_OF_SLANG.

33. Carolyn Osiek, "Did Early Christians Teach, or Merely Assume, Male Headship?" in *Does Christianity Teach Male Headship? The Equal-Regard Marriage and its Critics* (ed. David Blankenhorn, Don Browning, and Mary Steward Van Leeuwen; Grand Rapids: Eerdmans, 2004) 23–27, 27.

Paul writes in metaphor using the terms "head" and "body" several times in Ephesians, at first to describe Christ and the church (1:22; 4:15–17), and then to describe the husband and the wife. He will speak of a literal fleshly human body as well in Eph 5:28–31. Paul also uses "head" metaphorically and literally in 1 Cor 11:2–16 when speaking about specific practices related to male and female hair lengths and styles. To fully comprehend what Paul is doing in Eph 5:22–24, we must appreciate the communicative value of metaphor.

Before going further, we should understand what a metaphor is not. A metaphor is not something already known by the reader. It is not a fixed symbol, it is not a trick with words that can be dismissed as mere icing on a cake, and it is not a fancy or elitist way of communicating. Most importantly, a metaphor is not simply an alternative way of saying something that could just as easily be expressed literally. Instead, a metaphor is a language tool used to persuade or enlighten, a constituent part of the author's argument that seeks to demonstrate a new, novel, and creative perspective. The metaphor's power and meaning are attained by combining two different ideas, and it is their interaction and juxtaposition that creates the meaning.

In the September 2012 issue of *Christianity Today* James K. A. Smith wrote of the power of analogy, "Analogies have persuasive power, a suggestive force that operates on an almost unconscious level."[34] He cited two examples of analogy's capacity to create an emotional, cognitive, and imaginative image. Smith said that if he identifies American troops as "crusaders," the United States listener feels a negative tension, thinks about imperial atrocities, and creates an almost entirely negative picture. Smith cited as a second example identifying as a "prophet" or "martyr" someone who sides with one's own position. Thus to agree with the position makes one brilliant, prescient, and heroic.

In the Ephesian passage, Paul wants the reader to think differently about husband and wife and about church and Christ. Had Paul wanted to emphasize the husband's leadership in the family, he could have stated literally that the husband was the leader (*archōn*) of the wife. Instead, he pushes the Ephesians to think more organically and synthetically about their new reality as the body of Christ. Thus Paul pulled together two images, "head" and "body," and four concrete concepts: wife, husband, Christ, church, and invited the Ephesians to consider the latter four through the jarring juxtaposition of the former two.[35]

---

34. James K. A. Smith, "What Galileo's Telescope Can't See," *Christianity Today* (September 2012) 64.

35. Gregory W. Dawes (*The Body in Question: Metaphor and Meaning in the Interpretation of Ephesians 5:21-33* [Leiden: Brill, 1998] 26–40) traces the development of recent rhetorical thought,

Hermeneutics and the Principle of Reciprocity

Metaphors using "head" and "body" invite us to think creatively and expansively about life in the family and in the church. One hermeneutic that allows for such expansive reading is labeled by William Webb as the "redemptive movement" hermeneutic. He distinguishes his method from a static approach that "while [it] carefully measures the isolated words of the text in order to find suitable equivalents in the new setting, it fails to breathe into the new setting a measure of the empowering life force that made the text redemptive in its own day."[36] The redemptive movement approach suggests that within the biblical text one can discern a push or momentum generated by a particular teaching that grows and develops in the on-going life of the church. The classic example is the overturning of the institution of slavery—hinted at by the NT authors, but not fully realized within the church until centuries after the siren was sounded. I suggest that a similar alarm rings in our passage as it relates to the institution of marriage and the first century social patriarchy that supported the typical view of proper roles within that relationship. Paul set in motion an exegetical directive moving towards full functional parity between husbands and wives and between men and women generally.

With that far-reaching goal in mind, Paul employs the principle of reciprocity as exemplified in two statements. First, Paul states that a wife's body should be viewed by her husband as his own body, and second, that the two are one flesh. Added together these points suggest that a wife should view her husband's body as her own body. In fact, Paul connects these dots in 1 Cor 7:3-4. Here he notes that a husband does not have control of his own body, but his wife does. Paul's specific focus in 1 Cor 7:3-4 is sexual relations, an aspect of life that was generally viewed to be the exclusive domain of male prerogative. To give wives the authority (*exousia*) over their husband's decisions about whether or not to have marital relations was without precedent at this time. By giving the wife mutual authority in this area, Paul implies that all other areas of the marriage would be likewise governed in the same manner.

In Eph 5:21-24 the overarching point is one of distinction between believers in the church and between husband and wife, as a way to think about the distinctions between believers and Christ, who is the Savior of his body, the church. These social

---

highlighting I. A. Richards, *Philosophy of Rhetoric* (New York: Oxford University Press, 1936); and Max Black, *Models and Metaphors: Studies in Language and Philosophy* (Ithaca, NY: Cornell University Press, 1962), which stress the interplay between the terms used non-literally (focus) and those used literally (frame).

36. William J. Webb, *Slaves, Women and Homosexuals: Exploring the Hermeneutics of Cultural Analysis* (Downers Grove, IL: InterVarsity, 2001) 34, see also 186-88.

distinctions between people allow for both honor and submission to take place. The church honors Christ in its submission to its Savior, the wife honors her husband in her submission to him, the slave honors his or her (male or female) owner by submitting (Eph 5:24, 6:7), and all believers honor the emperor or monarch by submitting to him or, less frequently, her (1 Pet 2:13–17). Even as American believers do not see in 1 Peter a command to maintain a monarchial form of government and no longer adhere to the social structure that demanded a socially stratified culture such that honor could be given to those higher on the social ladder (slaves to owners), so too we need not support a gendered hierarchical system that assumes wives submit to husbands, based on inherent social inferiority.

Notice in Eph 5:25–33 that unity, not distinction, takes center stage. Moreover, the term "body" becomes dominant. It is used in a literal sense to speak about the conjugal relationship within marriage and in a figurative sense reflecting the relationship between members of the community of believers. The reciprocity experienced as each believer submits to the other (5:21) is found in a similar way among marriage partners who love each other as their own flesh/body (5:31–32). Paul links the mysterious oneness of marriage with the imponderable oneness that characterizes Christ and his church.

Is it possible, however, that Paul's *historical* context as described above is mitigated both by the *timeless* context of the topic, marriage, and by Paul's quotation of Gen 2:24? It is true that marriage (generally speaking) is a universal and global institution. Christians affirm that this social institution was established by God; indeed, some call marriage a sacrament. However, embracing these two truths does not give us immediate access into *how* Paul interpreted Gen 2:24, and we should be wary of anyone who says that God's word is self-evident. A quick glance at history demonstrates that "common sense" is often overturned by science, shown to harbor prejudice, or simply reflects one's cultural assumptions.

A clarifying example is evident in Sojourner Truth's implicitly referring to the code of chivalry, where the woman is delicate and without strength. One of my first and lasting images of Kenya, where my husband and I and our two children lived for three years, is of two young men and two young women walking along the grassy edge of a highway. The young men were muscular, striding along swinging their arms and clearly aware that females were present. By contrast, the two women hunched along under heavy loads of bundled firewood. My husband would have been mortified to walk beside me while I labored under such a load. But in Kenya, there is no cultural chivalry, and the views of proper behavior of men and women are markedly different from my own. My immediate point is to note that chivalry is not "common sense" or even "biblical," although I much prefer it when it comes to the task of collecting firewood! Therefore, we should not assume that Paul's quotation of Scripture makes its meaning more obvious.

In the context of Eph 5:22–33 Paul's quotation of Gen 2:24 serves to emphasize the unity that marriage brings, as he goes on to state, "This is a profound mystery—but I'm talking about Christ and the church" (5:32). That is, directly before the quotation of Gen 2:24, Paul stresses that we are members of Christ's body (5:30). The unity of the married couple, mysteriously created by God's decree in Gen 2:24, stands as an analogy for the unity of Christ and his church.

The central focus then of this passage and the remaining verses of Paul's revised household codes (Eph 6:1–9) is to use the assumptions of social and gender hierarchy firmly embedded in his culture to do two things: first, to explain more carefully the servant nature of Christian discipleship and, second, to highlight the mysterious new creation that is Christ's body, the church. However, Paul thoroughly undermines the social assumptions that placed men and women in hierarchical order and reinforced slavery (and by extension patronage). By addressing women and slaves first in this letter, Paul validates their worthiness as suitable examples of all believers, all males and all free people. Peter does something similar when he highlights slaves as modeling the suffering of Christ when they are unjustly beaten for their faithfulness to the gospel (1 Pet 2:18–25). To put this in more modern terms, Paul gives both wives and slaves (male and female) self-agency, thus honor. Moreover, Paul challenges the expansive authority that society gave adult males and slave owners (male and female). While some philosophers such as Musonius Rufus[37] and Plutarch[38] suggested education for women/wives is a good thing, the overall goal of such education is to reinforce the status quo, not to help women enter public life or pursue politics. Paul goes even further by commanding that the *agapē* love which characterizes Christ's servant heart and actions be the defining model for a husband's treatment of his wife, who is legally, culturally, and politically inferior to him, and thus more vulnerable in society.

Conclusion: Tyranny, Authority, and Service

In concluding I would like to look once more at my title, specifically to focus on the terms "tyranny," "authority," and "service." The common experience of government

---

37. Musonius Rufus, *Oration*. III; see discussion in Balch, *1 Peter*, 143–44.

38. Plutarch, *Advice to the Bride and Groom* 48, *Moralia* 145C; *Bravery of Women*, *Moralia* 242E–263C; see discussion in Keener, *Paul, Women and Wives*, 160.

at this time was that of tyranny. Jesus warned his disciples that in the church leaders should not "lord it over others," (Mark 10:42–45). Time and again Jesus reiterated that the disciples are to serve, and he pointed to himself as the key example as one who came to serve, not to be served. Yet clearly Jesus was their leader; he had the authority. "Authority" is a neutral, even positive, term when speaking about use of power. To those who say that Eph 5:21 cannot be speaking about everyone submitting to everyone else, because then nothing would get done, I respond that they are confusing submission and authority. Paul's point to the Ephesians is that each member of Christ's body is to respect and honor all others, and this is not based on social status or on "common sense" pronouncements of the day, but on the basis of Christ's work in each believer. Perhaps this meant that during the communion meal, owners would take turns serving their slaves, husbands would serve their wives, and parents would model service for their children, although I am less certain about where children were in these banquets. Leadership or taking authority in any given situation does not absolve one from being a servant and honoring all.

I suggest the issue of authority is at the heart of the contemporary discussion about the nature of men and women. In much of current Evangelical parlance the term "head" is linked with male authority, and a hierarchy of power between men and women results. I wonder if underneath the stress on hierarchical difference between men and women is a conviction that the essence of maleness is active (initiator) and the essence of femaleness is passive (responder or receiver). Those who stress male "headship" or male authority often argue that the leadership is one of initiative and not domination. Paul's view of marriage, with his focus on reciprocity, undercuts the active/passive model. As noted above, Paul insisted that a husband does not have authority over his body, but his wife does (1 Cor 7:3–4).

I contend that while the first century world saw the asymmetrical relationship between men and women as normal and based on common sense, Paul challenged that default assumption when the people in view are believers. Paul weakened the force of his world's social patriarchy by asking each believer to submit to the other. He challenged the authority differential within the marriage relationship by emphasizing reciprocity between the couple. Over all this, Paul stressed the profound mystery, the oneness of Christ and the church. This blessed relationship awaits its full consummation at the marriage supper of the Lamb, to which Christians down through the centuries have declared, "Maranatha! Come Lord Jesus."

RESPONSE TO COHICK

Dennis R. Edwards

I offer thanks to Lynn Cohick for her fresh and engaging discussion of leadership and headship in the NT with its emphasis on the letter to the Ephesians. My observations and questions will correspond to the sections of Cohick's paper.

Regarding custom and the laws of nature, Cohick uses the Jew/Gentile relationship to serve as a paradigm for the male/female and parent/child relationships found in Eph 5 and notes Paul's admonition in Gal 3:28. The occasion for Paul's letter to the Galatians was to check an attitude of Jewish religious superiority over Gentile converts that we refer to as *Judaizing*.[1] In Gal 3:28 the allegedly superior one in the relationship (i.e., the Jew) is being admonished while Gentiles are simultaneously affirmed. The cultural disadvantage of being Gentile is erased as those in the relatively superior position are told not to view themselves as having any special status in the eyes of God. Correspondingly, those in the relatively inferior position should be encouraged that their social status has no bearing on their relationship to God as they are all "in Christ."

There are similar challenges against Jewish hegemony in other NT passages, as Cohick makes clear, such as those found in Rom 14 and 1 Cor 8. Yet in the household codes, the challenge given to those in the relatively inferior position to maintain their culturally designated roles is explicit. I can imagine that a slave hearing Gal 3:28 would be grateful to God that her status as a slave in society would not be held against her in God's eyes or even in the eyes of the community, yet a slave hearing Eph 6:5–8 might think that his faith requires him to be content with his miserable station in life, and possibly even see slavery as God's will. Indeed, Eph 6:5–8 was used to keep American slaves docile by instilling a belief that their status was due to God's design. Consequently, I can see how the Jew/Gentile distinction is explicitly dismantled by Paul's teaching in Galatians and Ephesians, but I struggle to see how Paul's teaching in Eph 5 would "weaken the structure of social hierarchy."

As Cohick noted, some scholars (e.g., O'Brien and Hoehner) view the household codes as the direct application of 5:21, the outworking of the admonition, not just examples of it. Regarding Eph 5:22, the verbless verse that follows the injunction

---

1. For example, see Scot McKnight, *Galatians* (NIV Application Commentary; Grand Rapids: Zondervan, 1995) 21.

of mutual submission, O'Brien paraphrases the apostle Paul: "Submit to one another and what I mean is, wives submit to your husbands, children to your parents, and slaves to your masters."[2] For scholars such as O'Brien, the submission of wives, children, and slaves does not illustrate the mutual submission of v. 21 but defines it. O'Brien further notes, "The apostle is not speaking of *mutual* submission in the sense of a reciprocal subordination, but submission to those who are in authority over them."[3]

Cohick, however, suggests that Paul does advocate mutual subordination and is in effect saying, "Submit to one another; indeed, observe the way wives submit to their husbands." It may be that wives, as well as slaves and children, were to serve as examples of what mutual submission looked like. However, "Would Paul's readers have heard his admonition any differently than what they had heard all their lives?" If the submission of wives (as well as the obedience of slaves and children) was assumed at the time of the Ephesians letter, as Cohick notes, how is a wife's submission "in Christ" any different from her submission prior to her Christian faith?

Also, Eph 5:24 seems to teach that the example for wives is the church's submission to Christ. Paul says, "Just as the church is subject to Christ, so also wives ought to be, in everything, to their husbands." The church serves as an example for the wives as they are to be motivated by how all believers are subject to Christ. Yet it seems that Cohick would like the wives to serve as a model for the church, the idea being something like, "As wives submit, so should you all."

Regarding customs and the normalizing of prejudices, Paul's dual use of the concept of slavery—both figuratively and literally—showed how language that is typically oppressive could be flipped around in order to encourage godly behavior for those who are "in Christ." Cohick points out, "Paul places owners, metaphorically speaking, in the role of slaves," which is something he does for himself as well. This idea of putting oneself in the place of the "lesser" seems key to our understanding, if we are to think that Paul may have been subtly undermining some of the power structures of society. Indeed, any adjustment toward humility in thinking and acting on the part of the "greater" fills out the "principle of reciprocity" that Cohick discusses in her last section. Of course, I am left to wonder how many contemporary male preachers would figuratively refer to themselves as "women" as readily as they might call themselves "slaves," "servants," or even "children."

---

2. Peter T. O'Brien, *The Letter to the Ephesians* (Pillar New Testament Commentary; Grand Rapids: Eerdmans, 1999) 403.

3. Ibid., 404, emphasis original.

Cohick led me to realize that when Paul refers to Christ as the "head" of the church (Eph 5:23), but simultaneously describes the Lord as loving the church (v. 25), giving himself for the church (v. 25), cleansing and presenting the church (vv. 26–27), and nourishing and caring for the church (v. 29), our notion of "headship" must go beyond simple authority. It does seem likely that "head" is a metaphor to be explored more thoroughly.

Regarding metaphor and meaning, Cohick suggests, "A more likely figurative meaning [for *kephalē*] is 'honored part' or 'prominent.'" I have no difficulty applying this metaphor to Christ (Eph 5:23) and imagine it would have been quite acceptable to Paul's readers as a way to describe husbands. The issue seems to be how one reconciles "submission" even with this metaphorical understanding of "head." Wives, it appears, are still expected to show deference to the "honored" member of the family. Even though that honored member may not be depicted as a tyrant, he is still the leader. The responsibility for social change seems to rest with the leader, so the leader's behavior is of greater interest. Consequently, Cohick discusses in her conclusion how leadership and servanthood are not mutually exclusive. Even so, it appears that wives were still to play their prescribed societal role.

Regarding hermeneutics and the principle of reciprocity, I find myself thinking Cohick's "principle of reciprocity" could be explored even more deeply through examining the words directed toward the perceived "greater" member of the common relationships noted in the household codes. For example, Cohick observed how the concept of slavery was applied metaphorically to owners of slaves. The notion of slavery was given honor because even the apostle Paul applied the term to himself, and the context was one of Christian community. Even though Paul had authority as an apostle, he described his role in the life of the Christian community as one of service. One could easily think of Phil 2 at this point, especially the *Carmen Christi* found in vv. 5–11. Paul followed the example of the Lord Jesus Christ.

Surely this admonition to the more powerful in relationships was meant to ameliorate any opportunity for exploitation that society may have afforded them. It appears the supposed superior in the relationship (i.e., husband, master, parent) is being called to modify behaviors away from the accepted norm because they are "in Christ."

This is clearly the case with husbands. Cohick noted how husbands are to view their wives' bodies as their own and how 1 Cor 7:3–4 gives wives authority in decisions over marital relations. Toward the end of her paper Cohick mentions the command directed toward husbands to love their wives. As Klyne Snodgrass observes regarding Eph 5:25, "the stronger language is used of the husband's responsibility."[4] Certainly it seems more radical to challenge the member of society with greater status, but it is that challenge that is more likely to lead to social change (cf. Phlm 15–16).

Cohick's paper is stimulating and pushes me to reflect on the notions of power and metaphor. She refers to the mutual submission discussed in Eph 5 as the "principle of reciprocity." The case for this principle is enhanced when focus is placed on the metaphor of "head," allowing the term to signify "honored part" or "prominent" rather than "authority," and also focus is placed on the responsibilities of those in the more culturally powerful position.

In the American struggle for civil rights, the guns, dogs, and hoses of the more tyrannical leaders could have quashed African American protests. However, when members of the broader society, particularly those in the majority with greater status, began to add their voices, social change advanced with some greater efficiency. It seems that putting responsibility on the member of the community with greater status is more likely to lead to the dismantling of inequitable social structures.

---

4. Klyne Snodgrass, *Ephesians* (NIV Application Commentary; Grand Rapids: Zondervan, 1996) 296.

REVENGE, FORGIVENESS, AND SIBLING RIVALRY: A THEOLOGICAL DIALOGUE BETWEEN SCRIPTURE AND SCIENCE

Dennis Olson

A common view of the history of human development as it relates to revenge and forgiveness is that our ancient human ancestors were governed primarily by an animalistic law of revenge. According to this popular view, a full-blown ethic of forgiveness arrived relatively late on the human scene in late antiquity with the rise of the Jewish and Christian traditions. Forgiveness was the cure that helped to heal the deeply embedded barbarism of human vengeance that was dominant among our earliest human ancestors.[1] Such was a conventional viewpoint.

Certainly we can find texts in the NT that might be construed as supporting such a view. The apostle Paul writes, "Beloved, never avenge yourselves, but leave room for the wrath of God; for it is written, 'Vengeance is mine, I will repay, says the Lord'" (Rom 12:19, quoting Deut 32:35). Jesus' Sermon on the Mount cites the OT law of measure-for-measure retaliation or revenge, "An eye for an eye, a tooth for a tooth, a life for a life" (Exod 21:23–24; Lev 24:18–20; Deut 19:21; see also Gen 9:5–6). In contrast to this principle Jesus commands:

> You have heard that it was said, "An eye for an eye and a tooth for a tooth." But I say to you, Do not resist an evildoer. But if anyone strikes you on the right cheek, turn the other also; and if anyone wants to sue you and take your coat, give your cloak as well; and if anyone forces you to go one mile, go also the second mile.

The Sermon on the Mount pushes one step further:

> You have heard it said, "You shall love your neighbor [see Lev 19:18] and hate your enemy [perhaps loosely derived from an OT text like Ps 139:19–

---

1. Jordan Kiper, "The Evolution of Forgiveness and Its Implications," a paper presented at the Fifth Global Conference on "Forgiveness: Probing the Boundaries," at Mansfield College, Oxford University, UK (July 11–13, 2012) http://www.inter-disciplinary.net/probing-the-boundaries/persons/forgiveness/conference-programme-abstracts-and-papers/session-3-concepts-and-ideologies-of-forgiveness (accessed on 8/20/2012); J. W. Elder, "Expanding Our Options: The Challenges of Forgiveness," in *Exploring Forgiveness* (ed. R. D. Enright and J. North; Madison: University of Wisconsin Press, 1998).

22]." But I say to you, Love your enemies, and pray for those who persecute you so that you may be children of your Father in heaven. (Matt 5:43–44)

And how many times should followers of Christ forgive an enemy who has wronged them? Not seven times, Jesus tells his disciples, but seventy-seven times, meaning virtually without limit (Matt 18:21–22; see also Luke 17:4). Do these NT commands provide a realistic ethic by which to live—never exacting revenge on anyone, always forgiving every single wrong done to us?

How should we think about revenge and forgiveness in human relationships, especially with our brothers and sisters? And how do we define those family relationships, whether in terms of biology, faith community, or the broader human family? This is clearly a large topic, and we can do no more than begin to nibble around the edges in this essay. My goal is to look at selected insights regarding the overall topic of forgiveness, revenge, and sibling rivalry arising from two quite different points of view. Putting these two points of view alongside one another will be like looking through a pair of binoculars with two separate lenses by which we can examine the interplay of revenge and forgiveness among siblings. One lens in this set of binoculars is scientific nature. This first lens involves an array of recent studies by psychologists, anthropologists, and neuroscientists on revenge and forgiveness in human relationships, including within families. The second lens of our binoculars involves a close reading of selected biblical texts from the book of Genesis in which revenge and forgiveness within families play a significant role. We will ask what a perspective of biblical faith and theology might contribute to the dialogue on revenge and forgiveness in families. We will look through one lens at a time—first a set of scientific insights and studies and then a biblical and theological reading of Genesis. Then we will ask what we might see together and learn together as we put the two perspectives into conversation and dialogue. As we do so, we recognize that each lens has its own distinctive methods, assumptions, and ways of knowing. Nevertheless, the dialogue between them will hopefully prove fruitful and generative. We will note both marked differences of insight between the two lenses of science and theology as well as what we might call interesting "virtual parallels."[2] We begin by looking through the first lens of our binoculars.

2. The phrase "virtual parallels" is one used by William Brown to describe overlapping or strikingly similar elements when doing interdisciplinary comparisons between the worldview of the Bible regarding creation and nature and the worldview of modern natural sciences on the origins of the universe. To say they are "virtual parallels" is to affirm some striking similarities while also preserving the distinctive methods, assumptions, and modes of knowledge that are unique to the very different disciplines and interpretation of the Bible and theology as compared to the disciplines and interpreta-

The First Lens: What Do Recent Scientific Studies Teach Us about Revenge and Forgiveness in the Context of Sibling Rivalry and Family Relationships?

Across the wide spectrum of animal species (birds, insects, parasites, worms, fish, mammals, and the like), researchers have discovered a complex variety of both positive and negative relationships among siblings and within family groups.[3] On one hand, male and female siblings in some species of animals act very generously toward one another, sometimes in ways that are altruistic or self-sacrificing, even unto death. For example, worker bees defending a colony of honeybees go on suicide missions to attack large hornets who plague the honeybees' hive. Many of the worker bees will die when they attack the stronger and aggressive hornet, but they give their lives to protect the hive and the family of bees who are all descended from one queen mother.

On the other hand, some species feature intense fighting and competition among siblings. One extreme example involves a bird species called the black eagle. The mother black eagle regularly lays two and only two eggs in a nest during her reproductive cycle. The two eggs always hatch a few days apart. The firstborn chick has a head start and begins to eat earlier and grow stronger before the second egg hatches. When the second chick appears in the nest out of its egg, the older firstborn

---

tions of modern natural science. See William Brown, *The Seven Pillars of Creation: The Bible, Science, and the Ecology of Wonder* (New York: Oxford University Press, 2010). Further insights on the interdisciplinary relationship of theology and science are explored in Wentzel van Huyssteen, *Duet or Duel? Theology and Science in the Postmodern World* (Norwich: SCM, 1998). The metaphor we are using of the two parallel lenses of a pair of binoculars (the lens of modern science and the lens of Bible and theology) likewise seeks to preserve and honor the distinctive ways of knowing that operate in these two fields of inquiry while also allowing a meaningful dialogue between them.

Good science and good theology both share a certain epistemological humility, a confession of ignorance that drives our questions and motivates a blend of creativity and rigor as we face unresolved problems. Stuart Firestein, chair of the biological sciences department at Columbia University, argues that the heart and soul of scientific inquiry is not "the *Scientific Method*, an immutable set of precepts for devising experiments that churn out the cold hard facts.... [Science is] not facts and rules. It's black cats in dark rooms. As the Princeton mathematician Andrew Wiles describes it: It's groping and probing and poking, and some bumbling and bungling, and then a switch is discovered, often by accident, and the light is lit, and everyone says, 'Oh, wow, so that's how it looks,' and then it's off into the next dark room, looking for the next mysterious feline" (Stuart Firestein, *Ignorance: How It Drives Science* [New York: Oxford, 2012] 2). A similar acknowledgement of the driving force of ignorance may be salutary for theological inquiry as well.

3. A fascinating collection of studies of the enormous variety in sibling relationships and rivalry among diverse animal species is Douglas Mock, *More than Kin and Less than Kind: The Evolution of Family Conflict* (Cambridge: Harvard University Press, 2004).

"bully" chick begins to peck the younger sibling and actively prevent it from getting food from the parent. Remarkably, the mother eagle simply watches the bullying and never intervenes. Researchers documented how in one typical case the second younger chick sadly died within three days. In the course of those three days the little chick was assaulted by its older brother or sister on thirty-eight different occasions with a total of 1,569 blows by the older sibling's sharp beak.[4] Apparently the second egg functions as a kind of insurance in case the first egg fails to hatch. If the first egg does hatch, however, the second chick has little chance of survival because of the sibling's assaults. Researchers surmise that the food resources of the rugged mountainous terrain that the black eagle typically inhabits cannot support more than one hatchling per cycle.

So what about humans as a species? Psychologist Michael McCullough has recently collected the results of numerous studies on revenge and forgiveness from a variety of social, biological, and neuropsychological sciences in his book *Beyond Revenge: The Evolution of the Forgiveness Instinct*.[5] Using an array of psychological studies, empirical research, results of brain scans, evolutionary biology, and the study of our closest primate relatives, McCullough asks about the essence of human nature as it has evolved over millennia. Are we humans deep down loving, forgiving, and compassionate, or are we brutish and vengeful to the core? In order to answer that question we might begin with the argument by primatologist Frans de Waal in his book *Good Natured*. De Waal seeks to demonstrate from case studies and his own research that humans have inherited from our primitive and long extinct ancestors what many might consider "bad" traits like greed, deceit, and a lust for power and domination. However, he argues that humans have also inherited good and morally virtuous traits from our human ancestors, traits like having rules that benefit the group, sharing resources with those in need, helping and consoling those who suffer, and being generous with those who are generous to us. So, de Waal concluded, we humans are both fundamentally greedy, vengeful, and self-interested, *and* we are fundamentally kind, forgiving, and generous.[6] Such a view runs counter to some common views of the evolution of ancient humans as originally violent and vengeful, only later developing a greater capacity for kindness and forgiveness. In contrast to this popular view, De Waal would say humans have been both vengeful

---

4. Ibid., 51.

5. Michael McCullough, *Beyond Revenge: The Evolution of the Forgiveness Instinct* (San Francisco: Jossey-Bass, 2008).

6. Frans de Waal, *Good Natured: The Origins of Right and Wrong in Humans and Other Animals* (Cambridge: Harvard University Press, 2006).

and forgiving at the same time from their earliest stages of human development as a species.

Two Harvard anthropologists, Richard Wrangham and Dale Peterson, in their book *Demonic Males* added a further insight, based on work with chimpanzees.[7] They agreed with De Waal that chimpanzees exhibit positive moral attributes of generosity, forgiveness, compassion, and the like. However, the chimpanzees seem to exhibit these traits only with their own in-group, their immediate family and community. A different and harsher set of rules apply in relationships with chimpanzees from other communities. Male chimpanzees of the in-group often bonded together and formed patrol squads that roamed the borders of their group's territory. During these patrols the in-group chimpanzees brutally attacked and killed vulnerable males from other chimpanzee communities when they encountered them. The intense male bonding around vengeful attacks against would-be intruders served to protect the other members of the community and the food resources of their community's territory. This intense in-group bonding, however, also created a frequently aggressive and hostile stance toward outsiders.

A thorough review of a large number of scientific studies in human social psychology by Hewstone, Ruben, and Willis confirmed a similar trend within human groups and communities.[8] There is a consistent tendency for human beings to conform to a certain set of moral rules that are more compassionate and forgiving when humans relate to those within their own families and intimate in-group communities, especially with siblings. Like the chimps, humans tend to have a very different set of less generous and more hostile moral rules for relationships with outsiders. This seems to be generally true of human behavior in communities across diverse cultures and regions of the world, although the specifics of how this plays out can vary from culture to culture.

The first major conclusion that McCullough lifts up is that the desire for revenge is deeply ingrained in the human species. McCullough argues:

> ... scientific research demonstrates that the desire for revenge is a built-in feature of human nature. . . . Every neurologically intact human being on the planet has the biological hardware for experiencing it. . . . A readiness

---

7. Richard Wrangham and Dale Peterson, *Demonic Males: Apes and the Origins of Human Violence* (New York: Houghton Mifflin, 1996).

8. M. Hewstone, M. Ruben, and H. Willis, "Intergroup Bias," *Annual Review of Psychology* 53 (2002) 575–604.

to seek revenge served important functions for ancestral humans, and . . . it's still capable of serving many of those important functions today.[9]

Experiments in neuroscience and brain imaging demonstrate that human brains are hardwired to desire revenge, to feel good when revenge is achieved, and to feel frustrated when it is not carried out. It should be noted that studies consistently demonstrate that this desire for revenge is particularly pronounced in male human brains.[10] Humans, McCullough argues, have developed this revenge-desire mechanism because it serves two useful functions: protection and encouragement toward cooperation. The threat of revenge deters aggression by nonfamily members both within the larger community and outside the larger community (the protective function). The possibility of revenge also serves to promote and enforce cooperation among unrelated members of the community for the greater good (the cooperative function). Studies indicate that free loaders and slackers who do not contribute their fair share to the wellbeing of the larger community change their ways and begin to cooperate more for the common good when other members of the community inflict revenge on the slackers.[11] This capacity of strangers who are not related to one another to come together and cooperate for the long-term good of the community is one of the unique characteristics of the human species. Other species in the animal kingdom practice cooperation *within* families and colonies of relatives. A bee hive with one queen bee is an example. But, McCullough notes, ". . . cooperation among humans has a distinctive feature: we readily cooperate with non-relatives and even perfect strangers without promise of special consideration [or personal benefit] in the future. Indeed, human societies are built upon this sort of cooperation. Without cooperation . . . civilization as we know it would have been impossible."[12]

Studies show that we humans readily enforce cooperation among nonrelatives through revenge, even when the enforcement is costly to the enforcers.[13] Costly punishment and revenge, McCullough observes, "may indeed be one of the dynamics that allows generosity and cooperation to thrive within large groups of unrelated individuals."[14]

---

9. McCullough, *Beyond Revenge*, xvii.
10. Ibid., 137–46.
11. Ibid., 56–61.
12. Ibid., 56.
13. Ibid., 58.
14. Ibid., 78.

Clarifications should be made at this point. The need to act on these desires for revenge is lessened in modern developed societies to the extent that a reasonably effective and equitable system of law and order is in place: protective laws, police and law enforcement, courts, punishments, judges, shared economic sacrifice, and the like.[15] Furthermore, revenge (retaliating in some way against someone who has severely hurt you or the community) needs to be distinguished from cases of unprovoked aggression, violence by those who are mentally impaired, or excessive retaliation that harms the long-term wellbeing of large communities.[16]

A second major conclusion that McCullough draws from his survey of studies and experiments is that the capacity for forgiveness is also a built-in feature that is deeply ingrained in human nature. Like revenge, the human instinct for forgiveness helped to solve critical problems for our human ancestors and for human communities today.[17] This built-in capacity for forgiveness helped "ancestral humans get along with their genetic relatives," and it helped "establish and maintain cooperative relationships with nonrelatives or strangers."[18] In human development over millennia one's family and relatives were so essential to preserving one's life and well-being (providing protection, resources, education, and the like) that humans have been programmed to be much more forgiving and to engage in much less revenge when it comes to close family members like siblings. But humans also have the unique

15. Ibid., 24–25.

16. Ibid., 26–28.

17. Studies have shown that this instinct for forgiveness is a characteristic that is shared with several other group-living, social species (most primates, hyenas, dolphins, goats, and even fish). For example, a carefully controlled laboratory experiment observed the behavior of a species of fish called a guppy. Little guppies are quite susceptible to larger predator fish in their normal environments. Thus, the guppies regularly send out a small scouting party of two or more guppies to assess the threat level of any nearby predator fish like a sunfish. It is a dangerous mission. It proceeds with one guppy going out a little ahead of the other guppies in the scouting party and then retreating. Then it is the turn for another guppy to go out slightly ahead of the rest of the scouting party and then to retreat. So this back and forth dance occurs with each member of the scouting party taking turns until they get close enough to the sunfish to determine whether it is a threat or not. If the sunfish does not react, then all is fine. But if the sunfish does attack, some guppies are likely to be eaten and die.

Cooperation in this dangerous reconnaissance dance is enforced by revenge and forgiveness. If one of the guppies in the scouting party hangs back and does not take its turn at the head of the pack, the other guppies in the scouting party go behind the lagging guppy and force it to the front, exposing it to the predator fish. If the slacker guppy makes a good faith effort to redeem itself and moves forward toward the predator fish on its own as it is supposed to do, then the other guppies in effect forgive the slacker and allow the lagging guppy to resume its place and rotation in the scouting party. L. A. Dugatkin and M. Alfieri, "Interpopulation Differences in the Use of the Tit-for-Tat Strategy during Predator Inspection in the Guppy, Poecilia Reticulata," *Evolutionary Biology* 6 (1992) 519–526.

18. McCullough, *Beyond Revenge*, 89.

capacity to forgive and reconcile with nonfamily strangers under the right cultural, social, and contextual conditions that allow forgiveness to happen.[19]

A third major conclusion from McCullough's survey of studies is that humans have a deeply ingrained instinct to be adaptable and highly sensitive to context. McCullough observes that "human nature is flexible, multifarious, and exquisitely sensitive to context. The nature of human nature is to help people change their behavior to suit their changing circumstances!"[20] McCullough argues that an implication of this human flexibility and context-sensitivity is a hopeful one. The world can be made a less vengeful and more forgiving place if the environments in which we live and work contain more of the factors that promote forgiveness and less of the factors that promote revenge.

What are the conditions and factors that lessen revenge and make forgiveness more likely? Across cultures humans use three key signals to promote forgiveness rather than revenge in cases of severe hurt against another human being. These signals help to demonstrate that the offending party has truly changed so that they may now be considered worthy of the forgiver's care, they may be considered safe and no longer a threat, and they may be considered valuable in some way to the forgiver. These three key signals occur at every level of human relationship from families and siblings to communities and nations. The first signal consists of human words: a spoken and heartfelt apology.[21] Human words are powerful and can change a cycle of revenge into an experience of forgiveness and reconciliation. However, words can sometimes be cheap or insincere. Indeed, some cultures prefer more non-verbal gestures and actions in forgiveness rituals.

A second signal involves bodily gestures, displays, and movements that convey shame, guilt, and self-humiliation by the offender before the forgiver. The display

---

19. Ibid., xviii.

20. Ibid., xix.

21. McCullough, *Beyond* Revenge, 162–63. See also S. Blum-Kulka and E. Olshtain, "Requests and Apologies: A Cross-Cultural Study of Speech Act Realization Patterns," *Applied Linguistics* 5 (1984) 196–212; A. Lazare, *On Apology* (New York: Oxford University Press, 2004); S. J. Scher and J. M. Darley, "How Effective Are the Things That People Say to Apologize? Effects of the Realization of the Apology Speech Act," *Journal of Psycholinguistic Research* 26 (1997) 127–40. According to researchers five elements make up a good spoken apology: 1) acknowledging the offense and expressing humble remorse for one's role—"I am sorry," 2) admitting responsibility and fault—"I was wrong," 3) providing an explanation without turning it into an excuse—"let me clarify what happened, but this is in no way an excuse," 4) offering to pay or make amends—"what can I do to make it right?" and 5) promising never to repeat the wrong that has been done—"it'll never happen again." The research suggests that the more of these five elements that are present in a spoken apology, the more readily will the offended party be willing to forgive.

may be as subtle as facial blushing from shame. It may involve bowing down, crawling, or kneeling before the forgiver in some cultures.[22] The offender may volunteer to submit to some mild punishment as an act of showing sincerity.[23]

Interestingly, humans are not the only species to engage in such non-verbal bodily displays of self-debasement leading to what looks like forgiveness. After they have been involved in an intense conflict, especially when within their own family or community, chimpanzees similarly engage in certain bodily gestures. One chimpanzee will bow down in a submissive way to a former opponent. They will hold hands, kiss one another, and show affection to one another in a ritual of reconciliation.[24] The desire to forgive and reconcile with all its benefits of cooperation seems to run deep among certain highly social species, including humans.

A third signal alongside a verbal apology or bodily gestures of self-humiliation that makes forgiveness more possible is compensation. The offender pays some form of reparations to the victim or the victim's family. The compensation need not be total or at the same level as the original harm that was done. Even a modest and partial repayment or compensation is often sufficient to encourage the offended party to forgive and reconcile.[25]

Apart from these three signals that humans can give one another (verbal apology, bodily gestures, payment of compensation), other important elements further enhance the possibility of forgiving rather than avenging a wrong that has been done. One variable is the quality of the relationship. Forgiveness is more likely to happen and revenge less likely to occur when the two parties are intimate family members or siblings, close friends, or close colleagues at work. Our human brains are wired to

---

22. Kiper, "The Evolution of Forgiveness and Its Implications," 6. See C. Boehm, *Blood Revenge: The Enactment and Management of Conflict in Montenegro and Other Tribal Societies* (Philadelphia: University of Pennsylvania, 1987); Rolf Kuschel, *Vengeance Is Their Reply: Blood Feuds and Homicides on Bellona Island, Part I: Conditions Underlying Generations of Bloodshed* (Copenhagen: Dansk Psykologisk Forlay, 1988). Anthropologists have studied tribal societies in which blood vengeance and blood feuds are common. The cycle of killings stops only when a key member of the first murderer's family engages in a ritual of forgiveness. The ritual, anthropologists note, is nearly everywhere the same in these tribal societies. The ritual is public and involves public shaming of the one seeking forgiveness. The one seeking forgiveness often symbolically drops his weapon, makes himself vulnerable, lowers his body so he is in a subservient position that is lower than the one who is to forgive, and then allows the forgiver to intimately touch his head or hands.

23. McCullough, *Beyond Revenge*, 168–69.

24. Kiper, "The Evolution of Forgiveness and Its Implications," 6. See F. de Waal, *Chimpanzee Politics: Power and Sex Among Apes* (Baltimore: Johns Hopkins University Press, 1982).

25. McCullough, *Beyond Revenge*, 171–75. See W. T. Bottom, K. Gibson, S. E. Daniels, and J. K. Murnighan, "When Talk Is Not Cheap: Substantive Penance and Expressions of Intent in Rebuilding Cooperation," *Organizational Science* 13 (2002) 497–513.

encourage reconciliation and avoid revenge with siblings and other close relations. Another variable is the amount of time that has elapsed since the original harm occurred. The longer ago the incident happened the more likely the victim will be able to forgive.[26] A final variable in enhancing the likelihood of forgiveness is the increased age of the one being forgiven. The older you are the more likely it is that you will forgive the one who has offended you. As people grow older and become more vulnerable, they apparently have an incentive to reconcile with more people and thereby create a larger network of valuable relationships in old age.[27]

As we have looked through the first scientific lens of our binoculars, we have noted how deep both revenge and forgiveness are woven into our brains and our relationships. Revenge serves certain functions of protection and encouragement of cooperation among nonfamily strangers. Forgiveness is offered most readily with family members and siblings, but it can also occur under certain consistent factors and signals, even with former enemies or opponents.

The Second Lens: What Do the Stories of Genesis Teach Us about Revenge and Forgiveness in the Context of Sibling Rivalry and Family Relationships?

The second lens of our binoculars gives another angle of vision on the topic of revenge, forgiveness, and sibling rivalry. This lens is biblical and theological in nature with a focus on some key selected narrative texts from the book of Genesis. In all of Scripture Genesis contains the densest concentration of family stories involving human conflict and reconciliation. As such, the book of Genesis is a good place to start a theological conversation on sibling rivalry, revenge, and forgiveness in the Bible.

Before we enter the Genesis narratives, it may be helpful to pause and survey the OT usage of the vocabulary of revenge (Hebrew *nqm* "to avenge") and the extensive vocabulary of forgiveness (Hebrew *nś'* "to lift up, forgive," *kpr* "to cover over, atone," *ksh* "to cover [sin]," *ṭhr* "to cleanse, purify," *slḥ* "to forgive, pardon"). The language of revenge throughout the OT is applied quite evenly both to humans (fifteen of forty-one occurrences) and to God (twenty-six of forty-one occurrences). In contrast, the language of forgiveness and acts of forgiveness occur almost exclusively with God

26. Kiper, "The Evolution of Forgiveness and Its Implications," 6. See also G. Bono, J. Berry, M. McCullough, L. R. Luna and B. Tabak, "On the Form and Function of Forgiving: Modeling the Time-Forgiveness Relationship and Testing the Valuable Relationships Hypothesis," *Emotion* 10 (2003) 358–76.

27. Michele Girard and Etienne Mullet, "Forgiveness in Adolescents, Young, Middle-Aged, and Older Adults," *Journal of Adult Development* 4 (1997) 209–20.

as the subject and only rarely with humans as the active agent offering forgiveness. Of the approximately one hundred occurrences of the several words connected with forgiveness in the OT, only three of them involve humans forgiving other humans (Gen 50:17, Joseph forgiving his brothers; Exod 10:17, Pharaoh's request for forgiveness from Moses and Aaron as well as God; Prov 17:9, a proverb regarding forgiveness and human friendship). All other occurrences of explicit forgiveness language in the OT involve divine forgiveness of human sin and rebellion. However, as the social scientific literature suggested, often in more traditional societies the granting of forgiveness by one human to another is often expressed through customary actions and rituals rather than explicit words. We will see this at work in the Genesis stories to which we now turn.

Cain and Abel: Revenge and Forgiveness, Human and Divine (Gen 4)

The first story of sibling rivalry in the Bible is the story of Cain and Abel in Gen 4:1–16. It is immediately preceded by Gen 3 and the story of the serpent's temptation in the garden of Eden and Adam and Eve eating the forbidden fruit in order to become "like God" (Gen 3:5). Important parallels between the Adam and Eve story and the Cain and Abel story suggest that the two stories should be read together as a matching pair and thus be interpreted as a combined reflection on the nature of human sin. Examples of the parallels between Gen 3 and 4 include sin being associated with a crafty serpent in Gen 3 and with an animal lurking at the door in Gen 4 (3:1–5; 4:7). The woman's "desire" for the man is paralleled by sin's "desire" for Cain (3:16; 4:7). YHWH investigates a transgression in both stories and twice asks the humans "where?" (3:9; 4:9). Both Gen 3 and 4 contain similar phrases such as "cursed is/from the ground" (3:17; 4:11), "when you work the ground" (3:18; 4:12), and "east (of the garden) of Eden" (3:24; 4:16).[28] The broken relationship with God in Gen 3 is intertwined with the broken sibling relationship between Cain and Abel in Gen 4.

Cain and Abel were brothers, the first offspring of Adam and Eve. The brothers were joined by blood but divided by vocation: "Abel was a keeper of sheep, and Cain a tiller of the ground" (Gen 4:2). The two brothers brought an offering from the fruit of their respective labors. Abel brought sheep, and Cain brought an offering from his grain harvest. The LORD accepted Abel's offering but not Cain's offering. Out of jealousy Cain killed his brother Abel in anger. In response the LORD did not put Cain to death for the murder, as one might have expected based on a later text in Gen

---

28. Michael Fishbane, *Text and Texture, Close Readings of Selected Biblical Texts* (New York: Schocken, 1979) 26–27.

(Gen 9:5-6; see Exod 21:23; Deut 19:21). Instead, God banished Cain from his land and condemned him to wander as a fugitive for the rest of his life. The LORD also places a protective mark on Cain, warning any would-be avenger that they would receive a seven-fold retribution if they killed Cain (Gen 4:1-16).

The story of Cain's murder of his brother Abel raises many questions, but we will focus our attention on only a few aspects of the story. First of all, in light of the modern scientific discussions of revenge, we noted that in most human societies, revenge killing of one's own sibling is very rare. In other words, the story of Cain and Abel is not just about the entry of murder into the human condition. It represents the rare instance of the worst possible kind of murder, the murder of one's own brother or sister. We humans are generally not programmed to engage in such killing of our own family members, and so Cain has crossed an extreme line—homicide of one's own brother.

Just a few verses later in Gen 4, the reader comes upon an illustration not of revenge against a sibling (as with Cain killing Abel) but revenge against a stranger who is not a family member. The constant threat of an out-of-control spiral of increasingly violent revenge finds its first biblical expression as six generations later, a descendant of Cain named Lamech kills a man in revenge for hurting him. Lamech boastfully warns away anyone who would try to avenge his murder, "If Cain is avenged seven-fold, truly Lamech [will be avenged] seventy-seven fold" (Gen 4:24; cf. v. 15).[29] With Lamech revenge has spilled out into excess and threatens to create violent chaos rather than cooperation and community (see Gen 6:11). Although it may sound harsh to our modern ears, the OT law of equal retaliation—"an eye for an eye, tooth for tooth, and life for life" (Exod 21:23-24; Lev 24:18-20; Deut 19:21)—is designed to place a limit on such vengeful and escalating violence.

What might we observe about God's punishment of Cain, God's revenge for Cain's killing his own brother? Anthropological surveys of very diverse cultures around the world show that the inclination for a victim's family member to seek blood revenge against a murderer is present in most traditional and tribal human societies that do not have the mechanisms of modern law enforcement, courts, and police in developed societies. This was true in at least some traditions in ancient Israel. Blood revenge, however, also had a theological dimension. Blood in the OT was thought to carry the life force of an animal or human. Thus, consuming the blood of animals along with its meat was prohibited as a recognition that all life

---

29. The words of Jesus commanding his disciples to forgive not seven times but seventy-seven times (Matt 18:21-22; see also Luke 17:4) likely allude to these vengeful words of Lamech.

belonged to God (Gen 9:3-4; Lev 17:10-11, 14; Deut 12:15-16, 23-24). Any wrongful taking of a human life by another human or animal required a reckoning (Gen 9:5-6). Human life was considered sacred because it bore the image of God. Thus, a principle developed that illegal shedding of blood should normally be resolved through the shedding of the killer's blood (Gen 9:6).[30]

Interestingly, the Bible's first example of bloodguilt and vengeance—the story of Cain's murder of his brother Abel—undercuts this basic principle of life for a life. The victim's blood was portrayed as "crying out" to God from the ground (Gen 4:10).[31] In the case of Cain, God exercised a measure of mercy and forgiveness by not putting the murderer, Cain, to death as one may have expected. Cain was allowed to live. However, God's forgiveness was also accompanied by a measure of God's revenge or punishment. Cain, the tiller of the soil, was banished from his land and made to wander as a fugitive for the rest of his life. At the same time God also protected Cain from any other human who might seek blood vengeance for the murder by putting a protective mark on Cain (Gen 4:11-16). Moreover, anyone who killed Cain would "suffer a sevenfold vengeance" (Gen 4:15).

We noted at the beginning of the essay the commonly held but erroneous view that the human species was originally ruled by savage revenge and that only much later in human development did forgiveness arrive full-blown on the human scene with the rise of certain religious traditions, including Jewish and Christian traditions. We discovered in our survey of modern scientific studies of revenge and forgiveness compelling evidence that both revenge and forgiveness were deeply engrained in the human brain and in the long evolution of human beings, reaching back to earliest times. On its own theological terms the biblical story of Cain and Abel provides what we might call a "virtual parallel" to this modern scientific view.[32] The story of the earliest human beings in Gen 3 and 4 affirms the presence and complex interplay of both revenge and forgiveness at the earliest stages of interaction among humans and God. Of course, what is different in the Bible (as compared to a scientific perspective) is the role and reality of God, the Creator of the heavens and the earth and all that is within them. Although a scientific view of human evolution offers important insights, a Christian faith perspective would add that in a profound theological

---

30. This applied particularly in cases of intentional or premeditated killing (Num 35:16-18; Deut 19:5, 11; 1 Kgs 2:32).

31. This crying out of the blood of an innocent murder victim is a common motif in the OT (Isa 26:21; Ezek 24:7-9; Job 16:18).

32. On "virtual parallels" between scientific and biblical-theological perspectives, see footnote 2 above.

sense we confess that it is God who has ultimately formed our bodies and our brains to function as they do (Ps 139:13). The portrayal of sibling rivalry in the Bible adds a crucial new element to the experience of revenge and forgiveness in human relationships when it introduces the presence of God into the mix. The LORD's interaction with humans and Israel in the OT reveals the deep and complex character of God in whom revenge and forgiveness play a role. In the Old Testament's most definitive revelation of the divine character in Exod 34:6-7, the LORD reveals to Moses on Mount Sinai that the LORD is "a God merciful and gracious, slow to anger and abounding in steadfast love and faithfulness . . . forgiving iniquity and transgression and sin, yet by no means clearing the guilty, but visiting the iniquity of the parents upon the children and the children's children, to the third and fourth generation."

This holding together of mercy and judgment, compassion and consequences, and forgiveness and revenge characterizes the deep biblical character of God as well as the primal experience of humankind in the course of its long history. The biblical story of Cain and Abel testifies to the experience of revenge and forgiveness from humans' earliest beginnings.

Jacob and Esau: Revenge, Forgiveness and Sibling Rivalry Revisited (Gen 25–36)

The book of Genesis contains a number of sibling rivalry stories, many of which highlight the recurring theme of the younger sibling being elevated over the older sibling—Isaac over Ishmael, Jacob over Esau, Rachel over Leah, Joseph over his older brothers, and Judah over Reuben.[33] Each of these stories of sibling rivalry in Genesis contains its own distinctive plot and themes. We will briefly examine two of the sibling rivalries in Genesis, the rivalry between the twin brothers Jacob and Esau (Gen 25–33) and the rivalry between Leah and Rachel who were both sisters to one another and wives of Jacob (Gen 29–30).

The story of Jacob and Esau begins with their father Isaac and his wife, Rebekah, who became pregnant with twins. The two boys were already wrestling fiercely in-

---

33. Everett Fox, "Stalking the Younger Brother: Some Models for Understanding a Biblical Motif," *Journal for the Study of the Old Testament* 60 (1993) 45–68. Abraham's older son Ishmael is supplanted by the younger Isaac (Gen 17:15–22; 21:8–21). The younger Jacob is chosen by God and blessed by his father Isaac instead of his older brother Esau (Gen 25:21–28; 27:1–40; 28:10–22). The husband Jacob favors and loves the younger sister Rachel over her older sister Leah, both wives of Jacob (Gen 29:15–30). Among the twelve sons of Jacob the younger Joseph is favored by their father and ends up as the more powerful master over all his older brothers (Gen 37:1–11; 50:15–21). In Jacob's final blessing of his twelve sons before his death, the younger Judah is raised up with a special blessing (Gen 49:8–12) while the oldest son Reuben is demoted (Gen 49:3–4; see Gen 35:22).

side Rebekah's womb. The LORD reveals to her that these two sons are "two nations" who "shall be divided," the one stronger than the other and "the elder shall serve the younger" (Gen 25:19-23). When the twins were born (25:24-26), the first son came out "red" (Hebrew *'admoni*) which is a word play on "Edom" (which is used both for the color "red" and for the nation of "Edom" for which Esau is the ancestor, see 36:1). Edom was a nation on the eastern border of Canaan and thus a neighbor to Israel. The younger twin brother came out, "gripping Esau's heel," in effect, hitching a free ride through the birth canal. The younger twin is called "Jacob," meaning in Hebrew "he grabs by the heel" or "he supplants." Jacob will gain a reputation for swindling and conning whatever he can from his older brother Esau, stealing his blessing and his birthright as the eldest son. Esau grew up to become a skillful hunter and outdoorsman, and Jacob was a more "quiet" or civilized man, living in tents rather in the outdoors. The father Isaac loved Esau, while the mother Rebekah loved Jacob (Gen 25:27-28).

As adults the conflict between Jacob and Esau began with Jacob enticing Esau to give up his birthright as the eldest son for a bowl of red-colored stew (Gen 25:29-34). The sibling rivalry became most intense when Jacob and his mother Rachel trick the elderly and blind Isaac into giving to Jacob the blessing that rightfully belonged to the firstborn son Esau (Gen 27:1-29). After Esau discovered that Jacob had stolen his blessing, Esau angrily resolved, "I will kill my brother Jacob" (27:41). The Jacob-Esau relationship is a replay in many ways of the Cain-Abel story—two brothers, different vocations, an experience of perceived injustice by the elder brother, envy and anger, and a plan to kill the younger brother (Gen 4:1-16). Hearing of Esau's plans, Rebekah intervened and convinced Jacob to flee to Mesopotamia to avoid Esau's murderous plot.

After living in Mesopotamia in exile for twenty long years, Jacob decided to return from Mesopotamia to Canaan and to confront his brother Esau (31:38, 41). Jacob began by sending messengers to Esau to tell him that Jacob was returning with large herds of animals and many slaves (32:5). The messengers returned to Jacob, reporting that Esau was coming with an army of four hundred men to meet Jacob and his family. Jacob assumed Esau's intentions may be hostile and so decided to divide his family and herds into two groups so that if Esau destroyed one group, the other group might be able to escape (32:6-8).

God had encountered Jacob in a dream at Bethel twenty years earlier when Jacob was first leaving Canaan (28:10-22). Then God had been gracious and generous in offering promise and protection to Jacob. Now as Jacob was returning back to Canaan, God encountered Jacob again. However, this time God attacked Jacob in a wrestling match that left him wounded, limping, but also blessed (Gen 32:22–32). The morning after the wrestling match with God, Jacob looked up and saw Esau coming with his army of four hundred men. Jacob met his brother and bowed down to the ground seven times as a sign of humility as he approached Esau, hoping to save himself and his family from a vengeful death (33:1–3; see 27:41; 32:7–8, 11). Esau's reaction to seeing Jacob was not vengeance but forgiveness: "But Esau ran to meet him, and embraced him, and fell on his neck and kissed him, and they wept" (33:4).

We may note the ways in which many of Jacob's words and actions are "virtual parallels" to the range of signals and conditions that the scientific research on forgiveness suggests are necessary when an offender seeks forgiveness from someone they have hurt. This biblical scene of reconciliation appears to include three important conditions that, according to scientific research, would contribute to a willingness to forgive: the closeness of the relationship (they were brothers), the relatively long length of time that had passed since the injury (twenty years), and the increased age of the one offering forgiveness (Esau). Other motivations to forgive included the fact that Esau could feel safe (he was surrounded by his army of four hundred men, see Gen 33:1). There was potential value for Esau in restoring the relationship with Jacob and his herds of animals by merging their families and sharing resources (Gen 32:3–5; 33:12). Moreover, Jacob excelled at two key signals to Esau that may have turned any potential desire for revenge by Esau into a willingness to forgive: the paying of compensation and self-abasing bodily gestures. Jacob makes no verbal apology, and it may be that culturally a verbal apology was not expected. Instead, Jacob sent wave after wave of gifts as compensation to Esau (32:13–21; 33:8–11). The Hebrew word used in Gen 33:11 to describe the "gift/blessing" that Jacob gave to Esau—*berakah*—is the same Hebrew word used for the "blessing" of the eldest son that Jacob had originally stolen from Esau twenty years before (Gen 27:35–36, 41).

Jacob's bodily gestures also conform to what research suggests as appropriate cues. Jacob made himself vulnerable by gathering his family behind him and going alone ahead of them to meet Esau and his army of four hundred men (33:1–3). Jacob also demonstrated humility, "bowing himself to the ground seven times, until he came near his brother" (Gen 33:3). As a result Esau was overcome with emotion, and the two brothers intimately embrace and shed tears of deep emotion (Gen 33:4).

What implications might we draw as we look through the biblical and theological lens of the Jacob and Esau story of sibling rivalry alongside the other modern scientific lens regarding revenge, forgiveness, and sibling rivalry? Let me suggest seven brief insights.

First, From Families to Nations. The key dynamics of revenge and forgiveness that operate in smaller family and sibling relationships have important similarities to the dynamics of revenge and forgiveness that operate on a larger scale in neighborhoods, organizations, cities, and even nations. The LORD said to Rachel as the two babies in her womb were wrestling insider her, "Two nations are in your womb" (Gen 25:23). Scripture presents this story of sibling rivalry between brothers as in some way also reflective of the historical back-and-forth struggles of these two neighboring nations of ancient Israel and Edom. Modern scientific research confirms this insight. Many of the dynamics of revenge and forgiveness apply across the spectrum of human relationships from families to larger organizations and communities.[34]

Second, Who Is My Sister or My Brother? The biblical story of Esau and Jacob provides an example of flexibility in the definition of brother and sister. Esau and Jacob are biological siblings in Genesis. But Esau/Edom and Jacob/Israel are also representative of two different nations who worshipped different gods and who had distinct cultural identities. It is remarkable that throughout the rest of the OT, the nation of Edom is predominantly reviled as an enemy of Israel (Num 20:14–20; 1 Kgs 11:14–16; Amos 1:11). In particular, Edom was an ally with the enemy Babylon as its army destroyed the holy city of Jerusalem and the temple in 587 BCE (Jer 49:19–22; Ezek 25:12–14; 36:5; Ps 137:7). The entire book of the prophet Obadiah is devoted to God's judgment on the nation of Edom. Yet Genesis affirms that even this enemy-nation of Edom is a brother to Jacob/Israel. Indeed, the genealogies of Genesis trace all the world's families back to one common ancestral couple, Adam and Eve, affirming that all humans are in some sense brothers and sisters, bound together in the same family line as children of one Creator God.

Third, Enemies Can Teach Us about Forgiveness. In Gen 33 Esau the Edomite, Esau the enemy, is the compassionate forgiver. The forgiver is not Jacob the Israelite, not Jacob the chosen man of God. Jacob is the offender who must be brought low and humbled in order to be forgiven. Esau represents the people of Edom who were not worshipers of the God of Israel, and yet he is lifted up as the forgiving one in this narrative. Our survey of modern scientific research revealed that the capacity to forgive is a universal human quality. Even some nonhuman species carry out what seems to be something like forgiveness, especially in relationships within family groups. As Christians or other religious adherents, we may sometimes be tempted

---

34. McCullough, *Beyond Revenge*, 181–201.

to believe that we have a monopoly or superiority in our capacity to offer forgiveness and kindness. The scientific study of forgiveness and the biblical story of Esau forgiving Jacob, however, remind us that all humans have this deep and innate capacity to forgive as well as to take revenge.

Fourth, The Bible's Realism. Genesis is realistic about how revenge and forgiveness work in the real world. No matter how earnest we may be, sometimes attempts to forgive and reconcile break down or are only partial and not complete. When Esau offers to merge his family and resources with Jacob's family in what might have been a "happily ever after" ending, Jacob initially says "yes" but then acts to say "no." Jacob ensures that the merger of the two families does not happen by moving far away from Esau's territory (Gen 33:12–17).

After the encounter with Esau, Jacob immediately confronted another morally complex situation involving revenge and forgiveness when his daughter Dinah was raped by a Canaanite prince named Shechem (Gen 34). Although a powerful prince, Shechem humbled himself, asked for reconciliation, and offered compensation. As a precarious alien, Jacob seemed inclined to accept Shechem's offer. Jacob's sons, however, refused to forgive this outrage and devised a deceitful scheme to take revenge by killing all the males in the Canaanite city. The human desire for revenge is never too far beneath the surface, even among the people of God. Just as Jacob was wounded as he wrestled with God and limped away (Gen 32:22–32), so too Jacob will continue to walk, as we all do, with a limp as he struggles with the complex interplay of revenge and forgiveness in his life and the life of his family.

Fifth, The Bible's Key Contribution: The Central Role of God in the Interplay of Revenge and Forgiveness. The presence and activity of God in the Jacob-Esau story and in the reality of human life is a crucial element that usually plays little role in most modern scientific perspectives on revenge and forgiveness. When God is factored in, the dynamic of revenge and forgiveness changes. Jacob wrestles with God before he can be reconciled with Esau (Gen 32:22–32). Somehow wrestling with God prepares Jacob for his encounter with his enemy and his brother Esau. Jacob tells Esau after their reconciliation that "truly to see your face is like seeing the face of God" (Gen 33:10). Moreover, when Esau resists accepting all of Jacob's gifts and compensation, Jacob explains to Esau, "Please accept my gift that is brought to you, because God has dealt graciously with me, and because I have everything I want" (Gen 33:11). Jacob's sense of gratitude for the past generosity of God unleashed in him a generosity to his brother Esau. For the first time in his life Jacob was able to give a gift to someone else rather than steal or swindle it from them. As we noted earlier, human sin included both the disobedience against God in Gen 3 and the murder of a brother in Gen 4. Likewise, redemption for Jacob included both the wrestling and blessing from God in Gen 32 and the forgiveness and reconciliation with his brother in Gen 33. As the Scriptures testify, "We love because [God] first loved us" (1 John 4:19).

Sixth, Relinquishing the Human Desire for Revenge to the Justice of God. One of the significant ways in which the dynamic of revenge and forgiveness changes when God is factored into the equation is that the deeply ingrained human desire for revenge against those who have severely hurt us can be given up to God in prayer and lament. The portrait of Esau/Edom as a nation is an example. The Edomites outraged the people of Judah by collaborating with the Babylonians in the destruction of Jerusalem and the temple in the tragedy of 587 BCE. The prophets and psalmists join together in condemning the Edomites for their assistance and joy in Jerusalem's devastation. Thus, Ps 137:7 asks God to take revenge: "Remember, O LORD, against the Edomites the day of Jerusalem's fall, how they said, 'Tear it down! Tear it down! Down to its foundations!'" Science reminds us how deeply our desires for revenge are hardwired into our minds. The Bible offers us a way to relinquish these human desires and entrust them to the just judgment of God. Even as we do so, of course, we realize that God's ways may not always be our ways. The Psalms are saturated with laments about enemies and requests that God take revenge upon them. Words for "enemy" occur a total of 127 times throughout the Psalter. Some faithful followers of Christ may be reluctant to pray these prayers for revenge. They may seem "unspiritual" and thus unworthy to be prayed. If so, perhaps we have not as yet experienced the depths of pain from which these prayers arose. When the time arises when we do need them, the psalms are available as a vehicle for those who have been deeply, deeply hurt. The psalms allow the extreme sufferer to relinquish the desire for revenge to God. Letting such vengeful desires go can relieve us of the stress of holding on to toxic yearnings. In some instances entrusting our desire for revenge to God may open up an otherwise closed door to the possibility of forgiving a former enemy. The Apostle Paul's counsel works well in tandem with these psalms asking God for revenge on enemies. Paul urges us to lay our vengeful thoughts at God's throne and walk away: "Beloved, never avenge yourselves, but leave room for the wrath of God; for it is written, 'Vengeance is mine, I will repay, says the Lord'" (Rom 12:19).

Seventh, The Arc of God's Story Ultimately Tilts Away from Revenge and toward Forgiveness. The dual realities of revenge and forgiveness will remain a persistent part of human relationships and communities, even among the people of God. On this side of God's new heaven and new earth we will not be exempt from desiring revenge at times or suffering the revenge of others at other times. We noted earlier how the LORD tilted more strongly toward mercy and forgiveness even for the murderer Cain, although Cain suffered consequences for his deadly deed. Likewise, the LORD was merciful and kind to Jacob, promising to be "with you" and to "keep you wherever you go" (Gen 28:15). At the same time, God wrestled with Jacob through a dark night but, ultimately, through it all God blessed Jacob (Gen 32:22–32).

The arc of God's story with the world continues from Genesis forward into the OT and on to the NT. Eventually, God planted a stake in the ground in the shape of a Roman cross, an instrument of torture and pain. From that cross God's beloved Son resisted the desire for revenge (Matt 26:53). Instead, Jesus offered mercy: "Father, forgive them; for they do not know what they are doing" (Luke 23:34). The cross declares that God's forgiveness and compassion will have the final say in God's creation. In the meantime we continue to wrestle and struggle together in this messy, fallen world as brothers and sisters—in families, in faith communities, in nations, and in the world. We struggle with the help of God toward a future that finally only God can bring in all its fullness. But from time to time we are blessed to see these glimpses of God's kingdom coming—two enemies, two siblings walking toward one another, embracing after twenty years of hatred, weeping together in joy. For those precious glimpses, we give thanks.

Rachel and Leah: Sibling Rivalry and a Negotiated Alternative to Revenge (Gen 29–30)

Earlier we pointed to a number of social scientific studies that suggested that the intensity of the human desire for revenge against those who hurt or threaten us tends to be more pronounced as a whole among males as compared to females.[35] Psychological studies of the effect of gender on sibling relationships also tend to show that in the aggregate, "relationships between sisters are characteristically warmer" while "relationships between brothers are more likely to be characterized by both rivalry and/or camaraderie (although this is not invariant)."[36] An analysis of the biblical story of two sisters, Rachel and Leah, in Gen 29–30 provides an opportunity to discern whether the biblical portrait of these two sisters offers another

---

35. See footnote 10 above.

36. Robert Sanders, *Sibling Relationships: Theory and Issues for Practice* (New York: Palgrave Macmillan, 2004) 18.

"virtual parallel" to modern studies involving the interplay of revenge, sibling rivalry, and gender. As we consider possible parallels, we remain acutely aware of the complexities of sibling relationships, family structures, gender, cross-cultural differences, and the move from ancient to modern contexts. Whatever correlations we may discern between Genesis and our own time and context remain only suggestive and "virtual" in nature.

The narrative of Rachel and Leah begins when Jacob left his birthplace of Canaan and arrived in Haran in Mesopotamia among his mother's kin under the pretext of looking for a wife (Gen 27:41–28:5). Jacob encountered his future wife Rachel at a well watering her father's sheep. In conversation he discovered that she was the daughter of her mother's brother, Laban, and then "Jacob kissed her and wept aloud" (Gen 29:11–12). Rachel brought Jacob to meet her father Laban who "ran to meet him . . . embraced him and kissed him" (Gen 29:13), prefiguring Jacob's later encounter with his brother Esau with nearly identical language (Gen 33:4). Laban had two daughters, the elder Leah and the younger Rachel. In describing the two sisters the narrator contrasts the young Rachel who was "graceful and beautiful" with Leah whose eyes were *rakkôt* (Hebrew). In most contexts, the adjective *rakkôt* has a positive meaning of "tender/delicate/lovely" but in this context it may also mean "weak/feeble." Leah's outer beauty may be marred by "weak eyes," her eyes may be "lovely," or her eyes may reveal an inner disposition of delicate tenderness (Gen 29:17). In any case, Jacob falls in love with Rachel and not Leah. Jacob offers to work for her father Laban for seven years in order to earn the right to marry his daughter, Rachel (Gen 29:18–20). The intensity of Jacob's love for Rachel is clear; the seven years of labor "seemed to him but a few days because of the love" Jacob had for Rachel.

In an act of deceit, Rachel's father Laban secretly substituted his older daughter Leah on the wedding night when Jacob and Rachel were supposed to be wed. As a result Jacob was forced to accept Leah as his first wife and to work another seven years in order to marry his beloved Rachel as a second wife (Gen 29:21–29). The potential for sisterly rivalry is introduced by the narrator's comment: Jacob "loved Rachel more than Leah" (Gen 29:30). This imbalance in Jacob's affections for his two wives was matched by an imbalance in the other direction in regard to his wives' fertility and ability to bear children: "When the LORD saw that Leah was unloved, he opened her womb; but Rachel was barren" (Gen 29:31). The names that Leah gave to her sons express her hope that her ability to produce offspring for Jacob would cause Jacob to change his affections and to love Leah more than Rachel (Gen 29:32–35).

Meanwhile, the barren and desperate Rachel ("Give me children, or I shall die") devised a new scheme for Jacob to have children through Rachel's own maidservant Bilhah who bore two sons, Dan and Naphtali. Rachel interprets the name, Naphtali, as related to the Hebrew verb *niptaltî*, meaning "I wrestled": "With mighty wrestlings I have wrestled with my sister, and have prevailed" (Gen 30:8; see the allusion to God's wrestling with Jacob and not prevailing in Gen 32:28). For her part, Leah stopped having children after a time but continued the sisterly competition by following Rachel's example, allowing her own maidservant Zilpah to have two additional children with Jacob on her behalf (Gen 30:9–13).

The envy, jealousy, and escalating competition between the two sisters did not lead to physical violence and revenge. Instead, the narrative introduces a scene of negotiation, compromise, and fragile resolution. Leah's oldest son Reuben went out one day and gathered mandrakes, a fruit associated in the ancient world with fertility and feelings of love and romance (Song 7:13).[37] Rachel asked Leah for some of the mandrakes, and Leah initially resisted with a bitter remark: "Is it a small matter that you have taken away my husband? Would you take away my son's mandrakes also?" Rachel persisted and offered a win-win proposal. Rachel was Jacob's favored wife and thereby apparently had some say about when and if Leah could sleep with Jacob. Rachel proposed to Leah that Jacob "may lie with you tonight for your son's mandrakes" (Gen 30:15). Leah was given access to the marriage bed and gave birth to three more children (Gen 30:16–21). Rachel was given access to the fertility-enhancing fruit and ended up giving birth to her first biological child, Joseph (Gen 30:22–4). The compromise served both of their interests in building up their respective households and their status as Jacob's wives. Later, Rachel gave birth to one more son, Benjamin, but, tragically, she died in childbirth (Gen 35:16–21). Thereafter, Leah will be Jacob's only wife, but it is Rachel's sons (Joseph and Benjamin), not Leah's, who will remain the favored sons of Jacob (Gen 37:3; 44:18–34). Just as the reconciliation of Jacob and Esau did not end in a total and harmonious merger of their families (Gen 33:12–17), the stories of Leah and Rachel lead only to partial repair, a measure of healing but also tragedy, a sufficient resolution for a time but not happily-ever-after. Leah and Rachel did manage for a period to become close allies in their shared resentment of their father Laban and their shared support of Jacob's plans to travel from Mesopotamia to Canaan (Gen 31:14–18). What insights about sibling rivalry, revenge, and forgiveness might we derive from the Rachel-Leah story?

---

37. Claus Westermann, *Genesis 12–36* (trans. John Scullion; Minneapolis: Fortress, 1995) 475.

First, Women's Ways or Human Ways? Resolving Rivalry through Negotiated Compromise. Conflicts involving power, property, and status among kinship groups within ancient Israel form part of the background of this biblical tale of two sisters, Rachel and Leah, who are married to the same man, Jacob.[38] The interactions between these two sisters-wives-mothers provide a positive alternative in working through sibling envy, jealousy, and conflict. Instead of revenge they model compromise, negotiation, and seeking mutual self-interest. Such strategies are not confined to women characters in Genesis, of course. Abram and Lot agreed to a mutually beneficial arrangement of land division in Gen 13. Jacob and Laban negotiated a covenant of peace after their conflicts over property and Jacob's sudden departure for Canaan (Gen 31:43–54). The enemy-brothers Jacob and Esau reconciled (Gen 33:4). The whole Joseph narrative offers a powerful witness to forgiveness as an alternative to revenge among sibling rivals (Gen 45:4–15; 50:15–21).[39] Moreover, the narrative world of Genesis shows women are quite capable of acts of revenge against those whom they perceive as a threat to their status, access to resources, or honor in the community (e.g., Sarah and Hagar in Gen 16:3–6; 21:8–10; Potiphar's wife and Joseph in Gen 39:6–20). In the world of Genesis revenge is not exclusively a male or female capacity but a human one. Similarly, the capacity for forgiveness, reconciliation, negotiation, and working toward mutual self-interest are resources available to both men and women.

Yet, in a "virtual parallel" with modern social and behavioral sciences, the tendency to seek revenge, and particularly revenge through physical violence, seems more pronounced with male characters in the Bible than with female characters. This is not an "essentialist" claim regarding gender but an observation of generalized tendencies. As such, Rachel and Leah embody the human capacity to work through jealousy and conflict without resorting to revenge. They negotiated a compromise in which both find their needs and interests reasonably well served for the time being.

Second, God: Favoring One, Then the Other. We turn now to a question that is not usually on the radar of the modern scientific lens regarding sibling rivalry. What is God's role in the Rachel and Leah story? God opened and closed the wombs of the

---

38. Naomi Steinberg, *Kinship and Marriage in Genesis: A Household Economics Perspective* (Minneapolis: Fortress, 1993) 101–8.

39. The themes of sibling rivalry, opportunities for revenge, and the triumph of forgiveness permeate the extended story of Joseph and his brothers in Gen 37–50. The subtlety, complexity, and layers of interactions among the characters leading to reconciliation require a separate treatment from this essay. A suggestive study of anger as it relates to rivalry, revenge, and forgiveness in Genesis and the Joseph story is Matthew Schlimm, *From Fratricide to Forgiveness: The Language and Ethics of Anger in Genesis* (Siphrut 7; Winona Lake: Eisenbrauns, 2011), esp. 169–84.

two women (Gen 29:31; 30:2, 22–23). God heard, saw, and responded to the pain, prayers, and praise of Rachel and Leah (Gen 29:32, 35; 30:6, 17, 22). God did favor one woman for a time, but then God turned and acted to support the other woman in her time of need. When Jacob "loved Rachel more than Leah" and "the LORD saw that Leah was unloved," God tipped the scales of blessing back to Leah. God granted Leah children while Rachel remained barren (Gen 29:30–31, 33). After Leah bore four sons, Rachel interpreted the birth of her surrogate son through her maidservant Bilhah as God's judging again in her favor (Gen 31:6). After an interim period of barrenness for Leah, God again allowed Leah to give birth to two more sons and a daughter (Gen 30:18–21). Then God turned and granted Rachel the birth of a son named Joseph (Gen 30:24). God appears here balanced and evenhanded between Rachel and Leah, going back and forth in responding to the two sisters in their respective hours of need. The balance of God's interactions with Rachel and Leah correlate with the two women's own evenhandedness in attending to each other's needs as they negotiated their way toward a mutually satisfying resolution of their conflict.[40]

Third, "Now I Will Praise the LORD": The Subtle Intertwining of Divine Agency and Human Initiative. A third theological insight from the Rachel-Leah cycle of stories is how the narrative braids together strands of active human resourcefulness and creativity and strands of divine agency and activity in, with, and under human activity. On the human resourcefulness side, the barren Rachel devised a strategy to have children through her maidservant Bilhah. Later, Rachel's strong insistence on having access to the mandrakes as a fertility enhancer led to her giving birth to Joseph. Leah likewise had children through her maidservant Zilpah when she later became barren. Leah bartered her mandrakes for a chance to sleep with Jacob and gave birth to three more children. In the midst of all these human ventures, the human participants also prayed to God for divine aid. The voices of the narrator and the two women characters repeatedly affirm God's activity as a complement alongside the robust actions and enterprising strategies of the two women (Gen 29:31–33, 35; 30:2, 6, 17–20, 22–24).

The affirmation of the subtle intertwining of the human and the divine in the narratives of Genesis seems an appropriate place to conclude our binocular study of modern scientific and biblical-theological perspectives on sibling rivalry, revenge,

---

40. It should be noted that God's evenhanded justice in treating Rachel and Leah does not extend to their two respective maidservants, Bilhah and Zilpah. The maidservants appear in the narrative as pawns in the narrative, forced to sleep with the patriarch and to act as surrogate mothers for their mistresses.

and forgiveness. We have noted a number of "virtual parallels" and correlations between the insights from the natural and social sciences and the insights of the book of Genesis regarding sibling rivalry, conflict, revenge, and forgiveness. The various scientific insights into revenge and forgiveness brought certain elements of the biblical text into greater relief and clarity. We have also observed ways in which the two lenses of inquiry and wisdom depart, particularly in terms of the role and activity of God as related to humans and the world. As people of faith, we can appreciate the multiple realms of human inquiry and scholarly disciplines as gifts and resources that God has given. People of faith will negotiate their way through the insights of these human sciences, discerning and engaging those intellectual resources that help them better understand and participate in the often messy realities of the families, communities, and world in which God has placed us. At the same time, they will work in light of Scripture's overriding admonition that "the fear of the LORD is the beginning of wisdom" (Ps 111:10; Prov 1:7).

Appendix: A Brief Rejoinder to Professor Jack Lundblom's Response

I thank Professor Lundblom for his thoughtful response to my paper. I am not able to respond to all his points here, but let me offer the following as a partial response to one objection raised. Professor Lundblom believes that I use the term "revenge" too broadly. The definition that I offer is "retaliating in some way against someone who has severely hurt you or the community." Professor Lundblom does not believe that this definition covers some of the examples cited in the paper, including Cain's murder of his brother Abel, God's punishment of Cain, chimpanzees who attack other transgressing chimps, or the killing of a new-born black eagle by its older sibling. In my judgment Cain's murder of his brother seems clearly to fall within the definition of revenge. The narrative notes that Cain was "very angry" (Gen 4:5), an emotion often associated with revenge among humans. Cain's anger seems clearly directed against his brother Abel, and the retaliatory murder seems motivated by Cain's perception of having been harmed by Abel through the shame and dishonor of Abel's sacrifice being accepted but not Cain's. Perceived harm plus retaliation equals revenge.

God's punishment of Cain, it seems to me, also fits the definition of revenge. God retaliates against Cain for the harm done against God's new creational community. God describes Abel's blood as "crying out to me from the ground" (Gen 4:10). The statement echoes Gen 9:5-6 in which blood revenge (life for a life) is rooted in humans bearing God's own image so that killing a human is viewed as an attack on God's own image. Elsewhere, the vocabulary of revenge and punishment overlap. For example, Hebrew *nqm* ("to avenge") is used for human punishment (Exod 21:20) as well as divine punishment or judgment (Deut 32:41, 43; Mic 5:4; Ps 99:8).

In the case of the outsiders transgressing the chimpanzees' territory, the outsiders are perceived as having done harm in threatening the sense of safety and security of the chimpanzee community, and the chimps retaliate. I will concede that the pecking of the new-born black eagle by its older sibling is not precisely an act of revenge. However, in evolutionary terms the second new-born chick's very existence does pose a threatened harm to the older new-born black eagle as it represents a potential rival in an ecological context of very scarce resources. Perhaps we might call this more "revenge-like" in evolutionary terms. In any case, my purpose in raising this example in the paper was simply to illustrate the wide range of sibling relationships, sometimes extremely cooperative and self-sacrificing (the colony of bees) and sometimes quite brutish and harsh (the new-born black eagles). The black eagle was not meant as a parade example of revenge in the paper's argument.

RESPONSE TO OLSON

Jack R. Lundbom

I have three comments on the section of Olson's paper dealing with revenge and forgiveness in humans, animals, and other created species. First, I read with interest the studies on aggression in bees, black eagles, chimpanzees, and the rest, but I see no evolution from revenge to forgiveness in humans and other species. From comments in the relevant section and at the end of the paper, I do not think Olson does either. Second, one lens of Olson's binoculars needs adjustment if the paper is to have focus. You cannot compare a scientific, evolutionary view of the created order with two examples of sibling rivalry from Genesis. Third, the term "revenge" is used here and throughout the paper way too broadly. On this third point, revenge and vengeance can overlap in meaning, and the terms are often used interchangeably, but they are not the same. Revenge is punishment inflicted in return for injury, insult, or other indignity one has sustained. Olson gets the definition right when he brackets out three other forms of aggression, but that is not enough. The discussion as a whole is flawed because the term "revenge" is made to cover a range of violent actions, many of which are not revenge. Violent behavior of newborn black eagles toward younger siblings is not revenge, and I am not sure whether protective action by chimpanzees against outsiders can be called revenge.

I did appreciate the factors Olson cited for lessening the need to take revenge: verbal apologies; body language conveying shame, guilt, or self-humiliation; and compensation. All can convey forgiveness.

Regarding Cain and Abel, I do not find this example from Genesis convincing. Cain is guilty of jealousy, anger, and murder, but he is not exacting revenge in killing his brother. The problem here is the imprecise definition of "revenge" carried over from the first part of the paper. Also, there is neither revenge nor forgiveness on the part of God. God simply punishes Cain for the murder and then shows mercy after the punishment. I would omit this example from the discussion.

Regarding Jacob and Esau, I think this example is excellent. Esau forgives his brother and does not seek revenge for Jacob having bargained away his birthright and having taken his father's blessing. The reconciliation passage in Gen 33 is one of the great texts of forgiveness and grace in the OT. In my view it is the likely background for Jesus' parable of the Lost (Prodigal) Son in Luke 15:11–32.[1]

I see particular value in the observation that enemies are able to teach us about forgiveness. Olson points out that it was Esau, not Jacob, who forgave his brother, and this supports the claim that "all humans have the innate capacity to forgive as well as take revenge." I also find particular value in the paragraph about relinquishing the human desire for revenge and leaving justice to God (Deut 32:35; Rom 12:19). Jeremiah lived according to this rule, and his life was preserved (Jer 1:18–19; 15:20–21), but can we still pray for God to take vengeance on our enemies? Olson says this prayer is heard often in the Psalms. We hear it also from Jeremiah, where the prophet even asks God not to forgive those plotting against him (Jer 17:18).[2] We are taught by Jesus to love and forgive our enemies (Matt 5:43–48; Luke 23:34), enabling Christians to occupy the high moral ground against any detractors of our religion. Gandhi saw in the non-retaliation teaching of the Sermon on the Mount (Matt 5:38–41) the "highest form of religion" and said it is what "endeared Jesus to him."[3] But I think we can still pray for God to avenge wrongdoing done to us, for that leaves vengeance to him, and he may or may not take it.

---

1. See D. N. Freedman and J. R. Lundbom, *ḥnn* in *TDOT* 5:29.

2. See discussion in my *Jeremiah 1-20: A New Translation with Introduction and Commentary* (Anchor Yale Bible Commentaries; New York: Doubleday, 1999) 833.

3. M. K. Gandhi, *Gandhi's Autobiography* (trans. Mahadev Desai; Washington, DC: Public Affairs, 1960) 92; idem, *What Jesus Means to Me* (Ahmedabad: Navajivan, 1959) 4.

WIVES AND DAUGHTERS: WOMEN, SEX, AND VIOLENCE IN BIBLICAL TRADITION

Caryn A. Reeder

The men of her city will stone her with stones, and she will die, because she has done a foolish thing in Israel by prostituting the house of her father. And you will destroy the evil from your midst. (Deut 22:21, author's translation)

The series of laws in Deut 22:13–29 addresses various cases of sexual transgression. The section begins and ends with laws that identify men as the primary transgressors in certain cases of slander and assault, and these laws offer some protection for the women involved (vv. 13–19, 25–29).[1] In the three laws in the center of the series, however, the women involved in what is presented as sexual transgression are executed. If the parents of a slandered bride cannot provide evidence that she was a virgin at the time of her marriage, she is stoned at the door of her father's house (vv. 20–21). A wife caught in the act of lying with another man is executed along with the man (v. 22), and in the case of a man who lies with a betrothed young woman inside the city, both are executed (vv. 23–24).

These three laws have proved troubling for readers from at least the first century until our own day. Some of the questions raised by interpreters relate to the brevity of the laws. Many potential complexities and complications are not addressed, and since the women do not speak, their stories are unknown. Other questions reflect more fundamental concerns with the agency and complicity of the women in the cases. For modern readers in particular, the assumption of patriarchal control over the women in the three laws is itself suspect.

These concerns can lead to the outright rejection of the texts altogether, or the more passive omission of the texts from the life of the church.[2] After all, the laws of Deut 22:20–24 represent the values of a social and cultural context that modern

---

1. At least the women are protected by ancient Israelite standards, though later readers have had difficulties with the concept of marriage to a slandering husband or rapist as protection (e.g., Philo, *Spec. Laws* 3.70–71, 82).

2. Notably, the laws of Deut 22:13–29 are not part of *The Revised Common Lectionary*, *Lectionary for Mass*, or the lectionary of *The Book of Common Prayer*.

readers, at least in the Western world, may find incomprehensible or intolerable. Moreover, the story of the woman caught in adultery in John 7:53—8:11 provides Christian readers with reason to bypass these laws as relics of another time. It may seem unnecessary to read them in church today.

The three laws of Deut 22:20-24 are part of the canon, however. To reject or ignore them limits our understanding of Deuteronomy's vision of the covenant, and also participates in what Philip Jenkins calls the "holy amnesia" of the church.[3] This second charge is serious in light of the long world history of sexual violence against women and of physical violence against women in response to perceived sexual transgressions, a story that continues to unfold around the world (consider, for instance, the issue of "honor killings")—and in our own churches.[4] Readers committed both to the canon of Scripture and to pastoral care for the survivors of assault have a responsibility to seek to understand these laws in their ancient context and to interpret them for the church.

This paper begins with a definition of the key issues of "family" and "violence" in Deuteronomy and its literary and historical contexts before turning to the interpretation of the three focus laws. While these laws can be understood within the social and theological concerns of Deuteronomy, they remain problematic for readers, that is, for you and me. When we read these texts in the church today, we read them with people who have committed adultery, with women and men who will not be virgins on their wedding nights, with victims of sexual assault and assailants. The perspectives and needs of the community must be taken into account lest our interpretation of these texts cause pain or provoke violence.[5] The third section of the paper thus proposes ways in which Deut 22:20-24 can be interpreted for the church.

Family, Violence, and Deuteronomy

It is no surprise that the world of Deuteronomy is very different from the worlds of modern readers. The difference can be easy to overlook, however, when dealing

---

3. Philip Jenkins, *Laying Down the Sword: Why We Can't Ignore the Bible's Violent Verses* (New York: HarperOne, 2011) 13-15.

4. Cf. Susanne Scholz, "'Back Then It Was Legal': The Epistemological Imbalance in Readings of Biblical and Ancient Near Eastern Rape Legislation," *The Bible and Critical Theory* 1.4 (2005) 1-22, 2 (cited 25 August 2012; online: http://bibleandcriticaltheory.org/index.php/bct/article/viewFile/61/47); Cheryl A. Kirk-Duggan, *Violence and Theology* (Horizons in Theology; Nashville: Abingdon, 2006) 16; Carole R. Fontaine, *With Eyes of Flesh: The Bible, Gender and Human Rights* (The Bible in the Modern World 10; Amsterdam Studies in the Bible and Religion 2; Sheffield: Sheffield Phoenix, 2008) 175-77.

5. See further Fontaine, *With Eyes of Flesh*, 152-53.

with concepts as basic and pervasive as "family" and "violence." Before addressing the laws of Deut 22:20-24, it is necessary to establish an understanding of what these ideas represent in Deuteronomy and its ancient contexts.

Defining the Family

The women of Deut 22:20-24 are identified as "young woman," *naʿărāh* (vv. 20-21, 23-24), and "woman," *ʾīšāh* (v. 22). The young woman in vv. 20-21 is also by implication a daughter (cf. v. 16). The woman in v. 22 is "the one married to a husband" (or "the ruled-over of a lord"). The young woman in vv. 23-24 is a betrothed virgin and a neighbor's wife. These women are identified by "family" relationships, and to understand their stories it is important to understand how Deuteronomy constructs the "family."

In Deuteronomy family is often represented by the term "household" (*băʿit*). "Household" can specifically refer to a family lineage, as in Deut 25:9 (cf. "house of the father" in Gen 12:1; Exod 12:3; etc.). These households are patrilocal. Wives live with their husbands' families, and inheritance passes through the male line (Deut 21:15-17; 24:1). In Deut 12:7 and 12 the household includes the patriarch and his wife or wives (represented by "you"), their sons and daughters, and their slaves. The sons' wives and children would be part of the household, as could the patriarch's brothers and unmarried sisters (cf. 4:9; 7:3; 25:5). According to Deut 16:11 the household also incorporates otherwise unattached members of the community like Levites, sojourners, widows, and orphans. In the society depicted in Deuteronomy the family is composed of people connected by blood, marriage, or location.

This society is patriarchal. Deuteronomy's laws are addressed to, and represent the perspective of, the male head of household (note, for instance, 5:21; 13:7 [ET 6]; 20:5-7; 22:15-17). The patriarch's wife is also significant though. A mother is to be honored along with the father (5:16; 21:18-21; 27:16), and the wife is sometimes presented as a unit with the patriarch (as in 5:14; 6:2; 12:12).[6] Moreover, in Deuteronomy's historical context women and children were essential to the survival of the household.[7] Deuteronomy's households are part of settlements tightly con-

---

6. Cf. Christopher J. H. Wright, *God's People in God's Land: Family, Land, and Property in the Old Testament* (Grand Rapids: Eerdmans, 1990) 220; Tikva Frymer-Kensky, "The Family in the Hebrew Bible," in *Religion, Feminism, and the Family* (ed. Anne Carr and Mary Stewart Van Leeuwen; The Family, Religion, and Culture; Louisville: Westminster John Knox, 1996) 55-73, 59; J. G. McConville, *Deuteronomy* (Apollos Old Testament Commentary 5; Downers Grove: InterVarsity, 2002) 21, 26-29.

7. With respect to its history, the book has been placed in several different time periods, but it is most often assigned to the reign of Josiah over Judah (2 Kgs 22-23); see, e.g., Jeffrey H. Tigay,

nected to the land. In the agricultural economy represented here, all the members of the household—young and old, women and men, slaves and masters—would be required to work together in the home and fields to support their common life.[8] Women and children therefore have their own power in the household. A patriarch could not survive if he alienated his coworkers.

"Common life" is a key concept in Deuteronomy's historical setting. House design in ancient Israel incorporated shared courtyards, flat rooftops for daily activities, and common living spaces, and these houses were tightly connected spatially and socially to other households in the village or city.[9] Family members lived, worked, ate, played, and slept in the sight and hearing of their own household and their neighbors' households. In ancient Israel and in the community presented in Deuteronomy, family life was a public affair, and of public concern.

The public nature of family life includes sex. Household space in ancient Israel did not include private bedrooms for married couples. Moreover, sexual intercourse is a communal concern because it connects and thus affects multiple households. The language of Deut 22:13–29 reflects this setting: "I gave my daughter to this man as a wife" (v. 16); "a woman married to a husband" (v. 22) and "the wife of his neighbor" (v. 24); and the distinction between intercourse in the city and in the fields (vv. 23–27). In this context the prohibition of adultery in 5:18 and the cases of sexual transgression in 22:13–29 are not primarily about private or personal morality. These laws make sex an issue of covenantal faithfulness, an issue that thus affects the honor of the household and the welfare of the community.[10]

Within the narrative setting established in Deut 1:5, the people of Israel stand on the banks of the Jordan River, listening to one last speech from Moses before

---

Deuteronomy: The Traditional Hebrew Text with the New JPS Translation (JPS Torah Commentary; Philadelphia: Jewish Publication Society, 1996) xxi.

8. Carol Meyers, "The Family in Early Israel," in *Families in Ancient Israel* (Leo G. Perdue et al.; The Family, Religion, and Culture; Louisville: Westminster John Knox, 1997) 1–47, 24–31; J. David Schloen, *The House of the Father as Fact and Symbol: Patrimonialism in Ugarit and the Ancient Near East* (Studies in the Archaeology and History of the Levant; Harvard Semitic Museum Publications; Winona Lake: Eisenbrauns, 2001) 138–40; John S. Holladay, "'Home Economics 1407' and the Israelite Family and their Neighbors: An Anthropological/Archaeological Exploration," in *The Family in Life and Death: The Family in Ancient Israel: Sociological and Archaeological Perspectives* (ed. Patricia Dutcher-Walls; New York: T. & T. Clark, 2009) 61–88, 61–62.

9. Cf. Holladay, "'Home Economics 1407,'" 65–71; Meyers, "The Family in Early Israel," 16–17, 21; Schloen, *The House of the Father as Fact and Symbol*, 106–12, 136–38, 150–51.

10. Cf. Richard D. Nelson, *Deuteronomy: A Commentary* (Old Testament Library; Louisville: Westminster John Knox, 2002) 83; Christopher J. H. Wright, *Deuteronomy* (New International Biblical Commentary; Peabody, MA: Hendrickson, 1996) 80.

crossing into the promised land. In this context Deuteronomy's laws outline Israel's covenant identity, and the household has an important place in this identity. The responsibilities of an individual household—including caring for its members, caring for its land, and respecting communal and social traditions and expectations—are important to the success of the covenant as a whole. The disruption of a single household likewise can endanger the covenant and community.[11] The historical and narratival significance of family life provides a key context for interpreting the laws of Deut 22:13-29.

Defining Violence

In the Hebrew Bible the vocabulary of violence is primarily associated with unrighteous, oppressive, and illicit activities.[12] Though not every violent act is identified as such (e.g., Deut 19:11-13), the biblical definition of violence is nonetheless limited to wicked actions or behaviors like murder, false witness, robbery, and other injustices. This list can be extended to include sexual assault as in the rapes of Tamar in 2 Sam 13 and the Levite's concubine in Judg 19.[13] The sexual transgressions and capital punishment described in Deut 22:20-24, however, are not violence by biblical standards. The inclusion of violence in the title of this paper is a deliberate intrusion that reflects two concerns: first, the potential for sexual violence in the stories these laws tell, and second, the violence of execution.

---

11. So also, e.g., Wright, *Deuteronomy*, 80. Cf. Philip J. King and Lawrence E. Stager, *Life in Biblical Israel* (Library of Ancient Israel; Louisville: Westminster John Knox, 2001) 4-5; Schloen, *The House of the Father as Fact and Symbol*, 65-67.

12. *ḥāmās* in Gen 6:11; Deut 19:16; *pārîṣ* in Ps 17:4; Ezek 18:10; *šōd* in Isa 16:4; Ezek 45:9; etc.

13. I use the word "rape" advisedly. Whether or not "rape" is an appropriate descriptor for biblical stories has been debated in recent years. There is no single Hebrew word that expresses what a modern Western reader means by "rape," and Robert S. Kawashima suggests that since women in biblical Israel lacked the legal power of sexual consent, rape is essentially a legal impossibility ("Could a Woman Say 'No' in Biblical Israel? On the Genealogy of Legal Status in Biblical Law and Literature," *Association for Jewish Studies Review* 35.1 [2011] 1-22, 2). On the other hand, Tamar verbally objects and Amnon physically overpowers her (2 Sam 13:12-14), and the concubine is seized and tossed out by her husband and abused all night until she dies (Judg 19:25-26). These scenes are clear examples of sexual violence against the women involved. Cf. Sandie Gravett, "Reading 'Rape' in the Hebrew Bible: A Consideration of Language," *JSOT* 28.3 (2004) 279-99, 281, 284; Yael Shemesh, "Rape is Rape is Rape: The Story of Dinah and Shechem (Genesis 34)," *ZAW* 119.1 (2007) 2-21, 5; S. David Sperling, "Dinah, 'Innah, and Related Matters," in *Mishneh Todah: Studies in Deuteronomy and Its Cultural Environment* (ed. Nili Sacher Fox, David A. Glatt-Gilad, and Michael James Williams; Winona Lake: Eisenbrauns, 2009) 73-93, 85.

First, the ambiguity and brevity of the laws of Deut 22:20-24 leave open the possibility of sexual violence. The wife in v. 22 and the betrothed woman in vv. 23-24 are both objects of men's actions, and their willingness to participate in the intercourse is not addressed. While in the first law the woman is the actor, her story—how she gave up her status as a "virgin of Israel"—is unknown. The possibility of rape cannot be discounted in these laws (as interpreters have repeatedly noted).[14] From a pastoral perspective it is particularly important to note the potential for sexual violence in these texts. Following Carol Fontaine's passionate argument, to fail to do so participates in the oppression of victims of violence in the church today.[15]

Second, the execution decreed for the women and their male partners can be interpreted as violence. In the Hebrew Bible execution and punishment of wrongdoing is only described with the vocabulary of violence when it is on a large scale (the destruction of entire cities or peoples).[16] These instances, however, allow for the possibility of describing the punishment of an individual as violence as well.[17] The act of stoning decreed in Deut 22:21 and 24 is, in fact, inherently violent, involving members of the community in physically causing the death of the offender.[18] If the women were unwilling partners in the sexual intercourse, their execution becomes even more violent by modern standards—think of the outrage over the honor killing of a rape victim. Finally, the identification of the execution of women for perceived sexual transgression as violence also reflects a concern with the after-life of these texts, which could be used as justification for violence against women.[19] This potential must be kept in mind as the texts are read and interpreted.

This paper focuses on the representation of women in Deut 22:20-24. Men also face the violence of execution in these texts, and their stories are also unknown. (Perhaps the men involved did not know the marital status of the women with whom

14. Cf. Philo, *Spec. Laws* 3.73, 77-78; *m. Ketub.* 1:6-7; Cynthia Edenburg, "Ideology and Social Context of the Deuteronomic Women's Sex Laws (Deuteronomy 22:13-29)," *JBL* 128.1 (2009) 43-60, 52; Scholz, "Back Then It Was Legal," 6-7; Shemesh, "Rape is Rape is Rape," 6.

15. Fontaine, *With Eyes of Flesh*, 175-76; see also Scholz, "Back Then It Was Legal," 2, 8, 18.

16. See Isa 13:6; Jer 47:4, 51:55; etc.

17. See further Hector Avalos, *Fighting Words: The Origins of Religious Violence* (Amherst: Prometheus, 2005) 19; Ziony Zevit, "The Search for Violence in Israelite Culture and in the Bible," in *Religion and Violence: The Biblical Heritage* (ed. David A. Bernat and Jonathan Klawans; Sheffield: Sheffield Phoenix, 2007) 16-37, 16-17, 26-27.

18. J. J. Finkelstein, *The Ox That Gored* (Transactions of the American Philosophical Society 71.2; Philadelphia: American Philosophical Society, 1981) 27.

19. Cf. Sir 42:9-14; Cheryl B. Anderson, *Women, Ideology, and Violence: Critical Theory and the Construction of Gender in the Book of the Covenant and the Deuteronomic Law* (JSOTSup 394; London: T&T Clark International, 2004) 98-99.

they lay, or perhaps they were raped by the women[20]). In the world represented in Deuteronomy, though, men had more power and agency, as indeed the laws themselves reflect. Men are the actors here. The roles of the women in these laws are more ambiguous. In historical context women in general were more vulnerable to sexual violence, accusations of wrongdoing, and the shame of illicit intercourse, factors that remain true for the modern church. Because the three laws focus more attention on the women, and because of the potential danger of these laws for women around the world today, this discussion is primarily concerned with the wives and daughters of Deut 22:20–24.

Reading Deuteronomy 22:20–24

The laws of Deut 22:20–24 carry the demand for the execution of women involved in illicit sexual intercourse. Beyond the content the three laws have several similarities.[21] They are case laws, like the other laws in Deut 22:13–29: *if* a particular event occurs, *then* a particular result should ensue. The women are at various stages of marriage (betrothed, newly married, married), but they are all legally connected to a husband. In the first and last the method of execution is stoning. Each law ends with the refrain that the execution of the offenders eradicates "evil" from the people ("you," second person masculine singular, in vv. 21 and 24, and "Israel" in v. 22).

These laws are also similar in what they omit. In none do the offenders, male or female, speak; their stories are unknown. The second and third laws do not make mention of any sort of trial, nor, in contrast with Deut 22:13–21 and 28–29, are the families of the offenders or the offended explicitly involved. In the discussion of these three laws, attention will be paid to what they include and what they omit. Both are important for interpretation.

Deuteronomy 22:20–21

The first of the three laws is part of a larger section, which begins with a story. If a man marries a woman but then he "hates" her, he might claim (either officially or unofficially) that she was not a virgin at the time of their marriage.[22] This claim

---

20. Adele Berlin, "Sex and the Single Girl in Deuteronomy 22," in *Mishneh Todah: Studies in Deuteronomy and Its Cultural Environment* (ed. Nili Sacher Fox, David A. Glatt-Gilad, and Michael James Williams; Winona Lake: Eisenbrauns, 2009) 95–112, 101.

21. See also Edenburg, "Ideology and Social Context of the Deuteronomic Women's Sex Laws," 44–47; Nelson, *Deuteronomy*, 266.

22. On the husband's action see further Deborah L. Ellens, *Women in the Sex Texts of Leviticus*

is described as an accusation of "deeds of words" (Deut 22:13–14): it is a baseless charge. The accusation is significant enough though that the parents of the bride must address it before the elders of the city. As the parents' involvement indicates, the accusation against the young woman also affects them (cf. Philo, *Spec. Laws* 3.80–81).[23]

The case has two potential outcomes. The parents can produce "evidence of virginity" before the elders of the city, proving that their daughter was a virgin at marriage.[24] The husband is then disciplined for his slander (perhaps by a beating). He must pay a fine to the father (twice the bride-price listed in Deut 22:29), and he cannot divorce his wife. The young woman is thereby vindicated as a "virgin of Israel" (vv. 15–19).[25] If, however, "evidence of virginity is not found for the young woman," she is condemned to execution (vv. 20–21).

The necessary evidence of virginity is described in v. 17 as a cloth that can be spread out on the ground, most likely a sheet or garment stained with blood from the wedding night. The "evidence," as Tikva Frymer-Kensky notes, is rather flimsy. What would stop the parents from faking it?[26] The condemnation of the young woman on the absence of this evidence is even more troubling. According to v. 20 the woman is executed if the evidence is not "found" (cf. v. 14). This wording, which echoes the "finding out" of wrongdoing in various laws of Deuteronomy, highlights the unique nature of this law. Elsewhere witnesses are required (17:6–7), or wrongdoers must be discovered in the act (cf. 22:22, 24:7). In this law the young woman is condemned

---

and Deuteronomy: A Comparative Conceptual Analysis (New York: T&T Clark, 2008) 224–6; Caryn A. Reeder, *The Enemy in the Household: Family Violence in Deuteronomy and Beyond* (Grand Rapids: Baker, 2012) 45–47.

23. The issue is one of public honor since the daughter's behavior reflects on the father's house and also an economic matter relating to the bride-price. See further Berlin, "Sex and the Single Girl in Deuteronomy 22," 109, 111; Carolyn Pressler, *The View of Women Found in the Deuteronomic Family Laws* (BZAW 216; Berlin; Walter de Gruyter, 1993) 28–29; Tikva Frymer-Kensky, "Virginity in the Bible," in *Gender and Law in the Hebrew Bible and the Ancient Near East* (ed. Victor H. Matthews, Bernard M. Levinson, and Tikva Frymer-Kensky; London: T. & T. Clark, 2004 [1998]) 79–96, 93.

24. Gordon J. Wenham ["Bĕtûlāh 'A Girl of Marriageable Age,'" VT 22 (1972) 326–48, 326, 331–36] argues that the Hebrew word *bĕtûlāh* refers to a girl of an age to be married, not a virgin, and *bĕtûlîm* is evidence of regular menstruation. As Pressler, *The View of Women*, 26–27, notes, however, in legal codes *bĕtûlāh* carries the technical meaning "virgin" (cf. Lev. 21:13–14), and *bĕtûlîm* in this law refers to evidence of virginity (cf. Ellens, *Women in the Sex Texts of Leviticus and Deuteronomy*, 207–9; Berlin, "Sex and the Single Girl in Deuteronomy 22," 103).

25. Following her wedding night, of course, the woman is not physically a virgin. Rather, the ascription "virgin of Israel" replaces the evil name given to the young woman by her husband in Deut 22:14.

26. Frymer-Kensky, "Virginity in the Bible," 95; see also Tigay, *Deuteronomy*, 476.

on the word of a man presented as a false witness and on the absence of proof of innocence.[27]

Since the young woman is not given a voice in the proceedings, her story is unknown. Perhaps the sexual intercourse occurred before her betrothal, an act punished by marriage rather than execution in Deut 22:28-29. She may have been raped, which would potentially limit her culpability (cf. vv. 25-27). It is also the case that not all virgins bleed on their first sexual intercourse. These possibilities are not addressed in the law of Deut 22:20-21.[28]

Instead of an empty accusation, "deeds of words" (v. 14), if evidence is not provided, the "word" is true in v. 20. The young woman is taken to the door of her father's house and stoned to death by the men (or perhaps people) of the city (v. 21). Most other executions in Deuteronomy take place outside the city gates (17:5, 21:21, 22:24), indicating the removal of the threat from the community. That this young woman is executed at the door of her own home implicates her family in her transgression, punishing them as well as her.[29]

The unusual nature of this law receives some explanation in v. 21: the young woman has "prostituted the house of her father."[30] Engaging in sexual intercourse before marriage is an offense against a woman's future husband, but it is also—and more importantly, according to this charge—an offense against her father, and thus the patriarchal system. This young woman has challenged patriarchal authority over her body by having sex with an unapproved partner.[31] The description of her action as "foolishness" emphasizes the seriousness of the matter. Foolishness describes serious wrongdoings that endanger the entire community, wrongdoings that challenge communal authority structures and tradition (cf. Josh 7:15, Judg 19:23-24, 2 Sam 13:12, etc.).[32] The inclusion of this terminology in the law helps explain the unusual

---

27. Ancient interpreters addressed this problem by including requirements for evidence and witnesses of wrongdoing (see Josephus, *Ant.* 4.246; *Sipre Deut* 235-37).

28. Cf. *m. Ketub.* 1:6-7; Kawashima, "Could a Woman Say 'No' in Biblical Israel?" 19; Tigay, *Deuteronomy*, 476.

29. So also Tigay, *Deuteronomy*, 206; Timothy M. Willis, *The Elders of the City: A Study of the Elders-Laws in Deuteronomy* (SBL Monograph Series 55; Atlanta: Society of Biblical Literature, 2001) 226.

30. Prostitution, *znh*, here does not necessarily refer to selling sex for money but to illicit sexual activity in general.

31. See further Willis, *The Elders of the City*, 207-9; Pressler, *The View of Women*, 30-31.

32. Anthony Phillips, "*Nebalah*—A Term for Serious Disorderly and Unruly Conduct," *VT* 25 (1975) 237-42; Frymer-Kensky, "Virginity in the Bible," 95.

elements, and in turn the disruption of expectation in this law reinforces the seriousness of the problem.

Deuteronomy 22:22–24

The two laws in Deut 22:22–24 are concerned with adultery. Adultery, prohibited in the ten commandments (5:18), refers to sexual intercourse between a man and the wife of another man (cf. Lev. 20:10).[33] By its nature, then, adultery involves three people, and through them their households. Like the foolishness of the young woman in Deut 22:20–21, the two cases of adultery in vv. 22–24 disrupt communal expectations and authority.[34]

The law in v. 22 addresses the case of adultery between a man and another man's wife. The wife is described as the woman married to a husband (*běʿūlat bāʿal*; cf. Gen 20:3). Her identity is dependent on her husband, who has authority over her (as *bʿl*, which can mean to rule over or to marry, suggests).[35] The man who lies with her violates the husband's rights (cf. Deut 5:21).

This law is very specific. The two must be "found" in the act of intercourse. Rumors or suspicions of adultery are not part of Deut 22:22, as in Num 5:11–31. The evidence of transgression is obvious. A formal process of accusation or trial is not included, however, and the identity of the finders and the circumstances of the discovery are not specified.[36] These factors could be significant for the trustworthiness of the testimony, as 19:16–20 suggests. The nature of the woman's involvement is also unknown. She may have been raped, which could potentially mitigate her condemnation (as is the case for the betrothed woman in Deut 22:25–27).[37]

The brevity of Deut 22:22 allows for and at the same time displaces these important questions. According to the letter of this law the man and the wife caught

---

33. The marital status of the male adulterer is not of concern in the Torah. Cf. Tigay, *Deuteronomy*, 71; and Nelson, *Deuteronomy*, 83.

34. See especially Louis Stulman, "Sex and Familial Crimes in the D Code: A Witness to Mores in Transition," *JSOT* 53 (1992) 47–63, 59.

35. Cf. Pressler, *The View of Women*, 31. For Ellens, *Women in the Sex Texts of Leviticus and Deuteronomy*, 4–5, 210–13, this description and the place of the women in these laws in general indicates that the husband owns his wife (cf. Exod 21:28–36, 22:7; Deut 15:2); but see also Wright, *God's People in God's Land*, 220–21; and Wright, *Deuteronomy*, 88, 246. At least the language suggests that the wife owes fidelity to the husband as to a ruler or master.

36. A trial may be assumed by the law, but since trials are explicitly mentioned in several other capital cases in Deuteronomy (cf. 17:2–7, 21:18–21, 22:13–21), its omission here is notable.

37. Cf. Kawashima, "Could a Woman Say 'No' in Biblical Israel?" 17; Pressler, *The View of Women*, 32; and Scholz, "Back Then It Was Legal," 6–7.

in the act of committing adultery are executed no matter what the circumstances.[38] Notably, the executioners and the place and method of execution are also omitted, though it is possible that, as in the surrounding laws, they are stoned by the people of the city (see also 21:21).

The case of adultery in Deut 22:23-24 involves a man and a young woman betrothed to another man. Betrothal is a legally binding relationship. The young woman is already considered a wife (note v. 24, and, in contrast with vv. 28-29, the absence of the young woman's father from the story), and thus authority over her body belongs to her betrothed husband. When she engages in intercourse with another man, that union is an act of adultery.

According to vv. 23-24 the man "finds," "lies with," and "dishonors" the wife of his neighbor. This description could indicate the man's primary responsibility for the transgression. To dishonor, ʿnh, generally indicates mistreating, abusing, or shaming a person (cf. Gen 15:13; Exod 22:21-22 [ET 22-23]; and Deut 26:6), and in connection with intercourse specifically the verb has a distinctly negative overtone (cf. Ezek 22:10-22).[39] It is used to describe the case of rape in Deut 22:28-29 (see also Judg 20:5; 1 Sam 13:12, 14; Lam 5:11).[40] In conjunction with the lack of agency implied by "being found" in v. 23, the use of ʿnh in v. 24 allows for the possibility that the young woman is forced to have sex.[41]

According to rabbinic interpretation though, the "finding" of the young woman suggests that she has placed herself in a position to be found, thus increasing her culpability (*Sipre Deut* 242).[42] Moreover, "to dishonor" is used to describe rape only

38. So also Berlin, "Sex and the Single Girl in Deuteronomy 22," 101; Edenburg, "Ideology and Social Context of the Deuteronomic Women's Sex Laws," 52-53; Ellens, *Women in the Sex Texts of Leviticus and Deuteronomy*, 229.

39. As emphasized by Shemesh, "Rape is Rape is Rape," 5. See also Lyn M. Bechtel, "What if Dinah is not Raped? (Genesis 34)," *JSOT* 62 (1994) 19-36, 24; Sperling, "Dinah, ʿInnah, and Related Matters," 86.

40. Cf. Edenburg, "Ideology and Social Context of the Deuteronomic Women's Sex Laws," 45; Gravett, "Reading 'Rape' in the Hebrew Bible," 281-85.

41. So Edenburg, "Ideology and Social Context of the Deuteronomic Women's Sex Laws," 45; Scholz, "Back Then It Was Legal," 7. Ellen van Wolde, "Does ʿInnâ Denote Rape? A Semantic Analysis of a Controversial Word," *VT* 52.4 (2002) 528-44, 537, 542, argues that ʿnh cannot mean rape; it refers rather to the lowering of a woman's social position through illicit intercourse. While "to dishonor" on its own may not indicate rape though, it is used in the context of forced sexual intercourse (e.g., Judg 19:25-26, 20:5; 2 Sam 13:11-22); cf. Edenburg, "Ideology and Social Context of the Deuteronomic Women's Sex Laws," 45; Gravett, "Reading 'Rape' in the Hebrew Bible," 281, 285; Sperling, "Dinah, ʿInnah, and Related Matters," 85.

42. See further Edenburg, "Ideology and Social Context of the Deuteronomic Women's Sex Laws," 54; Ellens, *Women in the Sex Texts of Leviticus and Deuteronomy*, 219-20. In historical perspective the

in conjunction with other words, like "seizing" a woman in Deut 22:25 and 28. The verbs used in v. 23, finding and lying with, do not necessarily imply force.[43] Finally, their meeting occurs inside the city, that is, in public space which is frequented by potential helpers. In v. 24 the failure of the young woman to cry out in this public space is the reason for her execution. She is considered to be a culpable partner because she did not seek help (in contrast to vv. 25–27).[44]

Of course, as Philo notes, the man could have prevented her from crying out by force (*Spec. Laws* 3.73, 77–78). According to Deut 22:13–19 a woman's honor, and thus the honor of her household, rested on the control of her body. The social dishonor consequent upon admitting to intercourse, whether forced or not, could also effectively silence the woman.[45] In fact, in Deut 22:23–24 the young woman's only action is to be silent. She is the young woman who has been betrothed to one man, and she is the young woman with whom another man lies.[46] Her agency and consent in this encounter remain ambiguous.

Whether she consented or not, the young woman and the man are equally culpable in Deut 22:23–24. The man is culpable because he "dishonored" his neighbor's wife, and the young woman because "she did not cry out in the city."[47] The two are thus to be stoned to death at the city gates, presumably by the residents of the city.[48] The execution of the adulterers in vv. 22 and 24 indicates the danger of adultery within the community. To be sure, the husband's rights to the body of his wife are violated, but the covenant community itself is also violated by the disruption of household relationships and the challenge of patriarchal authority.[49]

---

young women in Deut 22:23–24, 25–27, would have good reason to be out and about in the city or countryside: they are carrying out their household work. The rabbinic interpretation reflects a different social setting in which women worked in the home rather than outside it (*m. Ketub.* 1.8, 7.6; cf. Philo, *Spec. Laws* 3.169–171).

43. See also Bechtel, "What if Dinah is not Raped?" 25; Gravett, "Reading 'Rape' in the Hebrew Bible," 289; McConville, *Deuteronomy*, 341.

44. Many commentators assume that the woman's failure to cry out means that she was a consensual partner; cf. McConville, *Deuteronomy*, 341; van Wolde, "Does ʿInnâ Denote Rape?" 536, etc.

45. See also Shemesh, "Rape is Rape is Rape," 6.

46. Cf. Nelson, *Deuteronomy*, 272.

47. Both Ellens, *Women in the Sex Texts of Leviticus and Deuteronomy*, 231; and Kawashima, "Could a Woman Say 'No' in Biblical Israel?" 16, argue that the woman's guilt is determined by location alone. If the encounter happened in the city, whether it is consensual or rape, the woman is guilty. Likewise, in the countryside the woman is innocent, whether the encounter is consensual or rape.

48. Like Deut 22:22 this law omits several key factors, including the discovery of the act and an official trial.

49. See further Philo, *Decal.* 126–27; Edenburg, "Ideology and Social Context of the Deuteronomic

Deuteronomy 22:20-24

Each law in Deut 22:20-24 ends with a common refrain: "and you will destroy the evil from your midst" ("from Israel" in v. 22). The rebellious son in Deut 21:18-21 provides a comparable example of this evil. According to this law, when the parents' authority in the household is threatened, the covenant itself is threatened.[50] The son is an evil, *ra'*, who must be excised from the community (cf. 17:12; 19:19; 21:21; 24:7). The women in 22:20-24 similarly challenge household authority by engaging in sexual intercourse with men to whom they have not been married by their fathers, and the evil of this disruption endangers the community (cf. Lev 18:20, 24-30; Jer 7:8-15).[51]

This evil also threatens the covenant. For Deuteronomy the covenant is maintained in and through the life of households (e.g., 6:1-9, 20-25), in which, of course, women are participants (note especially 5:14; 13:7-12 [ET 6-11]; 29:9-11 [ET 10-12]; etc.). In particular, women have the responsibility and right to provide an heir for their husbands (cf. 21:15-17; 25:5-10).[52] The execution of women for sexual transgression in Deut 22:20-24 relates in part to this responsibility. Ancient Jewish interpretations warn that a child born of an adulterous encounter could usurp a husband's inheritance.[53] Since the covenant itself is inherited in Deuteronomy (cf. 4:9-10), the legitimacy of children matters beyond the individual family affected. The safety of the covenant itself is endangered by women's "evil," and potential infractions are met in 22:20-24 with finality.[54]

Beyond concerns of communal authority and inheritance, the laws of Deut 22:20-24 also have theological significance, a connection suggested by the vocabulary of Deut 22:21. The "foolishness" of the daughter is echoed in ch. 32: Israel is a foolish people who foolishly despise and provoke Yahweh with their idolatry (vv. 6,

---

Women's Sex Laws," 57; and Wright, *Deuteronomy*, 88.

50. See Reeder, *The Enemy in the Household*, 39-45.

51. Cf. Josephus, *Ag. Ap.* 2.200-201; Edenburg, "Ideology and Social Context of the Deuteronomic Women's Sex Laws," 57; Frymer-Kensky, "Virginity in the Bible," 84-85, 95; Pressler, *The View of Women*, 42-43; and Tigay, *Deuteronomy*, 207.

52. In this sense sex is a good thing in Deuteronomy (cf. 24:5). Fertility is a blessing given by Yahweh, and infertility and the loss of children and wives are part of the covenant curses (7:12-14; 28:4, 11, 18, 30, 32).

53. Sir 23:22-27; Philo, *Decal.* 128, 130; Josephus, *Ant.* 3.274; *m. Yebam.* 4.13, 10.1; *m. Hor.* 1.4. Compare also Num 5:11-31, in which a wife who is guilty of otherwise unsubstantiated adultery is cursed in the womb and thus prevented from bearing an illegitimate heir to her husband.

54. Cf. Anderson, *Women, Ideology, and Violence*, 80; Ellens, *Women in the Sex Texts of Leviticus and Deuteronomy*, 324; Phillips, "Nebalah," 239; and Tigay, *Deuteronomy*, 71.

15). In Deut 31:16 idolatry is identified as committing prostitution against Yahweh. This description appears throughout the Torah and the prophets, who also equate idolatry with adultery.[55] Of course, Israel's prostitution and adultery with foreign gods results in destruction, defeat, and exile (cf. Deut 31:16–18; 32:19–25). Idolatry is an evil in Deuteronomy (4:25; 9:18; 17:2–5; 31:29). Faithfulness to Yahweh alone is a serious matter.

Through these verbal links the daughter's foolish prostitution and wives' adultery in Deut 22:20–24 become symbolic of the nation's unfaithfulness.[56] This connection is reinforced by the interplay of metaphorical and literal adultery as reason for national punishment in Jer 7:9–10 and Hos 1:2; 3:1.[57] Illicit intercourse is not only an evil for the community but for the covenant. The execution of daughters and wives in Deut 22:20–24 both reflects the punishment of Israel and removes the threat of punishment from the nation.

Interpreting Deuteronomy 22:20–24 for the Church

The literary and theological contexts of Deut 22:20–24 help to explain the deadly consequences of the three laws for the women involved. By engaging in sexual intercourse outside marriage, the wives and daughters threaten household authority, the inheritance of the covenant, and the very existence of Israel as the people of God. These women (and their partners) are evils that must be excised to protect the community.

This contextualization does not wholly alleviate the significant problems present in the laws, namely: the possibility of sexual violence, the execution of women and men on questionable evidence, and the potential for enacting violence against women on the basis of these laws. Interpreting these laws for readers today—particularly for readers who accept these texts as sacred Scripture—remains an important task. This section explores various balances to the violence of the Deut 22:20–24 in the literary and canonical contexts.

---

55. To prostitute in Exod 34:15–16; Lev 17:7; Jer 2:20; Ezek 6:9; etc.; to commit adultery in Isa 57:3; Jer 9:2; Ezek 23:37; etc.

56. See also Edenburg, "Ideology and Social Context of the Deuteronomic Women's Sex Laws," 58; and Tigay, *Deuteronomy*, 207.

57. Note also Gen 20:9; 26:10; Jer 20:10.

Reading within Deuteronomy

Deuteronomy contains many kinds of violence: warfare, the ban, covenant curses, and capital punishment. There are also, however, laws that protect the vulnerable and the promise of forgiveness granted to repentant Israel. These factors do not cancel out the violence, but they do offer alternatives to violence that provide readers with space for critical reflection.

First, a number of laws in Deuteronomy protect the socially vulnerable—including hated wives, captive brides, and unwanted levitical widows—from oppression or exploitation (e.g., 21:10–17; 23:15–16; 24:10–15, 17–22; 25:5–10). This concern is reflected in the immediate context of Deut 22:20–24 by laws that protect women from unjust accusation or condemnation.[58]

Verses 20–21 are part of a larger law in which a bride is protected from her husband's slander (vv. 13–19). The primary assumption of the bride's innocence in this lengthier section could be allowed to outweigh her condemnation in the final two verses (as happens in Philo, *Spec. Laws* 3.79–82). Likewise in Deut 22:25–27 a betrothed woman who is raped in the countryside, away from help, is not executed.[59] The conjunction of this law with vv. 23–24 allows the interpreter to read the mercy shown to the young woman in the countryside into the story of the young woman in the city.[60] These potential balances do not excuse the violence faced by women in vv. 20–24. However, reading these laws in the context of laws that protect vulnerable women, including in cases of illicit intercourse, provides readers with options and choices for interpretation.

Second, the theological metaphor of foolish, adulterous Israel provides another potential reprieve for the women of Deut 22:20–24. In Deuteronomy Israel's rebellion against Yahweh brings punishment: war, siege, famine, death, and captivity (e.g., 4:25–28; 28:15–68). As final as they may seem, however, these horrors are not

---

58. As case laws the laws of Deut 22:20–24 have a long history of interpretation as paradigmatic, and in fact, the first and last laws do have counter cases in which the women are not executed (vv. 13–19, 25–27). See Philo, *Spec. Laws* 3.77–78; *Sipre Deut* 243; McConville, *Deuteronomy*, 342; and Nelson, *Deuteronomy*, 272.

59. The case is compared to murder: like a murder victim the young woman is in no way liable for her rape. Unlike a murder victim, however, the fate of the young woman is not known. She may marry her betrothed (Berlin, "Sex and the Single Girl in Deuteronomy 22," 107), but the law itself does not comment on her future.

60. So McConville, *Deuteronomy*, 342. Pressler, *The View of Women*, 32, also suggests Deut 22:25–27 could influence the use of v. 22. For Philo, *Spec. Laws* 3.77, and *Sipre Deut* 243, the conjunction of the laws works both ways: the young woman in the city might be raped and thus not condemned, but the young woman in the countryside can be condemned if she consented.

the end of the story. When Israel repents and returns to Yahweh, Yahweh will forgive Israel's infidelity and restore the people to the covenant and the land (cf. 4:29-31; 30:1-10; 32:36, 43). If the foolish women in Deut 22:20-24 are symbolic of foolish Israel, then surely they can, like Israel, find forgiveness and restoration (e.g., Hos 1-3). In Deut 22:20-24, the execution of the women would (of course!) effectively prevent their forgiveness and restoration, but the reader is privileged to have this option available.

Reading in Conversation with Biblical Narratives

A number of texts in the Torah and throughout the Bible provide narrative examples of the situations addressed in Deut 22:20-24.[61] Notably in none of these stories are women executed for sexual transgression. Comparing the laws to the stories of Dinah, Tamar, Susanna, and Mary gives a reader space to consider the potential complexities of a situation that might mitigate the laws of Deuteronomy.[62]

The story of Dinah in Gen 34 has several verbal connections with the laws of Deut 22:13-29. When Dinah visits the local women, Shechem sees her, takes her, lies with her, and thus dishonors her (vv. 1-2). He then asks his father to arrange a marriage with Dinah (v. 4). So far the story follows the case described in Deut 22:28-29. Dinah's father and brothers though provide a different interpretation of events. From their perspective Shechem has defiled Dinah (v. 5). In so doing Shechem has committed a foolish act in Israel (v. 7), making Dinah into a prostitute (v. 31). Suddenly, despite Dinah's marital status, this story begins to sound more like Deut 22:20-21.

Of course, in contrast with Deut 22:20-21, in Gen 34 the man is the actor, not the woman, and only the man dies (along with all the men of the city). The reader is not privy to Dinah's desires in her encounter with Shechem.[63] In light of Deut

---

61. The potential literary relationships between the laws and the narratives are not of primary concern here. My interest is rather in reading the narratives and laws together within the interpretive context of the biblical canon.

62. The story of the woman caught in adultery in John 7:53-8:11 could be added to the list: the woman is not executed even though she is caught in the act, as in Deut 22:22. I have chosen not to discuss this story here because of its doubtful authenticity, but it is another example of the failure to put the laws of Deut 22:20-24 into use.

63. Bechtel, "What if Dinah is not Raped?" 28-31, argues that Dinah was not raped because Shechem loves her and wants to marry her. For Josephus, *Ant.* 1.337; Gravett, "Reading 'Rape' in the Hebrew Bible," 282-83; Shemesh, "Rape is Rape is Rape," 4; and Sperling, "Dinah, ʿInnah, and Related Matters," 89-93, Shechem's treatment of Dinah and the brothers' reaction to the incident identify this as a story of rape.

22:23–24 though, her complicity or lack thereof may be of little legal consequence if the encounter happened in public space, and that she initiated the contact by "going out" to the city could add to her culpability.[64] Notably, however, in Gen 34, Dinah is not punished. This story allows for a woman's innocence of wrongdoing even when she has participated in illicit intercourse according to the laws of Deut 22:20–24.

Dinah's story in Gen 34 makes no reference to the law in describing the punishment of Shechem, and according to v. 30 the slaughter carried out by Dinah's brothers is wrong (cf. 49:5–7). No laws are cited in Gen 38, but the story of Tamar seems more reflective of legal or traditional custom. Tamar is living as a widow in her own father's house, awaiting levirate marriage to her husband's brother, when she becomes pregnant. Judah, her father-in-law, is informed that she has prostituted herself.[65] In response he orders that she be brought out and burned (v. 24).[66] While Tamar's story is not an exact parallel to the laws of Deut 22:20–24, it rests on similar concerns. Though her husband has died, Tamar is expected to bear his heir (cf. Gen 38:8). To engage in sexual intercourse with someone other than her husband's brothers threatens her husband's inheritance.

The situation is complicated, however, by Tamar's revelation of the identity of the father of her baby: Judah himself. The execution is stopped, and Judah admits that Tamar was more right than he was (vv. 25–26). This denouement shifts the concern of the story to the woman's right to provide an heir for her husband.[67] Tamar's story is the only narrative example in the Hebrew Bible of the attempt to punish a woman for sexual transgression. That the execution is stayed due to the complexities of the situation is a significant witness against the violence of Deut 22:20–24.

The story of Susanna, part of Daniel in the Septuagint, centers on the accusation of a woman for adultery.[68] Two lustful elders approach Susanna while she is alone in the garden and demand that she have sex with them (v. 20). Though Susanna

---

64. Cf. *Gen. Rab.* 8:12; Gravett, "Reading 'Rape' in the Hebrew Bible," 283.

65. "To prostitute" here carries a double meaning: presumably Tamar's pregnancy is ascribed to illicit intercourse, but the reader also knows it has resulted from Judah's identification of her as a prostitute in vv. 13–19.

66. Judah condemns Tamar as her patriarch-by-marriage even though she is living under her own father's authority. See Mignon R. Jacobs, *Gender, Power, and Persuasion: The Genesis Narratives and Contemporary Portraits* (Grand Rapids: Baker, 2007) 194; and Willis, *The Elders of the City*, 218–19. Certainly for the purposes of the narrative it is important for Judah to be the one to pass judgment.

67. Cf. Jacobs, *Gender, Power, and Persuasion*, 185, 190.

68. The Old Greek version of the story is significantly shorter than Theodotion's version; cf. John J. Collins, *Daniel: A Commentary on the Book of Daniel* (Hermeneia; Minneapolis: Fortress, 1993) 427–28. Theodotion's version is followed here, with reference to the Old Greek.

is married, not betrothed, the setting of the story has obvious overtones of Deut 22:25. Following the expectation for the rape victim in that law, Susanna shouts in a loud voice (Sus 22-24; cf. Deut 22:24, 27).[69] Unfortunately the elders shout more loudly. They testify to the community that they witnessed a man lying with Susanna (Sus 37). The elders' story meets the requirements of Deut 22:22, and Susanna is condemned (Sus 41). Providentially, as Susanna is being taken to her death, Daniel intervenes and proves that the elders are false witnesses. The story ends with the execution of the elders and the vindication of Susanna (vv. 62-63).

Susanna's story shows several interesting developments in the traditions of Deuteronomy. First, as Jennifer Glancy notes, Susanna's speech to the elders in vv. 22-24 identifies victims of rape as guilty of sin, clarifying a message implicit in Deut 22:22, 23-24.[70] Second, the inclusion of an official trial with the two witnesses required by Deut 17:6 and 19:15 relieves some of the potential problems with the law of adultery. Of course, third, the trial scene also includes the serious problem of false witness (cf. Deut 19:16-20), a real danger for the socially and legally vulnerable victim of rape. It takes an act of divine intervention to save Susanna. Her acquittal in spite of these odds shows yet again the complexity of human experience, and the ways in which the laws of Deut 22:20-24 fall short of recognizing all the situations that might arise.

The same is true in the final story to be considered here. In Matt 1:18 Joseph and Mary are betrothed when she becomes pregnant. Since they do not yet live together, Joseph knows that the baby is not his. Mary has apparently committed adultery.[71] According to Deut 22:20-24 Mary should be executed, and Joseph, the righteous man, would know it (though, of course, Jews in Roman Palestine did not have the legal right to carry out an execution). Faced with this situation, Joseph decides to divorce Mary so that she will not be shamed (Matt 1:19; cf. 5:31-32, 19:9).[72] (How

---

69. The elders are attempting to rape Susanna, not to seduce her (cf. v. 19 in the Old Greek: the elders "force" Susanna). See further Jennifer A. Glancy, "The Accused: Susanna and her Readers," *JSOT* 58 (1993) 103-16, 104, 111-12.

70. Glancy, "The Accused," 113; cf. Ellens, *Women in the Sex Texts of Leviticus and Deuteronomy*, 231; and Kawashima, "Could a Woman Say 'No' in Biblical Israel?" 16.

71. In later traditions Mary is accused of adultery and promiscuity (*Protevangelium of James* 14:1; Origen, *Against Celsus* 1.28). See also W. D. Davies and Dale C. Allison, *Introduction and Commentary on Matthew I-VII* (vol. 1 of *A Critical and Exegetical Commentary on the Gospel according to Saint Matthew*; International Critical Commentary; London: T. & T. Clark, 1988) 203; Matthew J. Marohl, *Joseph's Dilemma: "Honor Killing" in the Birth Narrative of Matthew* (Eugene: Cascade, 2008) 64.

72. Davies and Allison, *Introduction and Commentary on Matthew I-VII*, 204, note that to shame, *deigmatizō*, appears as a rabbinic Hebrew loan word used for the trial of women for adultery in *m. Ed.* 5.6; *b. Ber.* 19a.

the divorce could be kept quiet, or how Mary could be protected from disgrace, is unclear in light of the public nature of life in Roman Palestine.) As in the story of Susanna though, by divine intervention Mary is saved from divorce and unwed pregnancy (Matt 1:24). Mary's story again indicates the need for flexibility in the laws of Deuteronomy. Even if a situation looks like adultery, it may not be.

These four stories provide a canonical balance to the violence of Deut 22:20–24. Reading the narratives alongside the laws provides an interpretive space for readers to engage with the problems of the laws and particularly to attend to the importance of situation and context. Moreover, what a text does not say can be as important as what it does say. In these four narratives the women are not punished for actual or perceived sexual misconduct, and in fact no biblical narratives tell of the punishment of women who are raped, like David's daughter Tamar, or who commit adultery by choice or force, like Bathsheba. The absence of narratives in which women are executed for sexual misconduct is itself an important biblical context for reading and interpreting Deut 22:20–24.

Reading Deuteronomy 22:20–24 in the Church

The laws of Deut 22:20–24 can be understood in their cultural and theological context. Control over women's bodies protects the community by maintaining household authority, protects the covenant by ensuring legitimate inheritance, and protects Israel as the people of God by excising the evil of infidelity. However, from an ethical standpoint these laws are unremittingly absolute and final. They leave no space for mitigating circumstances—in fact, there can be no mitigating circumstances according to these three laws. Deuteronomy 22:20–24 remains a problematic text for interpreters. How should we read and interpret these laws for the church today?

One option is to identify these laws as paradigmatic and to focus attention on the alternative cases in the literary context as the lasting paradigms. In the rest of the chapter, and indeed throughout Deuteronomy, vulnerable women are protected from slander, rape, and oppression in general. There is, in fact, no evidence that these laws were put into use: in biblical narratives of women caught in sexual transgression (adultery, rape, seduction) the women are never executed, even when they should be according to these laws. To set Deut 22:20–24 in this larger context does not cancel out the potential for violence in the three laws, but it does complicate their message. Readers of the canon can find space in the midst of this tension for critical reflection and interpretive choice.

It is important, however, to admit to the violence in these three laws. They present a black-and-white understanding of sex, in which women can be condemned to execution regardless of situation or choice. One needs only to call to mind the frequent news reports of "honor killings" around the world—including in Christian families in Europe and North America and including cases of adultery and rape or even simply talking to men—to know the reality of this danger. To ignore the potential for violence in the laws is dishonest and dangerous in a church that includes sinners, victims, and abusers. Honesty with our communities requires honesty with the text.

A second option is to read these laws for their underlying intent. In Deuteronomy's vision for the covenant identity of Israel individuals are called to choose the life of the community over personal pleasure or gain. In the three focus laws women and men are implicitly instructed to maintain sexual fidelity in order to protect the community as a whole. This message has value for the church today in a society in which sex has become a private matter of personal choice and gratification. It is good to be reminded, as these laws do, that we are a community, and what we do matters to the community as a whole (consider 1 Cor 6).

While this message is important, I would like to propose a third option for the interpretation and use of Deut 22:20–24 that incorporates and redirects their threat of violence. As we have seen, the violence in these laws, and the violence these laws could promote, contrasts sharply with the witness of Scripture. To read these laws and use them for the life of our communities, which include people who are suffering through the pain of sexual transgression and assault, can take advantage of the tension between law and narrative, text and reality. In this tension a reading of Deut 22:20–24 could teach us to recognize the victims of sexual violence and exploitation in our churches and communities. It could encourage us to incorporate the stories of men and women who have survived abuse into the life of our churches. It could lead us to participate in efforts to end sex trafficking. "So you shall purge the evil from your midst" (Deut 22:21 NRSV).

RESPONSE TO REEDER

Christopher B. Ansberry

I would like to express my gratitude to Caryn Reeder for her incisive evaluation of the hermeneutical, theological, and ethical issues inherent in certain Deuteronomic regulations regarding women, sex, and violence (Deut 22:20–24). Her sensitivity to the world out of which these prescriptions speak, as well as to the way in which other voices within the canon problematize a simplistic reading of these disturbing instructions, provides an interpretive paradigm for wrestling with difficult biblical texts. While this paradigm does not solve all of the ethical or theological questions raised by Deut 22:20–24, it helps us grasp the historical particularity of the biblical text and reflect on these covenantal principles as Christian Scripture.

In view of Reeder's invaluable contribution to our understanding of Deut 22:20–24, it is not my intention to reiterate the basic features of her argument. Rather, I would like to reflect on three specific issues within her argument, namely (1) the Deuteronomic vision of the family, (2) the function of Israel's constitutional literature, and (3) the place of Deut 22:20–24 in the life of the church.

The Deuteronomic Vision of the Family

The family laws within Deuteronomy and the socio-economic structure to which they bear witness confirm Reeder's conclusion that the Deuteronomic regulations reflect a patriarchal world. These regulations are not only addressed to male heads of households, but they also express male concerns and perspectives. Here we discover that the Deuteronomic program was not interested in tectonic shifts or Copernican revolutions. That is, it did not attempt to overturn the dominant androcentric social structure within the ancient Near Eastern world. The legal regulations assumed a standard, androcentric paradigm that governed interpersonal relations at every level of the social pyramid.

Reeder's reflections on patriarchal authority concretize the historical context of the family laws within Deuteronomy. Nonetheless, the nature of this authority may be qualified. It is important to recognize that the androcentric structure of Israelite society did not mean that men were free to abuse, colonize, or exploit more vulnerable members of the community. To the contrary, several family laws within

Deuteronomy indicate that the *paterfamilias* existed not to be served but to serve the interests of those entrusted to his care.[1] Admittedly, the interests of the patriarch overlapped significantly with the interests of the more vulnerable members within the household, since the family's security and identity was located in the well-being of the whole. Still, the interests of the *paterfamilias* were not to take precedence over the welfare of those within the domestic unit in general and women in particular. This notion is supported by the Deuteronomic regulations pertaining to coveting a neighbor's wife (5:21), the manumission of female slaves (15:12), the captive bride (21:10–14), the second-ranked wife (21:15–17), false accusations about a wife's virginity (22:13–19), the sexual violation of a betrothed woman (22:25–27), the degradation of a virgin who has not been engaged to a man (22:28–29), levirate marriage (25:5–10), and even the law concerning the divorced woman (24:1–4). These family laws do not necessarily seek to legitimize an androcentric social structure; they *assume* it. Instead, they seek to rein in the potential male abuse of power and to curb the household's degeneration into patriarchy.[2] Deuteronomy's attention to the welfare of the domestic unit, rather than to the tyrannical interests of its head, combined with its concern with the exploitation of male power, reorients our understanding of the nature of the familial regulations that punctuate the document. Whereas certain narrative accounts within the OT indicate that patriarchal exploitation was the reality in ancient Israel (Gen 20:10–20; Judg 11:34–40; 19:22–30; 21:19–24; 2 Sam 11:1–27; 13:1–19), the Deuteronomic family laws indicate that patricentrism was the ideal. In this case the family laws within Deuteronomy do not simply *assume* that fathers or husbands possessed exclusive "rights" to the sexuality of their daughters or wives. They also demonstrate that the protection of female sexual expression and, by implication, the honor of the household, the covenant fidelity of the family, as well as the stability of the community, were contingent upon a vision of domestic leadership governed by care and responsibility rather than the misogynistic exercise of power.[3]

This vision of male leadership does not solve the ethical problems that pervade Deut 22:20–24 or remove the moral offense evoked by the androcentric social

---

1. Daniel I. Block, "The Burden of Leadership: The Mosaic Paradigm of Kingship (Deut 17:14–20)," in *How I Love Your Torah, O Lord!: Studies in the Book of Deuteronomy* (Eugene, OR: Cascade, 2011) 138.

2. Daniel. I. Block, "'You Shall not Covet Your Neighbor's Wife': A Study in Deuteronomic Domestic Ideology," in *The Gospel According to Moses: Theological and Ethical Reflections on the Book of Deuteronomy* (Eugene, OR: Cascade, 2012) 137–68.

3. See Block, "The Burden of Leadership," 138–39.

structure expressed through these regulations. Nonetheless, this vision of leadership situates these ethical problems within a broader theological context. Within this context, regulations regarding illicit female sexual expression not only evince the reality of male control over the sexuality of wives and daughters, they also function to critique the nature of this control and censure male abuses of power. According to Deuteronomy the guys are the jerks, and the women must be protected from their abusive acts.

The Function of Israel's Constitutional Literature

This perspective on the function of certain family laws within Deuteronomy provides an entrée into questions concerning the function of the regulations within Deut 22:20–24. How did the law in general and the regulations within Deut 22:13–29 in particular function within ancient Israelite life? While Reeder notes that these Deuteronomic regulations have a long history of interpretation as paradigmatic, throughout her analysis she assumes that these prescriptions offered an invariable, hard-and-fast ruling on cases that were congruent with the hypothetical scenarios delineated in these laws. I wonder, however, whether the matter was this simple.

In light of the constitutional collections from the ancient world, it seems that casuistic laws served a didactic purpose; they functioned as models, paradigms, or exemplary verdicts that expressed communal values and shaped decisions in specific cases.[4] When viewed against this backdrop, it appears the Deuteronomic laws did not function as comprehensive judgments or as literal verdicts to be applied in specific cases. Instead, they functioned as a general guide that identified *some of* the ways in which covenant morality might be instituted in Israelite life. Put differently, these regulations represented model decisions that captured the essence or spirit of covenant ethics and justice.[5]

The ambiguity inherent in the regulations within Deut 22:20–24, as well as the way in which matters of female sexual transgression are treated in the narrative accounts reviewed by Reeder, seem to strengthen this conclusion. The brevity of these regulations, coupled with Deuteronomy's humanitarian ethos and the narrative accounts of Dinah, Tamar, Susanna, and Mary, creates a dialogical context that raises

---

4. See J. J. Finkelstein, *The Ox That Gored* (Transactions of the American Philosophical Society 71.2; Philadelphia: American Philosophical Society, 1981) 34–35, 45; John H. Walton, *Ancient Near Eastern Thought and the Old Testament: Introducing the Conceptual World of the Hebrew Bible* (Grand Rapids: Baker, 2006) 288–90.

5. Walton, *Ancient Near Eastern Thought*, 293.

several questions concerning their function. While Reeder isolates various questions raised by the glaring omissions in these laws and reflects on their potential contribution to our understanding of their judgments, she does not consider how these omissions may illuminate our understanding of the way in which these laws actually functioned. Similar to ancient Near Eastern regulations, if these laws functioned as model decisions or even extreme judgments upon women, were they to be applied in a literal fashion within every comparable situation regarding illicit female sexual activity? If these laws served as general guides that do not account for mitigating circumstances, then, by definition, do they create space to reflect on the way in which matters of agency and complicity may attenuate the violent judgments mentioned in these regulations? If the narrative accounts reviewed by Reeder indicate that the judgments within Deut 22:20–24 were never implemented in accordance with the letter of the law, should we assume these regulations functioned as a strict paradigm for adjudicating matters regarding illicit female sexual expression?

The brevity of these Deuteronomic laws demonstrates that they did not serve as a sufficient, legal foundation for governing the community; rather they served a didactic function. Far from displacing questions or interpretive possibilities, the terseness of these laws appears to invite consideration of these questions and interpretive possibilities.

This conclusion calls into question Reeder's assessment of the nature of the laws within Deut 22:20–24. Are these laws really "absolute and final?" Or, are they general models, even extreme decisions that highlight the seriousness of illicit sexual activity and its implications for the covenant stability of the family as well as the community? Do these laws "leave no space for mitigating circumstances?" Or, do they create space to reflect on mitigating circumstances? With Reeder, I agree that the Deuteronomic concern for the vulnerable, the promise of forgiveness to the repentant, and certain narrative accounts in the canon balance the violence in Deut 22:20–24 and provide options or choices for interpreting these laws. To this I would add that the brevity of these laws, their striking omissions, and their probable function in ancient Israel demanded the consideration of situational variability and mitigating circumstances. These regulations were not literal, hard-and-fast rulings; they were models or extreme paradigms designed to express the gravitas of sexual offenses and their socio-religious implications for the family as well as the Israelite community.

The Place of Deuteronomy 22:20–24 in the Life of the Church

So how do these disturbing regulations concerning woman, sex, and violence speak to the church? In light of the proposed nature and function of these laws, I would like to elaborate upon Reeder's compelling conclusions. If Deuteronomy bears witness to the way in which Israel's constitutional tradition was modified and reinterpreted in the face of new circumstances and contexts, then the church is obligated to take part in this ongoing tradition of interpretation and actualize the covenantal principles delineated in these laws in order to protect the well-being of the family as well as the community. If the laws within Deut 22:20–24 create room to reflect on situational variability or mitigating circumstances, then they force us, even compel us, to care for victims of sexual violence in our churches, to become the voice for the voiceless within these texts, to execute justice for the vulnerable, to rein in male abuses of power, and to purge forms of emotional and physical abuse within our communities. In short, these laws call us to be a community committed to the protection and restoration of the family. They call us to snap out of our "holy amnesia" and purge the evil from our midst by guarding the identity of the family and, by implication, the identity of the church. The theological principle communicated by these regulations is clear. Nonetheless, the place and use of "constructive violence" to actualize this principle within the church remains a subject that requires serious ethical and theological reflection.

GENERATIVITY, COVENANT WITNESS, AND JESUS' FINAL DISCOURSE

Jim Dekker

While on vacation in central Ontario and pondering this project, I came across a T-shirt that said "Courage is experienced just before reality hits and one realizes how stupid the idea really is." What I am proposing is not evident in much literature on Scripture or social science research, so I am well aware that this presentation is an exploration. Social science studies on generativity simply do not look to Scripture to find indications of the dynamic in the relationship with God and his people. Biblical scholars are not necessarily reading lifespan theory for inspiration either. Partnering the two is "courageous" and I will let you decide if I have bought the T-shirt.

In this paper I will first present the basic understanding of generativity according to lifespan theory. Second, I will turn our attention to Scripture and observe how God leans on a generative witness in Jesus' final discourse in John 17. I will address John 16 through the lens of generativity revealing Jesus' disposition at the close of his ministry and to set the backdrop for John 17 where I make the case that generativity between God the Father and the Son is God's modus operandi for the gospel witness for the world. In short, the final discourse of Jesus indicates a very generative disposition in Jesus for the disciples and in the relationship between God the Father and the Son and now carried on by the Spirit among us. I will then briefly suggest that this generative picture is consistent when looking back at covenant families in the OT. Finally, after some cautions, I will suggest that this picture creates many implications for ministries in the church.

Let me begin by saying I am almost fifty-years-old. I have been married for twenty-six years. My oldest daughter has graduated from college and now has "a real job" that can carry her into her long-term vocation. My youngest daughter is recently engaged and will be married sometime next year. I am in a season of generativity. My thinking has shifted from typical child rearing to asking, "How has my parenting prepared my children for their future?" I am well aware of my failings as a parent and wonder if my children will one day name me in a therapy session. At the same time I have so much hope for them that I actually think they will carry my lessons on and do amazing things. Believe it or not, I am not alone. Many parents enter a season where we know our children are moving on and that our time of influence is ending. We wonder how we have contributed to the future health of society through our efforts as parents.

This is the season of generativity. Although this happens with parents, it also happens among others as well. Marriage is not a prerequisite, nor is having your own children. Generativity occurs among people leaving long-standing vocations. It occurs among godparents for their godchildren, uncles and aunts with their nieces and nephews, and anywhere an older adult has invested in the lives of the next generation and is preparing to "let them go" in the face of the adult's diminishing influence on a world in need of change. This is generativity.

Generativity

Over sixty years ago Erik Erikson (1950) identified the concept of generativity within the study of lifespan theory. According to Erikson generativity "is primarily the concern in establishing and guiding the next generation.[1] Erikson's theory proposes that people move through life resolving particular personal tensions that arrive in stages. In early adulthood persons are challenged by "role confusion" and "identity formation" (stage five). From this stage a person is further challenged by isolation and the fostering of intimacy (stage six). Once a healthy resolve occurs to some extent on these issues, the person moves beyond the scope of the personal to more communal concerns. This is when generativity versus stagnation begins (stage seven). In this stage the middle adult either seeks to promote prosocial values in the next generation or gives up and succumbs to stagnant effects on the world around them.

Since the 1950s generativity has been studied, tested, and nuanced in many directions. Literature on generativity now exists in many fields. Dan P. McAdams, chair of the Psychology Department at Northwestern University and lead researcher at the Foley Center for the Study of Lives, with his team developed the Loyola Generativity Scale (LGS) and the Generative Behavior Checklist (GBC). Both of these instruments have been tested for degrees of validity and offer helpful data for discerning generativity. McAdams defines generativity as ". . . an adult's concern for the commitment to promoting the development and wellbeing of the future generations"[2] Generativity is a personal motivation or, as McAdams says, a concern, that engenders various actions and perspectives that promote the wellbeing of

---

1. Erik. H. Erikson, *Childhood and Society* (2nd ed.; New York: Norton, 1963) 267.

2. Dan McAdams, "The Redemptive Self: Generativity and the Stories Americans Live By," *Research in Human Development* 3 (2006) 81.

the next generation. Like most developmental stage theories, pressure from social scientists has pushed the description of generativity into more multidimensional characteristics. More specifically McAdams and St. Aubin add:

> Generativity has been variously described as a *need, drive, concern, task* and *issue*. It has been couched in terms of biological and instinctual imperatives (a drive to reproduce oneself), philosophical and religious longings (a search for transcendence and symbolic immortality), developmental tasks (a stage in normal growth), and societal demands (the integration of the adult into a productive niche). It has been identified with behavior (child rearing), with motives and values (concern for preserving what is good and making other things better), and with a general attitude toward life and the world (having a broad perspective and understanding one's place in the sequence of generations).[3]

McAdams and Aubin suggest that generativity functions not only as a psychological place but rather a multidimensional interaction within and between the person and society. As one experiences generativity, one begins to see the role of cultural concerns. These concerns foster a reflection upon one's own life and distill values and morals important to pass on to the next generation so as to address these cultural concerns. The person also fosters a particular belief in the ability of the next generation to make a difference. This perspective is also fueled by a sense of one's own finality. Generativity tries to leave a personal legacy in the lives of the next generation. McAdams and St. Aubin illustrate the seven components of a multidimensional construct of generativity in the following diagram.[4]

---

3. Dan P. McAdams and Ed de St. Aubin, "A Theory of Generativity and its Assessment Through Self-report, Behavioral Acts, and Narrative Themes in Autobiography," *Journal of Personality and Social Psychology* 62.6 (1992) 1003–1015, 1004.

4. Ibid., 1005.

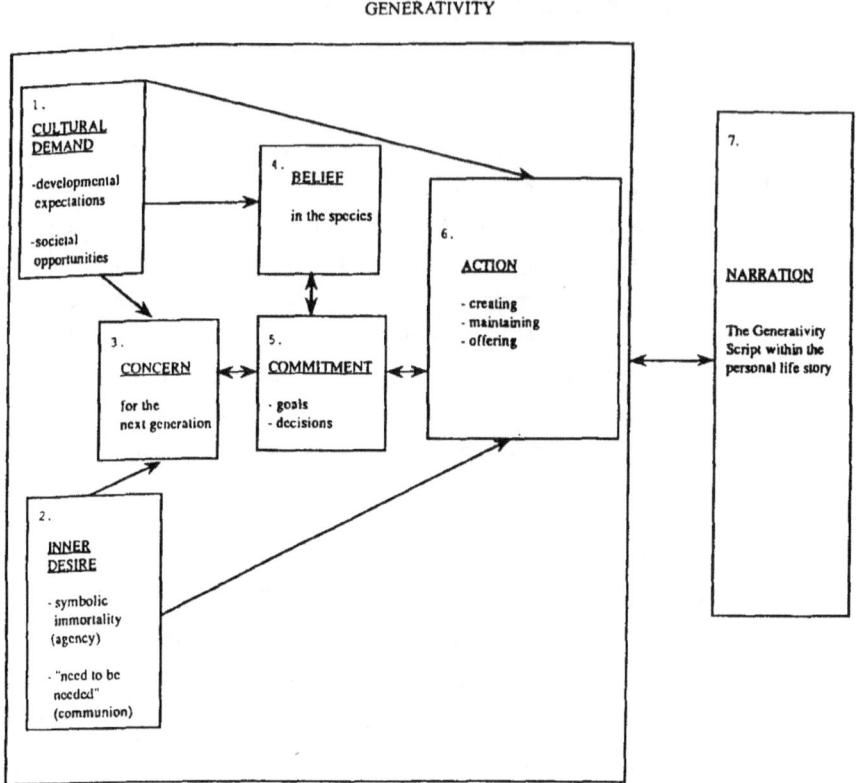

Figure 1. Seven features of generativity.

The first two components work together. "Cultural demand" identifies society's pressure on adults to contribute to the formation and/or resourcing of the next generation. "Inner desire" refers to one's "need, instinct, or drive...two kinds of desires have typically been identified: (a) a desire for symbolic immortality and (b) a desire to be needed by others."[5] These two dynamics generate a "concern" (3) for the next generation. "Belief" (4) often refers to one's commitment to the goodness or worthiness of human life in spite of countless evidences to the contrary. As the energy of "belief" encounters "concern," a commitment to making a difference in the next generation develops (5). At this point, generative action (6) emerges. One begins to generate actions that are more than prosocial or altruistic but carry with it a need for legacy building. It also carries with it a sense of empowering the next generation to take the helm. McAdams and St. Aubin astutely observe "generative behavior sometimes involves the seemingly selfless offering up of that which has been created

5. Ibid.

or maintained, passing something or someone onto the next generation as a gift, granting the gift its own autonomy and freedom."[6] They go on to say that a final component of the narrative script embraces a sense of finality, that the narrative provides freedom to end well, knowing the next generation has experienced your effort to provide what it will need for their future and the future of others.

Several aspects of these seven components have been nuanced by several scholars in a collaborative work.[7] Regarding narrative script they add that generative persons have "a tendency to see 'redemptive' sequences in one's own life, in which negative experiences are turned into positive outcomes."[8] Not only do generative adults use positive events from their past but they reinterpret the negative ones for positive uses in the lives of those that follow them. One other nuance offered is the notion that "Generativity in the domain of parenthood encompasses not only the nurturing of and provision for one's children, but also a timely encouragement and granting of autonomy to the developing child as he or she matures into an independent adult."[9] This "letting go process" is a launching of one's children into the world beyond the inner family. The granting of autonomy to the next generation is more like a statement of affirmation rather than permission: it affirms the fact that the next generation will be left independent of the previous as a natural due course.

From this quick survey of generativity particular elements emerge. First, there is a sense that culture is not where it should be, and it could be better through the lives of the next generation. Second, there is a distinct sense within the generative person that his or her own life has narrative themes or a script that can resource the next generation for the sake of a better future. This may come out as a symbolic immortality. Third, generative people have a sense for their limited time and narrowing window of opportunity to influence the next generation.

The Final Discourse

Space limitations prevent dealing with the host of commentaries on our text, so George Beasley-Murray's Word Biblical Commentary will stand as a foil for discus-

---

6. Ibid., 1006.

7. Michael W. Pratt, Henry A Danso, Mary Louise Arnold, Joan E. Norris, and Rebecca Filyer, "Adult Generativity and the Socialization of Adolescents: Relations to Mothers' and Fathers' Parenting Beliefs, Styles, and Practices," *Journal of Personality* 69.1 (2001) 89–120.

8. Ibid., 92.

9. Ibid.

sion of my thesis.[10] Although he does not speak in terms of generativity, which no one would expect, his work speaks clearly to it.

Beasley-Murray observes that John 15:1—16:33 as a farewell discourse has three parts: 15:1–17; 15:18–16:4a; and 16:4b–33. Two items from his discussion speak to possible generative themes. First, the statement "I have said these things to you" (15:11) has a sense of closure specifically to the previous section but to Jesus' sense of his closing ministry on earth.[11] A "final discourse" as a closing of one's ministry has a particular generative force. Jesus is not just teaching as he had in the past but is now actually passing something of himself on to the next generation in the face of his nearing departure, all of which indicates a distinctly generative disposition. Confirming this notion is Beasley-Murray's recognition that the parable of the Vine is an association with the last supper—a significant closure event in Jesus' relationship with the disciples:

> The discourse harks back directly to the introduction to the Last Supper in 13:1–30; the imagery of the Vine and its branches not unnaturally recalls the words of the Institution regarding "the fruit of the vine," which Jesus gave his disciples but which he would not again drink (Mark 14:23); the thought of sharing in the body and blood of Christ inevitably entails the concept of unity with the Christ in his dying and rising ... a theme which lies at the heart of the Vine parable.[12]

Second, in the section in 15:18–16:14a Beasley-Murray unwittingly pays attention to a particularly generative characteristic in Jesus. In the generative person or parent one tends to recognize the crazy world in which their children need to survive. The generative person offers principles and beliefs but also tries to provide hope and support for the future, knowing the children will have to proceed on their own. In generative fashion Jesus identifies the nasty world his followers will face but promises that the Paraclete will be with you. Beasley-Murray identifies the Paraclete saying (15:26–27) as an insertion from some other source and placed into Jesus' voice. He suggests that the purpose of the insertion is to remind the first century church that the Spirit is integral to their witness, unity with Jesus, and suffering in the face of Judaizing conflict in the first century.[13]

---

10. George R. Beasley-Murray, *John* (WBC; Waco TX: Word, 1987).
11. Ibid., 269.
12. Ibid., 269.
13. Ibid., 270.

This makes sense but I cannot help but think that Beasley-Murray is trying to solve a literary problem of an "insertion" by discussing first century drama in the church. This may serve the interests of the early church leaders; however, it makes direct sense to Jesus' disposition of generativity. Jesus is simply passing the baton to a new Paraclete for the church—the Holy Spirit. Generative specialists would immediately read this as Jesus seeking "symbolic immortality." Since he is in part of the Trinity, there is nothing symbolic about this distinctly generative dynamic. The Paraclete saying is a natural flow of generative passion within Jesus and need not be justified by a first century church agenda. This point comes up again in the next section of the discourse.

In the final section Beasley-Murray identifies several insertions of Paraclete sayings, but some are now associated with the ongoing revelation of Jesus' teachings long after he is gone. Now Beasley-Murray has made the association generative specialists would openly affirm. Jesus tries to encourage the disciples with the notion that there is a better day coming, and the Spirit will lead in the space between. It is the elder instilling hope in the face of pending struggle. The elder is encouraging hope that there will be a better day in spite of the elder not remaining with them. This hope is particularly true if one follows in the teaching of the elder. Beasley-Murray spends time identifying each insertion and the role the Spirit has in extending Jesus' message and presence among the disciples. Inserted or not, the sayings become a commentary on Jesus' generative desire to connect his autobiographical themes in the disciples long after he is gone. This view is indirectly affirmed by Beasley-Murray when he says:

> The final section of the discourse, vv. 25–33, contrasts the obscurity of the teaching of Jesus during his ministry with the plain speech that he will use in the future. This must refer to the instruction that Jesus will give to his disciples by means of the Paraclete after his death and resurrection. The implications of v. 25 are wide ranging; . . . it extends to the entire earthly teaching of Jesus, . . . an indirect allusion to the nature and purpose of this Gospel.[14]

I agree with Beasley-Murray here, and it affirms Jesus' generative energy where he captures his whole autobiographical theme and wishes to transfer it to the next generation with confidence and hope. Beasley-Murray is right that there is something different in the way Jesus is teaching. It is not just a teaching or an opportunity to endorse the Spirit's presence in the messages of the early church. This discourse

---

14. Ibid., 271.

captures Jesus' desire to commute his autobiographical themes to the next generation unlike any other mere teaching. Jesus is communicating the gospel in generative dynamic for his disciples.

John 17

The high priestly prayer of Jesus is a window into the relationship between the Father and the Son concerning Jesus' mission on earth which is now ending. With the backdrop of Jesus' generative disposition among his disciples in the preceding chapters, we now see generative characteristics present in Jesus' dialogue with the Father through a slightly different voice. In this prayer the Son speaks with his Father regarding the fulfillment of the mission. Jesus' autobiographical themes are now named before the Father as being fulfilled. It is as though a generative parent, after launching the children, has a conversation with his or her parents saying; "See, what you gave me, I have given them, and the story moves on."

In this prayer we see Jesus declaring the fulfillment of his mission as an obedience to the authority the Father has given him (v. 2). Not only did Jesus obey, but the disciples obeyed (vv. 6 and 8). The theme of obedience is communicated to the next generation through the witness of Jesus—the witness of God's glory. Here we see the passing down of obedience from one generation to the next.

Early in the prayer Jesus recognized that the completion of his mission brings God glory on earth, and Jesus anticipated receiving glory in these final days. However, this glory is not new to Jesus; it is the same glory he already had with the Father from the beginning (vv. 4–5). This "reciprocal glory," as Keener calls it,[15] does not end between the Father and the Son but is also shared with the disciples. In v. 10b Jesus receives glory because of the disciples, not just because it was given to him by the Father. In v. 22 Jesus recognizes that the disciples have been given the same glory Jesus has with the Father. Jesus in this final discourse identifies a successful generative passing on of the glory of God; this is not just a passing onto the next generation—Jesus remains as co-participant. Here again the symbolic immortality is not so symbolic but is instead the generative communicating of God's glory to and for the disciples.

In this prayer Jesus recognizes that the world does not know the Father, but because Jesus knows the Father and has made the Father known to the disciples this makes the disciples different from the world, even altering the disciples' access to

---

15. Craig Keener, *The Gospel of John* (Peabody, MA: Hendrickson, 2003) 1052.

the Father. In generative theory the elder knows things that the younger generation needs to know. That knowledge is passed on, making them different from others, in this case knowing the glory of God and being able to love others. This uniqueness is a key to surviving a rough world, and it becomes the legacy of the elder living in the younger. Such generative language is clear in the final passage of the prayer. Set with the backdrop of Jesus recognizing his time with the disciples is coming to an end, he says: "Righteous Father, though the world does not know you, I know you, and they know that you have sent me. I have made you known to them, and will continue to make you known in order that the love you have for me may be in them and that I myself may be in them" (17: 25–26).

As we have already seen in the comments on the final discourse, Jesus is concerned with his whole mission and as Beasley-Murray mentions, "The entire earthly teaching of Jesus . . .the nature and purpose of this Gospel."[16] Therefore, this prayer is a window into the relationship between the Father and the Son concerning Jesus' mission on earth. In both the final discourse and prayer we see generativity as God's modus operandi within Jesus for His disciples and those that follow after.

A look back

It is widely known that OT Scripture was an oral tradition passed on from one generation to the next. I suspect a degree of generativity in the very history of Israel developed through oral tradition. It seems to me that the message of God's love for his children runs through generative means.

Although we often talk of the covenanting God in terms of the suzerain-vassal relationship, we might turn our attention to the covenanting God communicated through generative efforts of one generation to the next in the autobiographical theme of "God with us." The covenant through Abraham likely did not pass to Isaac through a contract or mere teaching exercise or a declaration of inheritance. Rather, Abraham's journey is distilled in autobiographical stories for Isaac to see "God with us." The teaching or passing on of the inheritance is significant, but it must be more than an event. It is a presenting of autobiographical themes, values that the family bears from one generation to the next. Abraham's family lived the story together and saw God's providence of land, the giving of the animal that took Isaac's place on the altar, etc. These stories, in turn, empowered Isaac's family to move forward in that same story and pass their autobiographical narrative of "God with us" to the

---

16. Beasley-Murray, *John*, 271.

next generation. Emphasis on telling the story, remembering God's glory among us, becomes the story of the covenant throughout the OT.[17]

God's law clearly says: "You shall have no other Gods before me" (Exod 20:3). The first of the Ten Commandments implores the people to maintain the glory of God among them. Living the Torah of God is to ensure the awareness of God's glory in all of life. However, the people replace the glory of God with living strictly by the letter of the law. It makes sense that when the people of God break the first commandment, the stories of God's glory among them are broken. The generative passing on of God's stories in life to the next generation is now tainted. A possible example of this may be found in 1 Sam 2–4 where the Priest Eli was not successful in communicating respect for God's glory. This led to the deaths of his two sons, and even the birth of his grandson, Ichabod, incriminated the broken story. The generative effect continues, but now it has another's name written on it. Hebrews 8:6–13 indicates the weakness in our ability to carry the weight of glory from one generation to the next; however, in Christ a new glory is sustained in us by the Spirit (2 Cor 3:4–18).

There is need for caution. First, I do not wish to imply that we in our own efforts can pass on the new covenant by merely harnessing generative efforts for our children. For this reason my focus is not on a technique but about an appreciation for power that is present in families and how that power is also present in the final discourse indicating God's modus operandi with the gospel.

The literature on generativity indicates that we try to accomplish a kind of symbolic immortality of ourselves in the lives of the next generation. I think this tendency is true, and I would think that a generative gospel is about God's immortal presence among us. We autobiographically communicate the glory of God, and we are part of this story, but we are not the gospel. Jesus Christ is. The church ought to recognize this tendency in family generativity and help adults focus on fulfilling Jesus' prayer for the ongoing revelation of God's glory among us, rather than our own symbolic immortality. Generativity will happen, but the question remains whether the church will help families focus on the glory of God rather than our own symbolic immortality.

---

17. The book of Deuteronomy has been commonly identified as a covenant renewal document but, as Stephen Voorwinde notes, the book is also a farewell discourse having similarities to John 13–17. See his *Jesus' Emotions in the Fourth Gospel* (Library of New Testament Studies 284; London: T. & T. Clark, 2005) 98–101.

Implications

Generativity, as discussed in the social science literature, can be a resource for understanding a powerful dynamic that lives in our communities, not only among parents with children and grandchildren but among people who are invested in the lives of the next generation. Those studying generativity have looked at a wide variety of topics. John Ross looked at paternal identity in the nurturing of young men.[18] Dillon, Wink, and Fay looked at the differences between religious and spiritual generativity.[19] Dollahite looked at generativity and the fathering of children with special needs.[20] Lefell and others looked at a new construct they call "relational generativity."[21]

However, when it comes to speaking about a biblical theology of family, it is hard to find generativity as a theme. I find this odd. What we find are discussions of how the traditional family is or is not justified by Scripture. We hear how different the biblical definition and function of family are compared to today, making it difficult to even find help from Scripture. We hear of conversations about roles, rights, and relationships of love and parenting styles, all of which skirt this one powerful relational dynamic. In short, if generativity is the modus operandi of God's very communication of the gospel in Jesus Christ for the world, we might reconsider the significance of generativity in our church communities and begin deliberate shaping of our stories for the mission of God in our forms of Christian Education.

On one level, I believe we have always been working with parents. I do not know of a youth pastor or children's pastor who is able to dodge parental concerns in ministry. We often name the imperative to train the children in the way they go, but we reduce this to techniques. Yes, we look for children to embrace the presence of God at an early age, but then we develop cognitive and behavioral elements on which their faith is to take shape. We have done a great job at this; however, incrimi-

---

18. John Munder Ross, "The Development of Paternal Identity: A Critical Review of the Literature on Nurturance and Generativity in Boys and Men," *Journal of the American Psychoanalytic Association* 23 (1975) 783–817.

19. Michelle Dillon, Paul Wink, and Kristen Fay, "Is Spirituality Detrimental to Generativity?," *Journal for the Scientific Study of Religion* 42.3 (2003) 427–42.

20. David C. Dollahite, "Fathering for Eternity: Generative Spirituality in Later-day Saint Fathers of Children With Special Needs," *Review of Religious Research* 44.3 (2003) 237–51.

21. Michael Lefell, "Who Cares: Generativity and the Moral Emotions," *Journal of Psychology and Theology* 36.3 (2008) 161–221.

nating are the host of studies now identifying the fact that young people are leaving the church in droves.[22]

In our ministries we have parsed the life of Christ and the gospel in many ways. We have created curricula to address even the smallest jot and tittle of Scripture. In my field we speak a lot of cross-generational youth ministry or intergenerational-Christian education or family-based youth ministry, but is there direct attention given to the generative power that could fuel all this work?

I have a feeling we are just doing a lot of things and not deliberately fulfilling what Jesus prayed. James Poling, citing The Foley Center for the Study of Lives website states: "Dan McAdams, after hundreds of indepth interviews with adults concluded that redemption is the deepest meaning of generativity."[23] If a psychologist such as McAdams is recognizing the redemptive character of generative storytelling, I cannot help but think that the church should pay closer attention to what generativity looks like in Christian education and formation, not just to do something cross-generationally but to invest in the energy revealed in Jesus' prayer regarding his very mission on earth.

As one example we could gather those among us who are particularly generative in their understanding of culture and the next generation. In those gatherings we could begin hearing and practicing our stories of redemption. We could deliberately shape them in ways that the next generation can hear well. We could explicitly highlight the elements of John 17 in these stories (the glory of God, our unity in the Spirit, knowledge of God, hope in the future) and create a sense that our stories fulfill the very prayer of Jesus. We could then design opportunities to empower the next generation with these stories and call them to tell their stories in the same fashion.

Confirmation Sunday provides a second example. We often read the passage where Jesus calls the little children to himself; but this passage might be better placed at the beginning of confirmation. I suggest on Confirmation Sunday we read the final discourse of Jesus. After we have received our confirmands, we could read John 17 and place the gospel mantle on the shoulders of our children commissioning them to make sure their story is one that reveals the glory of God, knowledge of God, unity in the Spirit, etc. and so fulfill Jesus' prayer.

---

22. Barna and The National Study of Youth and Religion are resources of data being tapped by many identifying the exodus of youth from the church. One example is Kenda Creasy Dean, *Almost Christian: What the Faith of Our Teenagers is telling the American Church* (New York: Oxford University Press, 2010).

23. James Newton Poling, "Creativity, Generativity, and the Next Generation," *The Journal of Pastoral Theology* 19.2 (2009) 97.

If I take generativity seriously, I would see the generative energy of older adults as a God-given opportunity for the mission of the church. I would be sensitive and deliberate about shaping adult/adolescent relationships rather than putting older people with younger people and saying "chat a while." I would encourage the elders of our congregations to tell their stories, and I would find ways to commission elderly congregants to fulfill the prayer of Jesus, to tell the stories of God's glory in their lives in order to empower the next generation to bear the same mantle. I suspect we are happy to talk about war, economics, politicians, or "I was here when . . ." stories. These are all fine conversations but are there not deliberate efforts we might make for our church that harnesses God's modus operandi of generativity that we might fulfill Jesus' high priestly prayer? I would think so.

RESPONSE TO DEKKER

Linda Cannell

In the context of a Symposium on the family this theme could be taken only as a family obligation. Therefore, Jim Dekker makes the point that generativity is a developmental task and a human obligation.

He selected Erik Erikson's description of the tensions that have to be navigated in human experience—specifically generativity vs. stagnation. Following Erikson, the tension of old age then is integrity vs. despair. The logic of Erikson's theory is that successful navigation of the tensions of development lead to greater productivity in the subsequent stages of life. In other words, people who are generative are less likely to end life in despair.

To avoid simple definitions of generativity, Dekker suggests the link between the developmentalist's postulation of a stage of life characterized by generativity and the necessity to pass on values *in order that* the community or nation will perpetuate itself for a particular purpose. The significance of this link could be made more explicit in the paper. It is important to be clear about the relationship of purpose and generative practices.

Imagine the scene in Deut 31 where Moses and Joshua are called by God into the Tent of Meeting:

> [16]And the Lord said to Moses: You are going to rest with your ancestors, and these people will soon prostitute themselves to the foreign gods of the land they are entering. They will forsake me and break the covenant I made with them. [17]And in that day I will become angry with them and forsake them; I will hide my face from them, and they will be destroyed.... [18]And I will certainly hide my face in that day because of all their wickedness in turning to other gods. (Deut 31:16–18, NIV)

We do not know "how" Moses heard these words, but he had led thousands through a desert for decades and had faced untold suffering and disappointment. One could say that Moses was truly a generative human being. Here on the very edge of the new land it is almost as if God said, "Moses, this people that you have led all these years will fail. I just want you to know that before you die!" Put yourself on that last mountain and imagine the particular challenges of coming to terms with a long life of leadership that seems about to end in spectacular failure. Moses was generative not because he wanted simply to pass on something to *this* people; if that was the case, he would certainly have descended into despair! It is clear from the closing chapters of Deuteronomy and Heb 11 that Moses had come to understand God's purposes in a way that took him well beyond the immediate.

The only way generativity can be seen as an essential process in shaping enduring communities or in "ending well" is if it is not a skill to be developed but an expression of something larger. Dekker's explanation of the gospel is promising ground in that it helps us see generativity as derivative of something more fundamental: *telos*, hope, and the reign of God. While the use of the Gospel texts will be critiqued by NT specialists, it would be helpful to elaborate on the ways in which any biblical narrative takes us beyond the developmentalists' notion of generativity as simply a *stage* in *adult* experience.

Humans who have a strong sense of purpose about anything and a belief in the capacity and willingness of the next generation to carry on the values and practices they hold dear will be driven to find ways to communicate, educate, and nurture. In other words, we are generative because something of great importance has captured us. More elaboration on this aspect of generativity in the paper would seem necessary. This elaboration becomes important because of the dark side of generativity. The dark side, which is not elaborated over much in this paper, emerges when our desires for the future become *our* desire to be achieved at all cost, when we view our investment in the next generation through a narrow lens, and when we seek to control them through slogans or prooftexts and expect them to maintain what we have built.

The point has been made in other papers presented at this symposium that, while the normal intent is not the overthrow of an established system, the Scripture, Jesus' teaching, Paul's teaching, and so on, do challenge the social order and conventional family practice. What is an inference in the paper could be made more explicit: generativity is not simply passing on "what is." Generative people challenge and question established patterns and call the next generation to consider "what is" in light of "what ought to be." To do this effectively necessitates the development of certain capacities such as reflective observation, examination, interpretation, dialogue, grounded decision-making, confrontation, and so on. Generativity must be wedded to educational practices that will cultivate these capacities.

Regarding Dekker's third and final section—implications for the educational ministry of the church—I have three observations. First, generativity is *derived*. The people of God are generative only as they embody the character and behavior mandated by God throughout the Scriptures and only as they are committed to the kingdom of God. A major area of teaching, surprisingly lacking in many church educational experiences, is the distinction between the church as an institution and the church as the people of God. This distinction is important because the organizational aspirations of leaders and members can overwhelm or overshadow the "theological" expression of the church, the community that God creates. Dallas Willard once made the point that if we try to create community we are in a place where God cannot bless. *God* creates the community; our work is to discern the nature of that community and seek to assist its growth toward maturity. The distinction between institutional and theological expressions is such an important distinction that I would define the role of leadership as leading the congregation to understand and live out authentically their identity and purpose as the people of God. Only then can a community be truly generative.

Second, generativity is more than a developmental stage. Dekker's reference to the Holy Spirit is important. Some years ago I heard the late James Loder express his frustration with developmental theory—the tendency to "pigeon-hole" people in fixed stages. In my judgment he was correct in noting that the significant thing about human development is not the stage one is in but the transitions between stages. What is the Spirit of God doing as we negotiate the twists and turns of our developing lives? Loder averred that the Spirit of God is most obviously at work in the transitions of life—the space between the stages! The lessons we learn there are the lessons that give power to generativity.

Preoccupation with generativity as a stage could obscure the wholeness of the transforming work of the Spirit of God in life and community. Further, if seen as a developmental task of thirty-five to sixty-five-year old adults (Erikson's theory), it could prevent adults from seeing that even children can be generative in ways appropriate to their experience. It should also be noted that most developmental theories were built on experimentation in Western contexts.

Third, this paper suggests certain educational practices to help churches nurture generative people, but I would recommend pushing harder! A radical reformation of the church's educational ministry is needed. Many years ago the church gave away two critical functions to outside agencies: education and mission. Churches are beginning to recover their full responsibility in these areas through partnerships and a renewed understanding of their role in executing these functions.

In addition to the examples Dekker provides in the paper I would add the following considerations. First, for generations the church has relied on material that was never intended to *deepen* biblical understanding and practice of the Christian faith. It is not the fault of curriculum publishers that the church has not adequately invested in the development of teachers nor has become strategic about *congregational* learning. Today, with the diminishment of publishers Protestant churches used for generations, scores of publishing entities have emerged—from formal companies to homegrown or church grown enterprises. This creates considerable confusion among church leaders who have little understanding of the editorial guidelines, marketing policies, content orientation, and methodological rationale of these publishers. Curricular material can only serve as a baseline. It is where churches go from that baseline that matters.

Second, many churches tend toward an "answering pedagogy"—in other words, teaching tends toward transmission of information or the "right answer." Where it occurs, this tendency is built on the presumption that delivering content automatically results in right thinking or behavior. In relation to the curricular problem the church needs to do thorough work in understanding the nature of learning and transformation and how they are fostered.

Third, families are important. Many of today's families are nervous about their responsibility as the spiritual nurturers of their children. A welcome trend is that churches are becoming like "tribes" of families. The focus is shifting from the expectation that churches will do the spiritual formation and teaching *for* families to churches providing space and opportunities for families and clusters of families to learn how to carry out their responsibilities in this area.

Fourth, the church is probably the last truly intergenerational community on the planet (other than some tribal cultures). Churches miss the benefit of intergenerational relationships when educational ministry is viewed as program and age groups are divided. In fact, if generativity is desired, intergenerational learning is a necessity.

Fifth, a former theology professor once said that in the spiritual development of children we have the process backwards. We begin with teaching the Bible as information to children, we place them in worship services with little expectation of understanding, and then we expect from these practices that children will automatically understand and practice Christian faith and values. He suggested that we think first of how to include children in the authentic life of the Christian community (not just attaching them to the church through programs). Then teaching and worship has a meaningful context, children are more likely to ask questions and make connections in what they are receiving, and they will begin to "see" adults for whom faith is valued and life is altered, and they will view them as models.

Churches will plan programs and practices, but if the work of understanding the nature and purpose of the people of God is not done, programs and practices will not promote generativity in the way Dekker intends.

THE USE OF SCRIPTURE IN CATHOLIC SOCIAL TEACHING'S VISION OF THE FAMILY

Mary Veeneman

The Roman Catholic Church has made headlines over the past several months for its policies surrounding the use of artificial contraception. Its efforts to obtain an exemption from a government requirement that employer-provided health insurance cover prescription contraception have made the church's views of artificial contraception prominent. The church's stance on this issue is rooted in its social doctrine of the family. Catholic social teaching is grounded in natural law and, as a result, is not always associated with a particular view of Scripture. Since the Second Vatican Council, however, Scripture has become an important source in the church's social thought, and this is particularly the case in the writings of John Paul II. While the biblical text plays an important role in these texts, it is likely not a use that will fully satisfy readers who see the work of biblical exegesis as central to the work of theology.

What is Catholic Social Teaching? The Church's Best Kept Secret

One book recently released on Catholic social teaching is subtitled *Our Best Kept Secret*.[1] Sadly, one of the most apt critiques of Catholic social teaching is that it is not well known or widely discussed. When I introduce Catholic social teaching to students, one of the first reactions I receive from evangelical students is, "I didn't know the church taught this." Interestingly, this is the same type of response I often receive from Catholic students.

Modern Catholic social teaching is a body of documents that begins with Leo XIII's *Rerum Novarum*, which was promulgated in 1891 and includes a group of encyclicals and conciliar documents written since then.[2] One of the potential problems with tracing the origins of Modern Catholic social teaching to 1891 is that it could be taken to suggest that the church did not have anything to say about social

---

1. See Edward P. Deberri, James E. Hug, Peter J. Henriot, and Michael J. Schulthies, *Catholic Social Teaching: Our Best Kept Secret* (rev. ed.; Maryknoll, NY: Orbis, 2003).

2. Kenneth Himes, "Introduction," in *Modern Catholic Social Teaching: Commentaries and Interpretations* (ed. Kenneth Himes; Washington, DC: Georgetown University Press, 2005) 3.

concerns prior to 1891.[3] This is, of course, not the case. Catholic social teaching is based on ideas found in Augustine and Thomas Aquinas, and certainly Leo and a number of popes before him had things to say about social issues prior to 1891.

The roots of modern Catholic social teaching are found in the late-nineteenth century. It was written during a time of significant social and political unrest and change and came about in response to a growing sense that the church needed to weigh in on these issues.[4] During the nineteenth century the industrial revolution was causing significant change to the social fabric. While the majority of the European and North American population had previously lived in rural settings, the industrial revolution led to a rush to urban centers and the new jobs they offered. In addition to the upheaval generally caused by this change, the shift to industrial jobs along with laissez-faire capitalism led to questions about the rights and dignity of workers, as most industrial jobs required long hours for very little pay. It is this set of issues that *Rerum Novarum* set out to address.

In *Rerum Novarum* Leo XIII acknowledged the substantial changes that came with the Industrial Revolution. He noted that the changes in the nineteenth-century economy led to substantial changes in the nature and condition of labor. Leo particularly emphasized the relationship between capital and labor, or the employer and the employee, which ultimately gets to questions of the wealthy and the poor.[5] Many of the ideas discussed in the encyclical would be familiar to those involved in the occupy movements, even though the details of the conditions of workers are somewhat different because *Rerum Novarum* addresses workers in a slightly different time period.

One significant claim that Leo made, and which resonants throughout a number of the Catholic social teaching documents, concerns the purpose of work. The purpose of work is for the acquisition of private property (something Leo XIII defended). In his encyclical Leo discussed a number of current economic problems and took a stance opposed to socialism (a solution proposed by a number of other thinkers at the time). Leo criticized socialism for promoting class warfare and for opposing religion. As an alternative vision to socialism, Leo promoted class cooperation, the right use of money, and the dignity of the laborer.[6] In *Rerum Novarum*

---

3. Ibid.

4. Thomas A. Shannon, "Commentary on *Rerum Novarum*," in *Modern Catholic Social Teaching: Commentaries and Interpretations* (ed. Kenneth Himes; Washington, DC: Georgetown University Press, 2005) 127.

5. Ibid.

6. Ibid.

Leo offered both religious and social solutions to the problems he outlined. First, Leo argued that a return to a more medieval guild system and the Christian religion can offer some solutions to these problems. Additionally Leo noted a number of things that can be implemented by the state, employers, and workers, including a more just distribution of resources, a just wage, and the regulation of labor by children and women. It is also important to point out that Leo wanted to be clear on one thing. None of the problems or solutions he laid out should take away from the human being's quest for eternal happiness. Next to that quest, these problems are only short-term.[7]

Catholic social teaching covers a breadth of social issues. In *Rerurm Novarum* and the documents that follow, the various popes (along with the bishops at the Second Vatican Council) address issues such as the rights of workers, the nature of the family, war and peace, environmental degradation, economics, development, healthcare, immigration, and the beginning and end of life. Although the various documents address different topics, there are some key principles that run through the entire corpus. These principles as outlined by the United States Council of Catholic Bishops include the life and dignity of the human person, the call to family, community and participation in social life, the right to life and the corresponding responsibility to protect life, the option for the poor and vulnerable, the dignity of work and the rights of workers, and solidarity and care for God's creation.[8]

Catholic Social Teaching on the Family—The Compendium and *Familiaris Consortio*

The family is one of the key structures of society discussed repeatedly in Catholic social teaching. This can be seen in a number of papal documents, most prominently in John Paul II's apostolic exhortation *Familiaris Consortio*. In addition to this, the *Compendium of the Social Doctrine of the Church,* which seeks to gather and organize Catholic social teaching by topic, devotes a lengthy section to an examination

---

7. Ibid., 127–28.

8. Bernard Brady, *Essential Catholic Social Thought*, (Maryknoll, NY: Orbis, 2008) 10–13. He quotes the USCCB statement, "Sharing Catholic Social Teaching: Challenges and Directions," which is the summary report of the USCCB task force on Catholic social teaching and Catholic education. He also notes that the *Compendium of the Social Doctrine of the Church* (2004) holds to four "permanent principles" of Catholic social teaching: the dignity of the person, the common good, subsidiarity, and solidarity. In addition to these four principles the *Compendium* discusses four core values: truth, freedom, justice, and love. For another treatment of principles of Catholic social teaching, see Mark S. Latkovic, "Catholic Social Teaching: Eight Principles of Social Justice," in *The Josephinum Journal of Theology* 7.1–2 (2000) 54–70.

of the family (and there it relies quite heavily on *Familiaris Consortio*). As a sidenote, I recommend the *Compendium* as one good place to start exploring Catholic social teaching. The *Compendium* opens its section on the family by discussing the family and its place in Scripture. This discussion is initially rooted in Gen 1 and 2 and their dual accounts of creation. In the course of creation, according to the *Compendium*, one can see how the man and the woman serve as the first example of human relationality. Further, the woman is created like the man and as one who completes the man. Additionally they are both involved in the work of procreation, and it is this ability which makes them co-creators with the one who created them. The *Compendium* uses these claims as the foundation for its assertion that the family is seen as "the primary place of 'humanization' for the person and society."[9] As a result, Catholic social teaching sees the family as a fundamental unit of society and the primary place where children learn how to interact with the rest of society.

The role of the family is crucial to the well being of all people, according to Catholic social teaching, because it is in the family that humans are to learn about God and the importance of responding to the call God places upon all people. The family is where virtues are learned, and the family should offer a model for each human being on how to relate to the rest of the world.[10] In addition to this, because the family is the first "natural society" (as noted above), it should also be understood as functioning at the center of all other social life. To take it away from this place of prominence is to inflict harm on the evolution of society as a whole. The family has its own dimension and serves as the principal place of interpersonal relationships. As a result the *Compendium* argues that the family is "the first and vital cell of society."[11]

The family is important both for the growth of the person and for society as a whole. It is in the family where the human being is born and where the human being grows. Children come directly out of a mutual self-giving love of a man and a woman in marriage, and their love creates the environment in which children are nurtured and educated. This is the place where the child is to learn truth and goodness, and this is also where the child is to learn what it means to love and be loved. By learning these things the child then learns what it truly means to be human.[12]

---

9. Pontifical Council for Justice and Peace, *Compendium of the Social Doctrine of the Church*, (Washington, DC: USCCB Publishing, 2004) 95. Here I am quoting the *Compendium*, which quotes John Paul II's Apostolic Exhortation, *Christifideles Laici*, 40.

10. Pontifical Council for Justice and Peace, *Compendium*, 95.

11. Ibid., 95–96. The *Compendium* quotes Second Vatican Council *Apostolicam Actuositatem*, 11.

12. Ibid., 96.

Not only is the family important for the development of the individual, but the family plays a critical role for society as a whole. The family makes a crucial contribution to the good of society in that the family itself is a society, the first communion of persons. Societies built on the model of the family are the best kinds of societies because it is the family that best resists a move towards either radical individualism or collectivism. In the family humans are at the center, and they never function simply as a means to an end.[13] Because of this claim, Catholic social teaching affirms the priority of the family over society and the state. The family is the very condition for the existence of any larger society or state due to its procreative role. The family has fundamental rights that cannot be violated, and the grounds for these rights are in human nature itself rather than anything bestowed by the state or another institution. Because of this, the state cannot take away from the family any tasks that it can perform on its own or in cooperation with other families.[14] At the same time that the state cannot take away such tasks, the state has as one of its central tasks the duty to sustain the family and give it whatever is needed to properly fulfill its tasks.[15]

With this view of the family it will likely come as no surprise that the church considers marriage to be its foundational structure. The church emphasizes the free choice made by the spouses to enter into marriage and God as the one who gives it meaning.[16] Further, using natural law, the church argues that marriage is a natural right and an institution that cannot be changed in its characteristic or its intent. Marriage, according to Catholic social teaching, has its own "proper, innate and permanent characteristics."[17] These characteristics include totality, which refers to the extent to which spouses are to give themselves to one another, unity, indissolubility, fidelity, and fruitfulness. The varying forms of marriage that exist in our current reality cannot necessarily be used to define or explain marriage. The *Compendium* fleshes out this claim by noting that polygamy (to give an example) is a radical denial of God's original plan for marriage because it does not uphold the personal dignity of its participants, who are called to give themselves in love in an exclusive relationship.[18]

---

13. Ibid., 96–97.
14. Ibid., 97. Here the *Compendium* is citing John Paul II in *Familiaris Consortio*, 45.
15. Ibid., 97. Here the *Compendium* is citing *Gaudium et Spes*, 48.
16. Ibid.
17. Ibid., 98.
18. Ibid. It states, "a radical denial of God's original plan is found in polygamy, 'because it is contrary to the equal personal dignity of men and women who in matrimony give themselves with a love that is total and therefore unique and exclusive,'" quoting John Paul II, Apostolic Exhortation *Familiaris*

Fruitfulness is a critical element of the church's view of marriage, and it is this claim that lies behind some of the recent controversy about the Catholic Church's position on artificial contraception. The Vatican II document *Gaduium et Spes* holds that marriage is fundamentally intended to result in procreation and the education of children as described above. Marriage is to be fruitful, and the most important fruit of marriage is the children that come out of it.[19] Marriage must fundamentally be open to new life. Every new human being contributes to the common good, and that life becomes a significant gift to those who give life. This, along with the proper formation of resultant children, is the most significant way in which the family contributes to the common good.[20] Specific directives come out of these foundational claims for how family life is to be planned. The church first condemns abortion and sterilization, noting that abortion in particular is a "horrendous crime."[21] In addition to these prohibitions, the church also prohibits the use of most forms of artificial contraception. While the church rejects artificial contraception, it does hold that periodic abstinence in keeping with a method such as natural family planning is permissible. Why the distinction? The church argues that using only natural methods of regulating family size implies a choice of full acceptance and mutual respect of persons within the marriage.[22] To be clear, the church does not teach that married couples should have as many children as biologically possible, though some do miss this element of the church's teaching. Rather, judgment about how to time the arrival of children and the total number of children to have is left solely to couples. In making these judgments they are to consider the children they already have and their own larger obligations towards their family as a whole and towards society. While public authorities can provide information to couples and enact some suitable measures regarding demographics, they can never do so in a way that takes this fundamental choice away from couples. Furthermore, any state programs that seek to expand sterilization and contraception should be morally condemned, according to the church, as they are an affront to human dignity.[23]

Consortio, 19.

19. Ibid., 98–99.

20. Ibid., 104.

21. Ibid., 98–99.

22. Ibid., 106. Here the *Compendium* cites Paul VI, *Humane Vitae* 7, 16, and 17. Also helpful is Pius XI, *Casti Connubii*. The moral philosopher Janet E. Smith has written on the philosophical grounds for the church's opposition to artificial contraception and has also popularized the idea with a number of lay Catholics.

23. Ibid. Presumably, the church would not object to laws that regulate population density, for example, or the number of people that can live in a single dwelling, but it would object to laws that

Catholic social teaching also takes care to stress that marriage was not instituted solely for procreation.[24] This is an important claim to make and one that is sometimes deemphasized. If marriage were solely for the procreation of children, this would leave open a question about the legitimacy of marriage between couples that experience infertility or are past child-bearing age when they marry. As a result, the church argues that the enduring nature of marriage and the deep value of the relationship of the marriage partners hold true even when desired children do not result. In these types of cases, the church advocates the adoption of children who need homes or other types of self-giving service.[25]

What may come as a surprise to some is that Catholic social teaching also rejects the use of most reproductive technologies. Although a couple may deeply desire to procreate, there is no inherent right to a biological child. The church argues that the use of reproductive technologies such as surrogacy, in vitro fertilization, or artificial insemination is morally problematic. These technologies either deny a child the right to be born to one mother and one father, who are mother and father both biologically and legally, or they separate the unitive and procreative act by moving procreation into the realm of a laboratory.[26]

Despite these caveats on its claims about the procreation of children, procreation is a core part of the church's understanding of marriage. The potential for and openness to procreation is a key part of marriage, and no legitimate marriage can be without these things. The church makes use of this language when discussing gay marriage. The *Compendium* acknowledges that the question of gay marriage is gaining prominence in the public discourse. It argues that without a full understanding of the human person, a clear response is not possible. A full understanding of human anthropology, according to the church, both acknowledges the crucial role of the transmission of life in marriage and the importance of complementarity between men and women. These two things make it impossible for any same-sex relationships to be considered marriage. The church argues that people who are gay are endowed with full human dignity and are called to a life of celibacy.[27] The church

---

attempt to regulate the number of children couples may have.

24. Ibid., 98–99.

25. Ibid., 99.

26. Ibid., 106–7. An objection which could be raised regarding the former claim is that children who are adopted at birth have different biological and legal parents, and adoption is supported rather than prohibited by the church.

27. Ibid., 103. The *Compendium* uses the term "homosexual." I have chosen to use the word "gay" due to the stated preference of many gay persons. See GLAAD's Media Reference Guide http://www.

goes further than making this claim though. It also argues that if marriage between one man and one woman were seen as one possible form of marriage, the common good would be undermined. Putting gay marriage on a level equal with marriage between a man and a woman is something that the state cannot do, because it is in contradiction with its duties—its chief duty being to promote the common good.[28]

In addition to fruitfulness marriage is also characterized by its indissolubility. The church holds that the marriage relationship requires both stability and indissolubility. A lack of these things undermines the total and exclusive love that should characterize marriage and damages the children that marriage should bring forth. The stability of a marriage is not the sole responsibility of the marriage partners involved. Rather, the responsibility for this falls to all of society. This is why marriage must be a socially and legally recognized institution. The allowance for divorce in contemporary society further undermines the institution of marriage and damages society. Couples who persevere in marriage serve as a sign of the fidelity between God the Father and Christ.[29]

As many know, the church prohibits remarriage after a civil divorce in the absence of a church-granted annulment. Catholics who do remarry after divorce without an annulment are not separated from the church, but they are barred from the reception of communion.[30] The church wants to be clear that it does not abandon those who have remarried after divorce, and those who are in this situation should continue to attend mass, listen to the Word of God, engage in prayer and acts of charity, and raise their children in the faith. At the same time the reception of the Eucharist is not permitted for those who fall into this category. Further, the *Compendium* argues that reconciliation in the sacrament of Penance, which makes reception of the Eucharist again possible, cannot be given unless the recipient has repented and is "sincerely disposed to a new form of life that is no longer in contradiction to the indissolubility of marriage."[31]

---

glaad.org/reference/offensive. Interestingly, the Catholic Church calls upon those who are gay to commit to a life of celibacy, and yet it bars gay men from the priesthood even though Catholic priests take a vow of celibacy.

28. Ibid., 103–4.

29. Ibid., 101–2.

30. *Catechism of the Catholic Church* (2nd ed.; New York: Doubleday, 1995) 1665.

31. Pontifical Council for Justice and Peace, 102. Essentially, because the church does not believe in the legitimacy of divorce, the only way to end a marriage is through annulment. In the absence of this, one who has obtained a civil divorce and subsequently remarries commits adultery in the eyes of the church. See John Paul II, *Familiaris Consortio*, 84.

The Biblical Hermeneutic at Work

As stated above, the *Compendium* seeks to aggregate the breadth of Catholic teaching on social issues. It cites the various papal and conciliar documents that make up Catholic social teaching as well as the *Catechism of the Catholic Church*. For its discussion of marriage and the family, the *Compendium* primarily cites *Familiaris Consortio, Humanae Vitae, Populorum Progressio, Gaduium et Spes*, and the *Catechsim of the Catholic Church*. The most-cited document in this section is John Paul II's apostolic exhortation *Familiaris Consortio*.

Familiaris Consortio very quickly gets to the heart of problems plaguing marriage in the modern context. John Paul II wrote this text in 1980 shortly after a meeting of bishops in Rome on marriage and family issues. The document addresses the changing roles of women, the increase in divorce, and the growing acceptance of artificial contraception by many Catholics. John Paul II reiterates traditional Catholic teaching on marriage and family that sees indissoluble, procreative marriage as the only acceptable norm. This assumption, along with the claims in *Humane Vitae* (among other documents), undergirds John Paul II's arguments in *Familiaris Consortio*.[32]

In writing *Familiaris Consortio* John Paul II drew on inherited Catholic teaching, Scripture, and natural law. It is clear from the outset that John Paul II saw these sources as interdependent. Lisa Cahill notes that in the final sentence of the introduction, John Paul II both held that the family is under assault from various forces in the broader world and that it is the church's role to proclaim to all God's plan for marriage and the family. This claim implies that what follows will make use of distinctively Christian sources, but that they will be used to speak to the renewal of family life both inside and outside of the church.[33]

John Paul II cited figures such as Tertullian, John Chrysostom, Augustine, and Thomas Aquinas, but the bulk of citations of the church's tradition come from documents written during or after the Second Vatican Council. John Paul II frequently cited both the council and his own writings. Interestingly, although Pius XI's *Casti*

---

32. Lisa Sowle Cahill, "Commentary on *Familiaris Consortio* (*Apostolic Exhortation on the Family*)," in *Modern Catholic Social Teaching: Commentaries and Interpretations* (ed. Kenneth Himes; Washington, DC: Georgetown University Press, 2005) 363. For another helpful discussion of the overall claims in *Familiaris Consortio*, see Ivy A. Helman, *Woman and the Vatican: An Exploration of Official Documents* (Maryknoll, NY: Orbis, 2012) 89–95.

33. Cahill, "Commentary on *Familiaris Consortio*," 369–70.

Connubii sought to address issues of contraception and family planning, John Paul II did not cite it in *Familiaris Consortio*.[34]

An examination of John Paul II's citations in *Familiaris Consortio* quickly shows that allusions to Scripture are woven throughout the text. Further, John Paul II makes use not only of the NT, but also of the OT in several places. The place of Scripture in this text undermines any claims that Catholic social teaching does not appeal to Scripture. At the same time the way in which Scripture is used is important to note. John Paul II pointed readers to Scripture frequently, but *Familiaris Consortio* does not contain any extended exegesis and only contains a handful of direct quotations of Scripture. Far more common are various allusions to the biblical text.[35]

Cahill points out that the two most significant uses of Scripture in the document can be found in the grounding of unity of spouses in the creation account and the use of Eph 5:32–33 to undergird a sacramental understanding of marriage. She also argues that in John Paul II's thought, the account of creation of the man and the woman provides the foundation for indissoluble marriage. What this does is move the indissolubility of marriage from something that comes out of the Christian faith to something that is fundamentally part of human nature.[36] What is perhaps most significant is that Cahill points out that even in these two critical uses of Scripture some (though not all) of John Paul II's conclusions seem to come more from Catholic tradition than any strict interpretation of Scripture. The appeal to creation is also used somewhat to support prohibitions against artificial contraception. Further, Eph 5:32–33 is used to argue that marriage for Christians is a sacrament because among Christians the love of marriage is taken into the spousal love of Christ, which is sustained and fulfilled by his work.[37] All said, while John Paul II made extensive use of Scripture, his use of Scripture may not be satisfactory to all. While he alluded to themes and claims of Scripture, he did not spend any time on exegesis, and he really addresses only two passages in any detailed way.

The *Compendium*, unsurprisingly, follows this same pattern. References to Scripture can be found throughout the sections described above, but there is no extensive exegetical work to be found. The *Compendium* reflects a tradition that deeply values Scripture and sees Scripture as articulating fundamental truths. At the same time the extensive groundwork for many of the claims in this section of

34. Ibid., 370.
35. Ibid.
36. Ibid.
37. Ibid.

the *Compendium* is much more likely to be found in appeals to natural law and the central principles of Catholic social teaching, which themselves are often grounded in natural law.

Despite this, it is also crucial to note that this does represent some movement in the way in which Catholic teaching is conveyed. John Donahue points out that the second Vatican Council represents a significant shift in the way Catholic social teaching relates to Scripture. In the earliest encyclicals in the tradition some uses of Scripture could be found, but Scripture was not used nearly as extensively as it is in the writings of John Paul II. Vatican II called for Scripture to be at the core of theological work and held that this should particularly be the case for moral theology.[38] After Vatican II Catholic social teaching, while still grounding much of its work in the natural law, began to make more theological arguments and to use Scripture more extensively. Donahue points out that the documents do not engage in the work of exegesis, but they do seek to put Christ at the center of their arguments, and they frequently use Scripture to accomplish this.[39] A particularly interesting point made by Donahue is that Gen 1–2 is a common thread that runs through several of John Paul II's writings. John Paul II frequently appealed to those texts to provide the foundation for human dignity and the creation of the human being in the image of God.[40] In the end it is important to stress that Scripture runs through Catholic social teaching documents since Vatican II. When we examine texts on the family, Gen 1–2 is a foundational text that undergirds some of the most important claims Catholic social teaching makes on this subject. Ephesians 5:32–33 is also a critical text for *Familiaris Consortio*, though John Paul II very clearly read this through a Catholic lens in a way that may not be familiar to those outside of the Catholic tradition. While this represents a critical shift over and against earlier documents in the tradition, it is also important to acknowledge that the lack of exegetical work may be a source of dissatisfaction to some readers, particularly those from various Protestant traditions.

---

38. John R. Donahue, "The Bible and Catholic Social Teaching: Will This Engagement Lead to Marriage?" in *Modern Catholic Social Teaching: Commentaries and Interpretations* (ed. Kenneth Himes; Washington, DC: Georgetown University Press, 2005) 9.

39. Ibid., 9–10.

40. Ibid., 10.

Conclusion

John Paul II's *Familiaris Consortio* serves as a key foundation for the church's understanding of the family as seen in the *Compendium*, particularly in the areas of contraception, gay marriage, and divorce. The late pontiff's writings are notable within Catholic social teaching for their extensive use of Scripture, as called for in the Second Vatican Council. While this use of Scripture will be a welcome development to many Protestant writers, it will not be fully satisfactory because of the lack of exegetical work.[41]

At the same time evangelical audiences in particular will find much to appreciate. As relations between Catholics and Protestants have improved over the last half-century, Catholics and evangelicals have found common cause on a whole host of social issues. Issues relating to abortion, stem cell research, euthanasia, and gay marriage have been occasions for Catholics and evangelicals to come together to seek common goals. While evangelicals may not arrive at their shared conclusions on this issue in exactly the same way, these documents will be of interest, both because of their use of Scripture and because of the conclusions they reach on pressing social issues.

---

41. It is also important to note that many have argued that the Catholic Church's positions on the family have often been critiqued as addressing ideals rather than actual situations in life. Erica Olson-Bang notes this in her response to this paper. That claim is important for any discussion of these issues.

RESPONSE TO VEENEMAN

Erica Olson-Bang

Mary Veeneman clearly and helpfully outlines a brief history of Catholic social thought. She summarizes official Catholic teachings on family and the use of Scripture in those teachings. While there has been an increase in scriptural references in post-Vatican II Catholic social teaching, she concludes that these teachings rely little on extended engagements with Scripture. Instead, prior Catholic teaching and natural law ground these arguments. Veeneman notes that John Paul II does indeed integrate Scripture into his writings, as encouraged by the Second Vatican Council, but most often in the form of scriptural references, not extended exegesis. The noteworthy exceptions to this come from two biblical texts, Gen 1–3 and Eph 5:32–33. Given the absence of extended scriptural engagement, she concludes that few non-Catholics will find these teachings useful.

I would like to make one observation and ask one question. My observation is this: these two most-commonly-cited scriptural texts do not address the family as a whole. Instead, they address the married couple. While this distinction might seem a trifling one, along with a number of Catholic theologians who base their work on Catholic social teaching, I argue that it is in fact a significant difference.

Catholic moral theologian David Matzko McCarthy argues recent Catholic teaching, including that of John Paul II, in adopting a strongly interpersonal framework, falls into the common Western trap of idealizing, romanticizing, and isolating the married couple.[1] He argues that we Westerners problematically imagine the married couple as a free-floating dyad, a husband and wife in primary relation, separate from all others, largely isolated from the claims of extended family, kin, community, and society. This Western romantic vision of interpersonal ultimacy is unfortunately taken up by Christian thinkers as well. Indeed, might not focusing almost exclusively on the primordial pair of Adam and Eve, together, alone in the Garden of Eden, represent the perfect example of this idealizing and isolating tendency? Instead, McCarthy urges his readers to consider the family as a little social unit, an important one, but one that is embedded in larger social units, particularly the church and neighborhood.

---

1. David Matzko McCarthy, *Sex and Love in the Home: A Theology of the Household* (London: SCM, 2004) 5.

Catholic ethicist Julie Hanlon Rubio commends McCarthy's point and argues that, in fact, this idealization of the nuptial pair represents a deviation from the Catholic tradition's own emphasis on the social role of the family. She wrote in her recent book *Family Ethics*, "Within the Catholic narrative, marriages are not simply romantic relationships of two people finding mutual fulfillment in completion. Rather, marriage is situated within family, community, and church. Families are not isolated havens, but small, sacramental, grace-filled communities connected to and engaged in a larger world."[2] Rubio argues that the Catholic social tradition itself recognizes and emphasizes the importance of the family's role in and for society. Families are not to be oriented inwards toward their own good alone but outwards toward the common good. She turns to Catholic social teaching and affirms Pope John Paul's conviction that the Christian family be characterized by hospitality, social involvement, and a "special concern" for those who are in need.[3] The family is to be social.

This vision of the Christian family as a social body is an understanding of the family that Catholic ethicist Lisa Cahill also espouses. The family, she argues, is to be a school for compassion, love, and service. However, it is not enough to exercise those functions within the family circle and among similar families.[4] For the family to be Christian in mission it must open outward with an expansive and inclusive sense of community.[5] The Christian family must even displace the central role of the nuclear family in deference to an ever-broadening understanding of God's family as central.[6]

This open, kingdom-focused family is based on Jesus' own praxis. Jesus claimed that his family was not his biological kin but the members of the kingdom of God. In Mark Jesus' family sends for him, and when he gets word that they are looking for him, he asks, "Who are my mother and my brothers?" Indicating those who were sitting around him, he continues, "Here are my mother and my brothers! Whoever does the will of God is my brother and sister and mother" (Mark 3:33–35 NRSV).

---

2. Julie Hanlon Rubio, *Family Ethics: Practices for Christians* (Washington, DC: Georgetown University Press, 2010) 18.

3. Ibid., 55. Rubio is referencing John Paul II's *Familiaris Consortio*, On the Role of the Christian Family in the Modern World (1981), available at http://www.vatican.va/holy_father/john_paul_ii/apost_exhortations/ documents/hf_jp-ii_exh_19811122_familiaris-consortio_en.html (accessed Sept. 27, 2012) sec. 44–47.

4. Lisa Sowle Cahill, *Family: A Christian Social Perspective* (Minneapolis: Fortress, 2000) 11.

5. Ibid., 131.

6. Ibid., 45.

This redefinition of the people of God as family is important to any Christian understanding of the family. Understanding the family of God as the Christian family decenters the nuclear family and offers instead the church as family, an understanding that challenges social, familial, and domestic norms with its openness and sociality.

However, this social understanding of family, which these authors draw from Catholic social teaching, would profit from being scripturally rooted, not only in texts that focus on the marital relationship, but also in texts that explore a biblical understanding of family more broadly understood, texts that explore the family's complexity, multi-generationality, interdependence, dysfunctionality, dynamism, and sociality. This brings me to my question. If Catholic social teaching narrowly focuses on two biblical texts that deal with the marriage relationship alone, what other biblical texts are available to us that might offer a broader familial vision?

I want to suggest possible texts here, biblical texts that offer a broader, more social vision of the family. Unfortunately, stories of dysfunctional families predominate in Scripture. Perhaps as Rubio suggests in her symposium paper, we might profit from considering the many difficult family relationships that we encounter in these biblical texts, such as the messy narratives of the matriarchs and patriarchs, of Sarah, Rebekah, Leah, Rachel, Abraham, Isaac, and Jacob. Perhaps the narratives of these ancestors in faith consist primarily of examples of what we should not do; at the same time, God's ongoing, faithful presence with these messy family lives encourages us.

The families we encounter in biblical texts are *not* idealized, romanticized, or simple. Instead, they are embedded in the complexities of real life relationships and multi-layered familial networks. They were graced and sinful families. For both Catholics and Protestants, beginning with these complicated biblical accounts represents a better and more realistic starting point for ordinary families.

FAMILY WORSHIP (ISAIAH 58:1–12)

Luke A. Powery

I am a PK, a preacher's kid, and the heart of my Christian education pulsated at home. My parents loved us into the Christian faith, but they were not religious ascetic robots that only spoke Christianese. They were real people. My father loved to watch golf and boxing, and my quiet soft-spoken mother, believe it or not, loved to watch wrestling—the WWE kind. My parents helped us with homework, attended our sporting events, prepared dinner every evening so that we could sit around the table to eat and chat, and bandaged our wounds when we had them. Yet, they did not spare the rod of correction either. My mother was like John in the wilderness preparing the way of my father as she wore a belt around her neck, on her shoulders, and said, "Wait until your father gets home." My father used the belt, making the crooked ways straight and rough places smooth. Furthermore, my parents encouraged us in our educational pursuits.

However, what stands out from the historical ethos of the Powery family, led by Brother Byron and Sister Mitty, is the intergenerational passing on of the Christian tradition. I learned to memorize Scripture, sing hymns, pray the Lord's Prayer, and maybe even preach, at home. My father loved to pray, and he was one of those groaners in the midnight hour and early in the morning. Sometimes, I thought it was a method to wake us up. The sounds of his rich baritone voice from my adolescent years still resonate in the acoustical corridors of my soul. Prayer was the pulse.

At times it felt as if God was playing a bad timing trick on me because it seemed like whenever my baseball buddies would come to pick me up to go hang out, just as soon as that doorbell rang, I could hear Dad give his musical cue for gathering us for corporate prayer. "Don't forget the family prayer, Jesus Christ will meet you there, when the family gets together, pray until the Lord comes near." Family worship, family prayer, and a part of family prayer at times was the ancient spiritual discipline of fasting.

Israel engaged in fasting, a worship diet. They abstained from food and wore the *en vogue* sackcloth and ashes as a sign of mourning and penance. They were liturgically literate. They wanted to draw closer to God, and this is the way they know how to do it. This is how they have done worship for years—sing the right song, say the right prayer, do the right dance, and say "amen" at the right time. But, they seemed to move farther away from God as they dove deeper into themselves, deeper into their own worship style. They could not figure out why their fasting would not work. "Why do we fast, but you do not see? Why humble ourselves, but you do not notice?" (Isa 58:3). I have a full worship diet of Christianity. I go to an Evangelical Covenant Church, an Evangelical Covenant seminary, an Evangelical Covenant retreat center, and of course the annual North Park Symposium on the Theological Interpretation of Scripture. I sing beautiful hymns, say lovely prayers of confession, serve the communion elements from time to time, and serve special potluck fellowship meals after the worship service. I pray before my meals and even before I go to bed. I read my Bible in Greek everyday early in the morning and sometimes I even fast like Israel, but God where are you?

Israel could not figure out what was wrong with their worship until God spoke—"You serve your own interest on your fast day, and oppress all your workers. You fast only to quarrel and to fight and to strike with your fists. Is this the fast I choose, a day to humble oneself? Will you call this a fast, a day acceptable to the Lord?" (Isa 58:3–5). God brought a serious liturgical critique against Israel. Israel's fast diet was abstention, not just from food, but also from others in the human family. They prayed, fasted, and worshipped, but it did not include the entire family of God. They delighted in God but hated God's people. They abstained from loving their neighbor. They fed on a worship diet of selfish, self-serving, self-interested, individualistic living which regards no one else but "me, myself, and I"—the worship style that I like, the worship music that I like, the kind of preaching that I like, my kind of praying, my kind of carpet in the church, my kind of organ music, my kind of choir anthem, my kind of church architecture, my way of doing the bulletin, my way of ending the service, worship my way, "I did it my way." Israel was consumed with and worried only about themselves and "*my* personal relationship with God" as I praise and worship my God my way. They created God in their own image as if soon they would be singing "Crown me with many crowns."

They neglected serving others. Their spiritual liturgical diet was navel-gazing at their stomachs full of self. They served their own interests, while disregarding others. They were satisfied with a selfish, status quo Christian spirituality that has no impact on society. They were only concerned with the liturgy and not the liturgy after the liturgy. They beat down and tore down anyone and anything on their way up towards the pearly gates of heaven. "I'll fly away, oh glory, I'll fly away, when I die hallelujah bye and bye" as they waved bye-bye to their neighbor in need. But this is not just Israel's story. This is our story too. It is the mirror of our lives.

I know I teach and preach at a proper and pristine and privileged university of the South, but today I have to return to my Pentecostal roots and pump up the volume and raise the roof. I have to blare and crash and thunder like God's trombones. Today I have to listen to Isaiah and shout out and not hold back. A Gregorian chant-like, evening vespers sermon will not do. Today I have to take God's advice and lift up my voice like a trumpet.

In many ways Israel's liturgical approach has been the church's practical theology of worship. We actually think that just coming to a Sunday service or a Wednesday night prayer meeting or attending a Bible study or a Christian Education class is the totality of what it means to worship God, and if we do not like the preaching, the singing, the praying, the children's sermon, the choir robes, the way communion is administered, we can go somewhere else, window shopping for a church that we like because it suits us and our needs, shopping at what has been called the "worship mall."[1] In this consumeristic age we struggle with selfishness, being too self-interested and desiring what Christian Scharen calls "self-maximization."[2] Thus, our worship diet neglects others many times. It may look like worship and sound like worship and feel like worship, but if concrete love of neighbor is not included in our diet of worship, it ain't worship! I know this is not true for anyone at the symposium but for those whose worship diet is unhealthy and neglects others.

But how can we neglect others when there are people enchained by a prison industrial complex just because of the color of their skin? How can we neglect others, as we climb up the ladder of socioeconomic success, when there are still inadequate resources in so many inner city schools? How can we neglect others when there are those who are so lonely or who are in such deep depression that they commit suicide because life becomes too much for them to bear? How can we neglect others with our worship if pain is the "matrix"[3] of praise? How can we neglect the friendless, the jobless, the homeless, and the hopeless? How?

I know how. We are only worshiping ourselves! Immortal, invisible, I am only wise. We're on the wrong kind of worship diet. It is not family worship. We are on a destructive diet that distances ourselves from others when in fact our Sunday worship of God is only authenticated by how we live for God on Monday through

---

1. Bryan Spinks, *The Worship Mall: Contemporary Reponses to Contemporary Culture* (New York: Church, 2011).

2. Christian Scharen, *Faith as a Way of Life: A Vision for Pastoral Leadership* (Grand Rapids: Eerdmans, 2008).

3. Walter Brueggemann, *Israel's Praise: Doxology Against Idolatry and Ideology* (Philadelphia: Fortress, 1988) 136.

Saturday in the world. Instead of Dr. Martin Luther King's dream, we are living a nightmare—not "coming together," not realizing that our lives are interdependent, but seeing, in the words of the Nigerian novel, *Things Fall Apart*.[4] They are falling apart because we serve our own interests even when it comes to worship. We get liturgical fast food only for ourselves in the drive through of oppressive selfishness. As we look at the menu, we experience theological amnesia and forget that someone else is hungry. We only buy the type of fast food we like. Our lives only incorporate a diet that will benefit us. We enroll in the "Me, myself, and I" diet plan and enter the darkness of destructive selfishness. We ask, like those in Isaiah, "Why do we fast, but you do not see?"

God sees but God runs a different worship diet program. God calls for selfless giving. God calls for worship as service in the world. God tells Israel "Your fasting is about abstention, even abstaining from doing justice, but my worship is about participation, engagement, doing justice for others, walking in love towards another. My worship is having your life service match your lip service. My worship includes social witness and social justice. My worship diet incorporates your entire life. My worship diet plan will help the world, not a Constantinian church that is only interested in endorsing imperial political power."

God pulls up in his automobile of justice and mercy and places his doxological diet food order before the children of Israel. "Is not this the fast that I choose? I'll have a juicy burger that looses the bonds of injustice, a thick chocolate milkshake that will undo the thongs of the choking yoke, and some hot, salty fries to set the oppressed free. Let me have a side order of chicken nuggets so I can share it with the hungry homeless person I saw downtown the other day. I had better buy some ice cream so I can give it to my bothersome, next-door neighbor. Have your McDonald T-shirts come out yet? I want to get one so I can cover the naked. God's doxological diet is for others, about others, for the common good. It is selfless. God is other-interested. God is other-wise. God cares for all of humanity, including your biological family that you may be stuck with. God includes them in the definition of worship and fasting.

God says to not neglect, ignore, or disregard your kin, your family. Our worship watches over one's family, but it is bigger and broader than that. There is a sense that justice-oriented worship has to do with care, not solely for one's blood family, but the entire human global family in need (Isa 66:22–23). This is family worship. God cares for all of creation. God cares for you and me, but especially the helpless

---

4. Chinua Achebe, *Things Fall Apart* (New York: Anchor, 1994).

outcasts. Family worship will lead you to volunteer at that soup kitchen you know about. Family worship will cause you to buy some clothes for a homeless shelter. Family worship will lead you to visit a widow with AIDS and befriend an orphan locked in prison and resist violence of any kind and be reminded that "I can never be what I ought to be until you are what you ought to be,"[5] even if I don't speak your language.

It does not matter if you have a Ph.D., Th.D., D.D., J.D., M.D., GED or no D at all. You can serve. "You don't have to make your subject and your verb agree to serve."[6] Dr. King, a man with a Ph.D., a Nobel Peace Prize winner, a man who had access to kings and queens, died fighting on behalf of sanitation workers in Memphis, Tennessee. He was on God's worship diet. King said, "Life's most persistent and urgent question is, what are you doing for others?"[7] That is the question of the hour as we check ourselves before we wreck ourselves liturgically. What are you doing for others? This is an invitation and opportunity to get off the pew of individualistic, pietistic, narcissistic, Sunday worship only matters, Jesus and me spirituality and to begin to give selflessly and love our neighbor—to show our Christianity, to show Jesus, to demonstrate our worship in the world, and to enroll in God's liturgical diet program and do family worship.

God did not say that they had to be Christian in order to be helped. God did not say that they had to have the same skin color to be helped. God did not say that they had to believe the same thing you believe or like the same things you like to be helped. Need is no respecter of persons! God just said that the food for my liturgical fast diet is to loose the bonds of injustice, undo the thongs of the yoke, let the oppressed go free, give bread to the hungry, a home to the homeless, clothes to the naked, and love to somebody. Family worship is a verb. The good news is that God is right there, inhabiting our worship as we serve. In fact, Jesus said "I was hungry and you gave me food, I was thirsty and you gave me something to drink, I was a stranger and you welcomed me, I was naked and you gave me clothing, I was sick and you took care of me, I was in prison and you visited me . . . just as you did it to one of the least of these who are members of my family, you did it to me"(Matt 25:35–40).

God actually can be found among the oppressed, for after redefining the meaning of fast, the meaning of worship, God told Israel, "Here I am." You've been search-

---

5. Martin Luther King Jr., "The American Dream," *A Testament of Hope: Essential Writings and Speeches of Martin Luther King, Jr.* (ed. James Washington; San Francisco: Harper & Row, 1986) 210.

6. King, "The Drum Major Instinct," in *A Testament of Hope*, 265.

7. King, "The Three Dimensions of a Complete Life," http://mlk-kppo1.stanford.edu/index.php/encyclopedia/multimediaentry/doc_the_three_dimensions_of_a_complete_life/.

ing the Internet all day long, befriending people on Facebook, whom you do not even know, forwarding mass emails, watching shows on YouTube, texting, and even tweeting right now. You have been attending your church for your whole life and still have not found me. But "Here I am" right with the least of these, right with the oppressed, the hungry, the naked, the outcast, demonized, dehumanized, and ostracized; right with that person you do not want to touch and want to ignore; right on the margins. That is where you will find me if you start my worship diet.

"Here I am." God is in the doing of justice for others. God is in community, the human community, the beloved community; you cannot find God when you neglect others. "Here I am" right there with you in the liturgy of liberation. Remember, I am Immanuel; I am with you. "Here I am." You will not be alone in your service. "Here I am," putting in the proper ingredients in your diet of justice and mission. "Here I am," still making my liturgical fast food for the poor, orphans, and widows. "Here I am" with the least, the last, and the left out. "Here I am," still bringing people out of Exodus into a promised land of hope. "Here I am," not in the ivory tower of cushiony Christianity, worried about the color of the new sanctuary carpet, but in the trenches of trouble trying to save some folks from suicide and dealing drugs and death row. "Here I am" on death row. "Here I am" in an orphanage. "Here I am" with the grieving widow. "Here I am" with a divorced man. "Here I am" with the lonely young adult single. "Here I am" with the couple that wants to have children but cannot. "Here I am" with the wife suffering under the headship of her husband. "Here I am" in the midst of sibling rivalry and guppies going at it. "Here I am" with women who have been sexually abused. "Here I am" with a young couple that has just discovered that a fancy wedding does not necessarily make a fruitful marriage. "Here I am" with those yearning for happiness in family life. "Here I am" on the crucible of the cross. "Here I am." You thought you were serving me, but I am serving you. I am meeting your need. Your healing is linked with the healing of others for the common good; this is how we rebuild society. "Then your light shall break forth like the dawn and your healing shall spring up quickly. Your gloom will be like the noonday. You shall be like a watered garden, like a spring of water whose waters never fail. Your ancient ruins shall be rebuilt" (Isa 58:8–12). That cannot happen without me, God says. You will call and cry for help and I will answer, "Here I am."

A set of pictures from the Indian Ocean tsunami in 2004 shows the gigantic swallowing waves rushing to shore while many people frantically flee for their lives in the opposite direction. But off in the distance, you can see one figure doing something very strange, running towards the deadly wicked waves. In the next shot you see a couple of other figures right by the mouth of the waves. A mother was desperately running to rescue her children. They survived. She risked death to give life. She was interested in others. She understood family worship.

God was right there because God inhabits family worship as we shed the weight of selfishness and self-preoccupation. God's liturgical fast food is still being served from heaven for all God's children. Dad was right—"Don't forget the family prayer, Jesus Christ will meet you there, when the human family of God gets together, pray, worship, work to repair the breach of brokenness, until the Lord comes near." God will be there. "Here I am," God says.

I do not know what your plans are after you leave this symposium, but I have a feeling that it is family worship time.

ANNOTATED BIBLIOGRAPHY ON THE FAMILY

Anderson, Cheryl B. *Women, Ideology, and Violence: Critical Theory and the Construction of Gender in the Book of the Covenant and the Deuteronomic Law.* Journal for the Study of the Old Testament: Supplement Series 394. London: T. & T. Clark, 2004. This study suggests that in some of the laws concerned with women in Exodus and Deuteronomy women are presented as subjects of male control. It is argued that these laws are inherently violent towards women and perpetuate violence against women.

Anderson, Herbert, and Susan Johnson. *Regarding Children: A New Respect for Childhood and Families.* Louisville: Westminster John Knox, 1994. This book begins with the foundation that "children are people." Society needs to base its theology of family and parenting on this foundation, and Anderson and Johnson discuss the importance of children's needs and how parents and the church can better address them.

Balch, David L. *Let Wives Be Submissive. The Domestic Code in 1 Peter.* Atlanta: Scholars, 1981. This monograph represents a breakthrough in the study of the so-called "household codes" in the NT and in 1 Peter in particular. It demonstrates that the household codes draw on ancient philosophical reflection on household management and use it for apologetic purposes to show that Christian faith was not seeking to undermine the family.

Balch, David L., and Carolyn Osiek, eds. *Early Christian Families in Context: An Interdisciplinary Dialogue.* Grand Rapids: Eerdmans, 2003. As the subtitle indicates, this is a collection of interdisciplinary essays by experts in biblical and classical studies. The six main parts cover archaeology, domestic values, women, slaves, children, and implications for theological education.

Balswick, Jack O., and Judith K. Balswick. *The Family: A Christian Perspective on the Contemporary Home.* 3rd ed. Grand Rapids: Baker, 2007. The book covers major issues which affect family life: marriage, parenting, sexuality, communication, social dynamics, and family life in modern society. The authors integrate a Christian perspective with insights from psychological and sociological studies.

Bartchy, S. Scott. "Undermining Ancient Patriarchy: The Apostle Paul's Vision of a Society of Siblings." *BTB* 29 (1999) 68–78. The closest family tie in the ancient Mediterranean society was experienced among siblings. The article argues that Paul followed Jesus in his attempts to undermine the authority and social cohesiveness of the patriarchal family, to offer an alternative surrogate family, and to make viable the choice of living in such a trust-based form of social relations by redefining the code of honor into which all males had been socialized. The goal was not to create an egalitarian society but a well-functioning family without fathers in which the strong would use their power for the weak.

Barton, Stephen C. *Discipleship and Family Ties in Mark and Matthew.* Society of New Testament Studies Monograph Series 80. Cambridge: Cambridge University Press, 1994.

This is a study of the so-called "anti-family" sayings of Jesus and their interpretation in Mark and Matthew, and it argues that the sayings of Jesus make sense in the context of his mission and that the relativization of family ties has strong precedent in Jewish and Greco-Roman traditions.

———. "The Epistles and Christian Ethics." Pages 63–73 in *The Cambridge Companion to Christian Ethics.* 2d ed. Edited by Robin Gill. Cambridge: Cambridge University Press, 2012. Barton's essay concludes with a discussion about the way the Epistles inform Christian ethics in the sphere of family life. He suggests that the patriarchal household codes should not be understood as divinely ordained patterns of hierarchical family relations under male authority but as models how the already given structures of personal and social existence are to be renewed in the light of membership in the body of Christ.

———, ed. *The Family in Theological Perspective.* Edinburgh: T. & T. Clark, 1996. This multidisciplinary collection of essays by leading British scholars has two main parts. The first covers biblical and historical perspectives, and the second covers issues relating to faith, family, and the modern world.

Bauckham, Richard. *Gospel Women: Studies of Named Women in the Gospels.* Grand Rapids: Eerdmans, 2002. In addition to treating women in the Gospels, Bauckham has an opening chapter on Ruth which explains how the Bible can be read from a female perspective. Later he argues that Joanna (Luke 8:3) is probably the same person as Junia (Rom 16:7) and that the women who saw the resurrected Christ were authoritative witnesses in the early church.

Beck, James R., and Craig L. Blomberg, eds. *Two Views on Women in Ministry.* Grand Rapids: Zondervan, 2001. The book explores the issue of women in ministry by creating a conversation between two egalitarian and two complementarian scholars, the egalitarians being Linda L. Belleville and Craig S. Keener and the complementarians Craig L. Blomberg and Thomas R. Schreiner.

Becker, Carol E. *Becoming Colleagues: Women and Men Serving Together in Faith.* San Francisco: Jossey-Bass, 2000. Interviews with mixed-gender teams provide the basis for insight and learning, and the result is a practical and useful book. Becker's goal is to educate and call mixed-gender teams to reflection and action in order to be effective in ministry.

Bennett, Jana. *Water is Thicker than Blood: An Augustinian Theology of Marriage and Singleness.* New York: Oxford University Press, 2008. This study discusses the relation of domestic life to the church. Are households the "woman's sphere," and are women barred from full participation in the church? The author finds that Augustine of Hippo is the source of very fruitful reflection on these topics, showing us that both marriage and singleness are best set in the context of the salvation story.

Bilezikian, Gilbert G. *Beyond Sex Roles: A Guide for the Study of Female Roles in the Bible.* Grand Rapids: Baker, 1985. Bilezikian examines key biblical texts pertinent to understanding female roles. He affirms the full equality of the sexes in family and church.

Annotated Bibliography

Birkey, Del. *The Fall of Patriarchy: Its Broken Legacy Judged by Jesus and the Apostolic House Church Communities.* Tucson, AZ: Fenestra, 2005. The book challenges the assumption that male dominance is dictated by the Bible. The author claims that patriarchy is the result of the Fall and leads to devaluation of and violence against women worldwide. Both Jesus and Paul were against patriarchy.

Blankenhorn, David, et al. *Does Christianity Teach Male Headship? The Equal-Regard Marriage and Its Critics.* Grand Rapids: Eerdmans, 2004. This collection of essays offers a variety of perspectives concerning biblical interpretation of male headship. The differing opinions on gender roles and leadership provide an avenue to thorough investigation of this theological issue.

Blessing, Kamila. *Families of the Bible: A New Perspective.* Santa Barbara, CA: Praeger, 2010. Blessing discusses the transformation of male-dominated patriarchy of the OT into a "spiritual family" of the NT. She argues that the spiritual family of Jesus is not heterosexual and therefore should not lead to heteronormativity and hegemony which excludes people from the family.

Brown, Jeannine K. "Silent Wives, Verbal Believers: Ethical and Hermeneutical Considerations in 1 Peter 3: 1–6 and Its Context." *Word & World* 24 (2004) 395–403. This article investigates the ethics in 1 Peter 3:1–6 and the apparently different ethics meant for believers and unbelievers. Brown examines the call given to believing wives married to unbelieving men, how they are to live, and how submission is demonstrated.

Bunge, Marcia J., et al., eds. *The Child In The Bible.* Grand Rapids: Eerdmans, 2008. This book looks at Old and New Testament texts and themes through the lens of children and childhood. It offers insights into religious, cultural, and ethical issues.

Burke, Patricia C. *Interpreting Life: Christian Women's Roles in the Church and Home.* Eugene, OR: Pickwick, 2011. The book depicts one Christian woman's struggle to determine her place in the home and church as the traditional roles of the 1950s gave way to the chaos created by the social movements of the 1960s and 1970s. Excerpts from over thirty years of writing reveals the strategies the author employed to remain positive and productive as family and church priorities took precedence over her own dreams.

Cahill, Lisa Sowle. *Family: A Christian Social Perspective.* Minneapolis: Fortress, 2000. Cahill argues that the usual religious agenda of restoring the traditional nuclear family is misinformed and misguided since it bolsters oppressive social, economic, and racial mechanisms that are destroying families. She claims that counter-cultural NT and early-church notions of family were very different from modern family values.

Calef, Susan A. "The Radicalism of Jesus the Prophet: Implications for Christian Family." In *Marriage in the Catholic Tradition: Scripture, Tradition, and Experience,* edited by Todd A. Salzman, et al., 53–65. New York: Crossroad, 2004. Calef criticizes how Christians try to answer the breakdown of families by reading the Bible selectively to find prooftexts for patriarchy. She suggests that the Gospel tradition paints a different view of the Christian family by looking at life through kingdom values and priorities. Christian families participate in the larger eschatological family of God, strive to respond to the promptings of the Spirit, are called to seek justice, share their possessions with others, practice corporal and spiritual works of mercy, and are called more deeply to the paschal mystery of suffering.

Clapp, Rodney. *Families at the Crossroads. Beyond Traditional and Modern Options.* Downers Grove, IL: InterVarsity, 1993. Many evangelicals have tried to respond to the postmodern challenge by defending the so-called "traditional" family. Clapp argues both that the "traditional" family is a reflection more of the nineteenth-century middle-class family than of any family in the Bible and that many modern and postmodern options are not acceptable to Christians.

Clark, Stephen B. *Man And Woman In Christ: An Examination of the Roles of Men and Women in Light of Scripture and the Social Sciences.* Ann Arbor, MI: Servant, 1980. Clark, writing from a complementarian perspective, finds that key biblical texts prove patriarchal gender roles and claims that Christian thinking has been infiltrated by modern ideologies. In the concluding part of the book he calls Christians back to base men's and women's roles on brother-sister love and make the home a center of care and service. This means that men and women need to have different areas of responsibility and that the expressions of their roles need to be culturally different.

Cohick, Lynn H. *Ephesians: The New Covenant Commentary.* Eugene, Oregon: Cascade, 2010. This commentary provides a practical explanation and appropriation of the letter by bringing historical and sociological information to bear on the text and its interpretation. It includes a prolegomena to the household codes.

———. *Women in the World of the Earliest Christians: Illuminating Ancient Ways of Life.* Grand Rapids: Baker, 2009. Cohick examines literary, epigraphic, iconographic, and archeological evidence concerning women during the time of the earliest Christians. She argues the evidence should be divided into two categories, prescriptive and descriptive, and that the social location of women is paramount in sorting the dissonance of the evidence. As long as the woman was viewed as a benefactor she was shielded from public charges of unwomanly character. Cohick does not suggest an egalitarian early church but argues that questions of female participation in the church were negotiated based on local situations.

Coles, Robert., et al. *Listening to Children: A Moral Journey with Robert Coles.* PBS Video, 1995. Child psychiatrist Robert Coles looks deeply into children's lives and how they respond to emotions, crises, and everyday modern family life in this documentary that engages children and their feelings about life's circumstances.

Cook, Kaye V., and Lance Lee. *Man and Woman: Alone and Together.* Wheaton, IL: Victor, 1992. This book dissects modern gender roles and how they shape culture and have been shaped by culture. The authors investigate the unique roles that singleness and marriage play in the dynamics of multigender relationships. They hope to refocus Christian society by offering a biblical perspective on gender and relationships.

Curran, Dolores. *Traits of a Healthy Family.* New York: Ballatine Books, 1983. Curran looks at fifteen strengths found in healthy families and urges readers to live into as many as possible. She acknowledges that families cannot exhibit all fifteen but seeks to draw attention to the positive aspects of healthy families.

Daley-Harris, Shannon, and Jeffrey Keenan. *Our Day to End Poverty: 24 Ways You Can Make a Difference*. San Francisco: Berrett-Koehler, 2007. This sensible guide empowers individuals to make a difference in our world in seemingly small ways. Practical tips for real issues enable one to see differences in his/her family and community and to feel part of a solution.

Davidson, Richard M. *Flame of Yahweh: Sexuality in the Old Testament*. Peabody, MA: Hendrickson, 2007. Davidson offers a detailed treatment of human sexuality and gender as revealed in the OT. He shows how the Edenic ideals of human sexuality, love, and relationship were plunged into discord after the Fall and how the OT provides a renewed vision of the true and the right. He also outlines the implications for the NT understanding of human sexuality and gender that grew out of the OT literature.

De Neui, Paul H., ed. *Family and Faith in Asia: The Missional Impact of Social Networks*. Pasadena, CA: William Carey Library, 2010. This collection of essays from the 2009 South, East, and Southeast Asia Network conference seeks to address "critical missiological issues relevant to the practice of mission in Asian and many other non-Western contexts." By speaking to the importance of family systems in many cultures, the essays focus on ways one is able to have a better missional impact.

Deasy, Jo Ann. "Called to This Image? How Discourses About Gender and Ministry Impact the Potential for Young Women to Develop a Pastoral Identity." PhD diss., Garrett-Evangelical Theological Seminary, 2009. This dissertation focuses on how the discourses within a local congregation in a "progressively evangelical" denomination function to both encourage and hinder the potential of young women to develop a pastoral identity.

Dempsey, Carol, and Elayne Shapiro. *Reading the Bible, Transforming Conflict*. Maryknoll, NY: Orbis, 2011. This book of "practical theology" studies several conflict stories in both Testaments and brings them into conversation with contemporary events and current strategies for conflict resolution, reconciliation, and forgiveness. Each chapter is meant for group study and includes questions for discussion.

Edenburg, Cynthia. "Ideology and Social Context of the Deuteronomic Women's Sex Laws (Deuteronomy 22:13–29)." *JBL* 128 (2009): 43–60. This article offers a careful structural analysis of Deut 22:13–29, a comparison of these laws with ancient Near Eastern parallels, and a reconstruction and critique of the "value system" the laws represent.

Elkind, David. *Ties that Stress: The New Family Imbalance*. Boston: Harvard University Press, 1998. This book seeks reconsideration of the family and unpacks specific family dynamics like family values, family imbalance, and navigating childhood and youth so as to educate and empower parents.

Ellens, Deborah L. *Women in the Sex Texts of Leviticus and Deuteronomy: A Comparative Conceptual Analysis*. New York: T. & T. Clark, 2008 This detailed study of the laws concerning women and sex in Leviticus and Deuteronomy analyzes the laws with respect to literary structure, social context, and ideology and argues that the laws of Deuteronomy in particular treat women as property.

Elliott, John H. "Jesus Was Not an Egalitarian. A Critique of an Anachronistic and Idealist Theory." *BTB* 32 (2002) 75–91. The currently-advanced theory that Jesus was an egalitarian who founded a "community of equals" is devoid of social and political plausibility and, more importantly, of textual and historical evidence. Jesus and his followers did not engage in social revolution, equality, and the eradication of the traditional family but in establishing a form of community modelled on the family as redefined by Jesus and united by familial values, norms, and modes of conduct.

Fontaine, Carole R. *With Eyes of Flesh: The Bible, Gender and Human Rights*. The Bible in the Modern World 10. Amsterdam Studies in the Bible and Religion 2. Sheffield: Sheffield Phoenix, 2008. This book includes essays that address a variety of issues related to gender and the Bible. Fontaine is particularly concerned pastorally with the ways violence and gender in biblical texts affect readers in the world (especially chs. 5 and 7).

Fox-Genovese, Elizabeth, et al. *Women and the Future of the Family*. Grand Rapids: Baker, 2000. Fox-Genovese analyzes the "slow dissolution of the family" and the many factors that have contributed to it. She also includes three responses to her work that offer different perspectives to the issue of familial relationships and her own replies in order to offer the reader a well-rounded discussion of the issue.

Fretheim, Terence E., and Beverly Roberts Gaventa, eds. *The Child in the Bible*. Grand Rapids: Eerdmans, 2008. The most recent collection of essays on a growth area in biblical and theological study, this volume contains eighteen essays covering texts from the Hebrew Bible, texts from the NT, and thematic essays.

Garland, David E. *1 Corinthians*. Baker Exegetical Commentary on the New Testament. Grand Rapids: Baker, 2003. In addition to being a very good commentary on pertinent texts, this commentary includes a helpful discussion on the meaning of "head" (Greek *kephalē*).

Garland, Diana. *Church Agencies: Caring for Children and Families in Crisis*. Washington, DC: Child Welfare League of America, 1994. This thorough work looks at the role the church has previously played in social welfare issues and in advocating for a more active response to the injustice and crisis many children and families face today.

———. *Family Ministry: A Comprehensive Guide*. 2nd ed. Downers Grove, IL: InterVarsity, 2012. This book examines and integrates the historical, sociological, theological, and biblical contexts to understand the role and meaning of family in the life of Christians and the church. It takes a three-pronged approach to family ministry, which includes developing families grounded in Christian faith, helping families live the teachings of Jesus with one another, and equipping and supporting families as they learn to serve others.

Garland, Diana, S. Richmond, and David E. Garland. *Beyond Companionship: Christians in Marriage*. Eugene, OR: Wipf & Stock, 2003. The authors examine prevailing ideas about marriage held by many church leaders, social scientists, counselors, and therapists.

Beyond discussion of the marriage myths, the authors look at current biblical interpretations of marriage, being married in America, the character of a good marriage, the role of anger and conflict, sexuality, and, finally, the unresolved differences that can lead to divorce.

Gowan, Donald. *The Bible on Forgiveness.* Princeton Theological Monograph. Eugene, OR: Pickwick, 2010. This is a biblical-theological survey of forgiveness throughout both OT and NT, including the stories of Jacob and Esau and Joseph and his brothers in the book of Genesis.

Gravett, Sandie. "Reading 'Rape' in the Hebrew Bible: A Consideration of Language." *JSOT* 28 (2004): 279–99. This article explores the lexical and narrative evidence for rape in biblical stories and laws and argues that while ancient Hebrew society may not have understood "rape" as a legal or social concern, it is appropriate to interpret texts in which "power and sexual aggression" are present as cases of rape.

Greenman, Jeffrey, et al. *The Sermon on the Mount through the Centuries: From the Early Church through John Paul II.* Grand Rapids: Brazos, 2007. This collection of essays shows how the Sermon on the Mount has been read throughout time. Contributors include among others Stanley Hauerwas, David Lyle Jeffrey, Margaret M. Mitchell, Mark A. Noll, Stephen Spencer, and Robert L. Wilken.

Harwood, Adam. *The Spiritual Condition of Infants: A Biblical-Historical Survey and Systematic Proposal.* Eugene, OR: Wipf and Stock, 2011. Harwood's work is an exegetical look at ten biblical passages relevant to the topic of infant spirituality. His biblical and historical survey allows one to wrestle with the critical issue of original sin and its implications for faith and salvation.

Hellerman, Joseph H. "Brothers and Friends in Philippi: Family Honor in the Roman World and in Paul's Letter to Philippians." *BTB* 39 (2009) 15–25. The essay seeks to demonstrate the value of insights from the social sciences for NT interpretation. It suggests that Paul established a relational ethos (surrogate family) among Christians in Philippi which would forcefully discourage competition for honor among persons who took seriously their identity as brothers and sisters in Christ.

———. *The Ancient Church as Family.* Minneapolis: Fortress, 2001. Hellerman argues that the social matrix most central to the first, second, and third century Christian conceptions of community was the surrogate kinship group of siblings who understood themselves to be the sons and daughters of God. The church was seen as a family.

———. *When the Church Was a Family: Recapturing Jesus' Vision for Authentic Christian Community.* Nashville: Broadman and Holman, 2009. Here Hellerman examines the early Christian church from a sociohistorical perspective and shows how Jesus' original vision for authentic Christian community can satisfy the relational longings of modern Christians who are affected by individualism.

Helman, Ivy A. *Woman and the Vatican: An Exploration of Official Documents.* Maryknoll, NY: Orbis, 2012. Helman examines documents from the 1960s to the present and deals with them thematically to explain the Roman Catholic theology of womanhood.

Hess, Richard, and M. Daniel Carroll, eds. *Family in the Bible: Exploring Customs, Culture, and Context.* Grand Rapids: Baker, 2003. A survey of the role of the family in the various literary sections of both Testaments by a number of evangelical scholars of the Bible. It lifts up the diversity of families and family issues found throughout the narratives, laws, and poetry of Scripture.

Hiers, Richard H., and Lisa Sowle Cahill. *Women's Rights and the Bible: Implications for Christian Ethics and Social Policy.* Eugene, OR: Pickwick, 2012. This book discusses the teaching of biblical law on women's rights and how that teaching should influence women's roles in society and the family.

Himes, Kenneth, ed., *Modern Catholic Social Teaching: Commentaries and Interpretations.* Washington, DC.: Georgetown University Press, 2005. This book explores the foundations of Catholic social teaching (interpretation of biblical texts, natural law, and ecclesiological foundations), includes a commentary on fourteen key documents, and discusses the reception of Catholic social teaching in the United States along with the future of the tradition.

Hodge, Carolyn Johnson. "Married to an Unbeliever: Households, Hierarchies, and Holiness in 1 Corinthian 7:12–16." *HTR* 103 (2010) 1–25. This article looks at how Paul's teaching in 1 Cor 7:12–16 might have been applied to different family structures in the ancient world. Her purpose is not to analyze Paul and his teaching but rather the practical response of those who heard it. She is especially curious as to how divided households would interpret Paul's words.

Horn, Cornelia B., and Phenix, Robert R., eds. *Children in Late Ancient Christianity.* Studien und Texte zu Antike und Christentum 58. Tübingen: Mohr Siebeck, 2009. Social, cultural, theological, and economic analyses of children offer important clues to understanding the development of Christianity and society in Late Antiquity. This volume brings together studies of a diverse collection of sources. The contributors address the existence of children's culture, medicine and healing of children, disability and deformed children, the economic condition of orphans, theological appropriations of children, the presentations of family relationships in Christian thought, monasticism and family obligations, early Christian response to pedophilia, the formation of Christian ethical identity, and the role of children in apocryphal texts.

Houston, James M., and Michael Parker. *A Vision for the Aging Church: Renewing Ministry for and by Seniors.* Downers Grove, IL: InterVarsity, 2011. With the conviction that the need to reconceive the place and part of the elderly in the local church is urgent, the authors offer biblical and historical views of aging and offer solutions for the aging chuch. They confront the idea that the aging are a burden, address the moral issues related to caring, provide examples of successful care-giving programs, and challenge the church to restore broken connections across the generations. Seniors are not the problem but the solution.

Hsu, Albert. *Singles at the Crossroads: A Fresh Perspective on Christian Singleness.* Chicago: InterVarsity, 1997. Many Christian singles feel marginalized or alienated because most churches emphasize marriage and family. The book argues that Christian singles do not need tips on finding a mate or advice on suffering through the single life. What they need is a biblically grounded and theologically informed perspective that honors singleness equally with marriage and family.

John Paul II. *On the Family: Familiaris consortio*. Washington, DC: United States Conference of Catholic Bishops, 1981. Pope John Paul II addresses the role of the family in society as a believing and evangelizing community. He addresses God's plan for marriage and family, the role of the Christian family as a community of persons, a community participating in the development of society and a sharer in the life and mission of the church. He also discusses the issues of pastoral care of the family.

Joiner, Reggie. *Think Orange: Imagine the Impact When Church and Family Collide*. Colorado Springs, CO: David C. Cook, 2009. Joiner argues for the cooperation and synchronization of homes and churches in building faith in children. The author asks what the church can do to empower the family and how the family can emphasize the work of the church. The synchronized effort is called "orange thinking."

Jones, Timothy Paul. *Perspectives on Family Ministry: Three Views*. Broadman and Holman, 2009. Every church is called to some form of family ministry. According to Jones most effective family ministries involve refocusing every church process to engage parents in discipling their children and to draw family members together instead of pulling them apart. The book includes three views on how to do this through family-integrated, family-based, or family-equipping ministry.

Jowers, Dennis W., and H. Wayne House, eds. *The New Evangelical Subordinationism? Perspectives on the Equality of God the Father and God the Son*. Eugene, OR: Pickwick, 2012. The debated topic of female subordination has raised another discussion among evangelical scholars. This collection includes essays from evangelical scholars who argue either for or against the notion that the Son eternally submits to his Father. Among the writers are Michael Bird, Bruce Ware, Linda Belleville, Kevin Giles, Wayne Grudem, and Craig Keener.

Kasper, Walter. *Theology of Christian Marriage*. Translated by David Smith. New York: Crossroad, 1983. The book focuses on the goodness of marriage by looking at the historical development of Christian attitudes toward sex and sanctity in marriage. The themes include marriage and sin, marriage as the ideal life, and the nature of marriage.

Keener, Craig S. *Paul, Women and Wives: Marriage and Women's Ministry in the Letters of Paul*. Peabody, MA: Hendrickson, 1992. Keener discusses historical, lexical, cultural, and exegetical details behind Paul's words about female roles in ministry and family. While taking the biblical text seriously, the author acknowledges that Paul's letters were written in a specific time and place for specific purposes. Especially interesting is his model for interpreting wives' submission through the lens of slaves in Eph 6:5–9.

Kiper, Jordan. "Forgiveness is Costly: The Evolution of Forgiveness and its Philosophical Implications." Papers from the Fifth Global Conference on "Forgiveness: Probing the Boundaries" at Oxford University July 11–13, 2012. No pages. Online: http://

www.inter-disciplinary.net/probing-the-boundaries/persons/forgiveness/project-archives/5th/session-3-concepts-and-ideologies-of-forgiveness/. This paper brings scientific study of forgiveness into dialogue with theology and philosophy and argues that forgiveness is neither a cultural innovation nor a behaviour that is beneficial in many circumstances, especially those where reconciliation gestures are absent.

Koskenniemi, Erkki. *The Exposure of Infants Among Jews and Christianity in Antiquity*. Sheffield: Phoenix, 2009. This study reviews the evidence for the practice of exposing infants from Graeco-Roman, Jewish and Christian sources and examines the rejection of the custom by Jewish authors like Philo and Josephus and by Christian writers such as Clement, Justin, Tertullian, Origen, Chrysostom, and Augustine.

Kroeger, Catherine Clark, and Nancy Nason-Clark. *No Place for Abuse: Biblical and Practical Resources To Counteract Domestic Violence*. Downers Grove, IL: InterVarsity, 2001. This informative work tackles the difficult topic of violence in the home. Through haunting statistics, biblical exegesis, and a call to action, the authors show the effect of abuse on individuals and family systems and seek to counteract the abuse in our society.

Köstenberger, Andreas, and David W. Jones. *Marriage and the Family: Biblical Essentials*. Wheaton, IL: Crossway, 2012. The authors argue for a traditional understanding of marriage, family, and gender roles. Other issues discussed are sex, reproduction, parenting, singleness, homosexuality, divorce, remarriage, and the church.

Lampe, Peter. "'Family' in Church and Society of New Testament Times." *Affirmation* 5 (1992) 1–20. The meaning of "familia" was wider than kinship in the Roman Empire. The article discusses how private households met the social, educational, economic, and juridical tasks and needs of the Empire. These tasks and needs are then discussed in comparison with the tasks and needs of the early church that were met by the private households.

Launderville, Dale. *Celibacy in the Ancient World: Its Ideal and Practice in Pre-Hellenistic Israel, Mesopotamia, and Greece*. Collegeville, MN: Liturgical, 2010. Launderville situates virginity, chastity, and celibacy within the larger social structure of the patriarchal household in Mesopotamia, Israel, and Greece. In this study celibacy emerges as an effort to separate from customary social-sexual relations with a human partner in order to connect with the divine in a manner that would transcend death. Launderville hopes to offer a more holistic view of sexuality for modern readers.

Lester, Barry, and Joshua Sparrow. *Nurturing Children and Families: Building on the Legacy of T. Berry Brazelton*. Malden, MA: Wiley-Blackwell, 2012. This compilation of essays looks at family dynamics through a scientific and practical lens. The authors urge others to focus on research-driven evidence and offer treatment of various topics to bring important perspectives on parenting, marriages, and other relationships.

MacDonald, Margaret Y. *Early Christian Women and Pagan Opinion: The Power of the Hysterical Woman*. New York: Cambridge, 1996. This book is a study of how Christian women were viewed in the public arena from NT times to the second century CE. The author shows the conviction of pagan writers that women were inclined toward excesses in religion and that female initiative was central to Christianity's development. Concern in the NT and early Christian texts about the respectability of women is seen in a new light when one appreciates that outsiders focused on early church women and their activities as a reflection of the group as a whole.

McCullough, Michael. *Beyond Revenge: The Evolution of the Forgiveness Instinct.* San Francisco: Jossey-Bass, 2008. McCullough gathers evidence from a wide range of disciplines (neuroscience, anthropology, psychology, and evolutionary biology) to understand how revenge and forgiveness developed and functioned in our early human ancestors and how they function today. McCullough argues that the instincts for revenge and forgiveness are "hard wired" into the brain and function somewhat differently among siblings and family members as opposed to those considered strangers or outsiders.

Moxnes, Halvor, ed. *Constructing Early Christian Families. Family as Social Reality and Metaphor.* London and New York: Routledge, 1997. This is a collection of essays on the family in early Christianity and its cultural milieu by an international group of scholars. Issues of sexuality and asceticism are also dealt with. Particularly valuable is the essay by Moxnes on "What is Family? Problems in Constructing Early Christian Families."

Neufeld, Dietmar, and Richard E. DeMaris, eds. *Understanding the Social World of the New Testament.* New York: Routledge, 2010. The authors bring expertise in the social sciences to develop interpretative models for understanding such values as collectivism, kinship, memory, ethnicity, and honour and to demonstrate how to apply these models to the NT texts.

Osiek, Carolyn, et al. *A Woman's Place: House Churches in Earliest Christianity.* Minneapolis: Fortress, 2006. The book looks at women in the household context and discusses the importance of issues of space and visibility in shaping the lives of early Christian women. Among the aspects discussed are the lives of wives, widows, women with children, female slaves, women as patrons, household leaders, and teachers. In addition several key themes emerge: hospitality, dining practices, and the extent of female segregation.

Osiek, Carolyn, and David L. Balch. *Families in the New Testament World: Households and House Churches.* The Family, Religion, and Culture. Louisville: Westminster John Knox, 1997. The authors explore the material and social environment of the Greco-Roman household through archeological evidence. This evidence is then viewed in relation to early Christian families and house churches. The authors show that few Christian writers were interested in the family as such but rather in family and household as image and proving ground for the church.

Padgett, Alan G. *As Christ Submits to the Church: A Biblical Understanding of Leadership and Mutual Submission.* Grand Rapids: Baker, 2011. This work argues for lives characterized by mutual submission because of the model Christ has set for us. Padgett explains the implications of a mutual submission ethic and its relationship to gender roles, leadership, and the Christian family.

Perdue, Leo G., et al. *Families In Ancient Israel.* Louisville: Westminster John Knox, 1997. The four authors examine the ancient historical and social development of the family in ancient Israel at various points in ancient Israel's history from early village society until later Second Temple Judaism.

Piper, John, and Wayne A. Grudem, eds. *Recovering Biblical Manhood and Womanhood: A Response to Evangelical Feminism.* Wheaton, IL: Crossway, 1991. This collection of essays discusses the roles of women in ministry and in the home from a complementarian perspective (female subordination). It includes essays on manhood and womanhood, key biblical texts, church history, biology, psychology, sociology, and the implications of the whole study. Chapter two is a helpful overview of their central concerns. Appendices include Wayne Grudem's lenghty response to the recent studies on the meaning of "head" (Greek *kephalē*).

Pressler, Carolyn. *The View of Women Found in the Deuteronomic Family Laws.* Beihefte zur Zeitschrift für die alttestamentliche Wissenschaft 216. Berlin: Walter de Gruyter, 1993. This brief study addresses the construction of women in the "family laws" of Deuteronomy as subordinates within patriarchal households. Pressler argues that the laws of Deuteronomy may protect subordinates, but they do not challenge or disrupt the patriarchal system.

Pierce, Ronald W., et al., eds. *Discovering Biblical Equality: Complementarity Without Hierarchy.* Downers Grove, IL: InterVarsity, 2004. This collection of essays from twenty-six evangelical scholars analyzes gender roles by looking at historical aspects of the discussion, biblical texts, theological perspectives, hermeneutical issues, and practical applications. The authors argue for a complementarity of the sexes which does not require a hierarchy of roles. These articles provide the best presentation of an evangelical, egalitarian approach.

Rawson, Beryl, ed. *A Companion to Families in the Greek and Roman Worlds.* Oxford: Blackwell, 2011. This is a major compendium of the most up-to-date classical scholarship on the family in antiquity. It represents the state of the art and includes essays on early Christianity.

Reeder, Caryn A. *The Enemy in the Household: Family Violence in Deuteronomy and Beyond.* Grand Rapids: Baker, 2012. This study of Deut 13:7–11, 21:18–21, and 22:13–21 examines the place of family violence in Deuteronomy and the interpretation of these three laws in later traditions. The conclusion offers suggestions for the ethical interpretation and embodiment of these laws in the church today.

Rubio, Julie Hanlon. *A Christian Theology of Marriage and Family.* Mahwah, NJ: Paulist, 2003. Hanlon Rubio discusses the calling of Christian families in contemporary society. She weaves together theology, social science, and her experience as a wife and mother as she explores the Catholic marriage liturgy, the NT, and Christian tradition. She also reflects on the ways Christian husbands and wives, fathers and mothers, and children can live out their vocations in changing times. The book concludes with chapters on divorce and the mission of the family.

Sanders, James. A. "The Family in the Bible." *BTB* 32 (2002) 117–128. Both the Israelite society and the early church were family-oriented but in different ways. The author shows that there is a shift from one culture to another, from emphasis on the worth and responsibilities of the tribe or clan to embracing the idea that anyone anywhere could be part of the new family of Christ. He argues that today's Christians should take the family seriously and not hide behind the conservative idea of drawing lines between different biblical and secular cultures.

Sanders, Robert. *Sibling Relationships: Theory and Issues for Practice.* New York: Palgrave Macmillian, 2004. This book is a thorough survey of issues related to sibling relationships and rivalries within families from infants to adulthood from the perspective of psychology and sociology. It includes research-based and practical strategies for addressing problems associated with sibling relationships.

Sandnes, Karl Olav. *A New Family: Conversion and Ecclesiology in the Early Church with Cross-Cultural Comparisons.* Studien zur Interkulturellen Geschichte des Christentums 91. Bern: Peter Lang, 1994. Sandnes argues that the early Christians presented themselves as a household of faith, a family-like community in which social and racial unequals shared and lived together.

Schlimm, Matthew. *From Fratricide to Forgiveness: The Language and Ethics of Anger in Genesis.* Winona Lake, IN: Eisenbrauns, 2011. Schlimm studies the language of anger in the book of Genesis, beginning with the story of Cain and Abel in Gen 4 and ending with Joseph's forgiveness of his brothers in Gen 50.

Scholz, Suzanne. *Sacred Witness: Rape in the Hebrew Bible.* Minneapolis: Fortress, 2010. This study addresses different categories of rape in the narratives and laws of the Hebrew Bible through the lens of women's experiences of rape throughout time, thus forcing the reader to confront the significance of the biblical texts for women in the world today.

Schroeder, Joy A. *Dinah's Lament: The Biblical Legacy of Sexual Violence in Christian Interpretation.* Minneapolis: Fortress, 2007. Schroeder studies the ways Christians have read six biblical narratives about sexual violence. She uses biblical commentaries, homilies, and devotional writings as a window into the history of the church's attitudes about rape. She raises questions about the way Christian readers continue to shield the Bible from criticism and to reinforce patterns of subjugation, silencing, and violence against women.

Scott, Kenneth, and Michael Warren, eds. *Perspectives on Marriage: A Reader.* Oxford: Oxford University Press, 1993. This book is a multidisciplinary anthology on the theology and spirituality of marriage. It explores marriage in its historical context, current views on the theology of marriage, the meanings and transitions of marriage, attitudes toward sexuality, communication, conflict and change, commitment, divorce and annulment, the spirituality of marriage, same-sex marriage, cohabitation, the theology of dating, counseling, and various issues that affect marriage.

Sims, David. *The Child in American Evangelicalism and the Problem of Affluence: A Theological Anthropology of the Affluent American-Evangelical Child in Late Modernity.* Eugene, OR: Pickwick, 2009. Sims is concerned with an evangelical theology of the child nurtured in the context of American evangelicalism and affluence. He argues that affluence is an impediment to the nurture of children. It affects their spiritual and moral formation and creates delusional beliefs about a life that consists in an abundance of possessions. Furthermore, affluence hinders the liberation of the poor.

Smith, Suzanne R., and Raeann R. Hamon. *Exploring Family Theories*. Oxford: Oxford University Press, 2009. This combined text and reader offers a diverse variety of perspectives that integrate theory with research and applications. Each principal family theory is presented in a concise manner with the relevant history, scholarship, and critiques.

Stearns, Peter N. *Growing Up: The History of Childhood in Global Context*. Waco, TX: Baylor University Press, 2005. This compilation of two lectures discusses the connection between "world history and childhood history" and how one's context impacts his or her youth.

Thistelton, Anthony C. *The First Epistle to the Corinthians*. New International Greek Testament Commentary. Grand Rapids: Eerdmans, 2000. This superb commentary not only includes helpful treatment of relevant passages in 1 Corinthians, but it also includes a helpful discussion on the meaning of "head" (Greek *kephalē*).

Trebilco, Paul. *Self-designations and Group Identity in the New Testament*. Cambridge: Cambridge University Press, 2012. Trebilco investigates the origin, use, and function of seven key self-designations of early Christians (brothers and sisters, believers, saints, the assembly, disciples, the Way, and Christian) and discovers what they reveal about the identity, self-understanding, and character of the early Christian movement. The treatment of brothers and sisters is especially important. Trebilco argues against the view that the early Christian community was egalitarian.

Van Henten, Jan Willem, and Athalya Brenner, eds. *Families and Family Relations as Represented in Early Judaisms and Early Christianities: Texts and Fictions*. Leiden: Deo, 2000. This is a volume of scholarly essays on various aspects of the realities of family life in Judaism and Christianity. Subjects include marriage metaphors, gender and gender roles, sibling relations, family nomenclature, kinship and identity, and the women in the Gospel of John.

Van Huyssteen, Wentzel. *Duet or Duel? Theology and Science in the Postmodern World*. Norwich: SCM, 1998. Van Huyssteen argues that the interdisciplinary relationship of theology and science can be a fruitful dialogue from which both disciplines can learn. While there is overlap, there are also distinctive modes of investigation, ways of knowing, differences about what counts for evidence, and rules for making arguments. Even so, theology can learn from science and similarly, science can learn from theology.

Van Leeuwen, Mary Stewart. *Gender & Grace: Love, Work and Parenting in a Changing World*. Downers Grove, IL: InterVarsity, 1990. Written from a Christian "social scientist" perspective, this book analyzes the role gender plays in marriage, parenting, and other relationships. Van Leeuwen also investigates the role that nurture plays in one's identity. This monograph is a thorough exploration of the household as a subject of instruction as well as a metaphor for the church in the Pastoral Epistles.

———. *My Brother's Keeper: What the Social Sciences Do (and Don't) Tell Us About Masculinity.* Downers Grove, IL: InterVarsity, 2002. Van Leeuwen investigates what it means to be male, especially looking at how males function in the context of relationships and society. She includes a chapter on male parenting in her work.

Waters, Brent. *The Family in Christian Social and Political Thought.* Oxford: Oxford University Press, 2007. This is a major contribution to a theology of the family written by a leading theological ethicist. It is wide-ranging and comprehensive and offers valuable critiques of other contributors to the field as well as offering its own constructive proposals.

Webb, William J. *Slaves, Women and Homosexuals: Exploring the Hermeneutics of Cultural Analysis.* Downers Grove, IL: InterVarsity, 2001. The book is intended as a tool for the application process in hermeneutics. The author argues that the transcultural homosexual texts are fundamentally different from the women and slavery texts which are heavily bound by culture.

Wright, Christopher J. H. *God's People in God's Land: Family, Land, and Property in the Old Testament.* Grand Rapids: Eerdmans, 1990. This analysis addresses "family" as connected to land ownership, and thus membership in the covenant. It is argued that women in the family laws are not possessions or property but dependents whose own dignity is protected by the laws.

Zenger, Erich. *A God of Vengeance? Understanding the Psalms of Divine Wrath.* Louisville: Westminster John Knox, 1995. Many of the Psalms ask God to take revenge upon the enemy of the one praying the psalm. Zenger wrestles with vengeance, both human and divine, through the book of Psalms and offers ways by which we may better understand the role and function of the Psalms that ask God to punish our enemies.

Zimmerman, Martha. *Celebrating the Christian Year: Building Family Traditions Around all the Major Christian Holidays.* Minneapolis: Bethany, 1993. Zimmerman gives useful instructions for families to celebrate holy days together. Each chapter focuses on one holiday and gives the background, resources for celebrations, recipes, and Bible verses to read as a family.

———. *Celebrate the Feasts of the Old Testament in Your Own Home or Church.* Minneapolis: Bethany, 1981. This "Christian education in the home" provides resources for family conversations about biblical holidays and feasts that may be difficult for children to understand. She includes background information, activities to do together, and recipes for each festival.

NORTH PARK THEOLOGICAL SEMINARY SYMPOSIUM ON THE THEOLOGICAL INTERPRETATION OF SCRIPTURE

SEPTEMBER 27–SEPTEMBER 29, 2012

Family

PRESENTERS

STEPHEN BARTON
Reader in New Testament, Durham University

JANA MARGUERITE BENNETT
Assistant Professor of Religious Studies, University of Dayton

LYNN COHICK
Professor of New Testament, Wheaton College

JIM DEKKER
Associate Professor of Youth Ministry, North Park University

DENNIS OLSON
Charles T. Haley Professor of Old Testament Theology, Princeton Theological Seminary

LUKE POWERY
Dean of Duke Chapel, Duke University

CARYN REEDER
Assistant Professor of Religious Studies, Westmont College

JULIE RUBIO
Associate Professor of Theological Studies, St. Louis University

MARY VEENEMAN
Assistant Professor of Biblical and Theological Studies, North Park University

RESPONDENTS

CHRISTOPHER ANSBERRY
    Visiting Assistant Professor of Old Testament, Wheaton College

LINDA CANNELL
    Adjunct Professor of Christian Education, North Park Theological Seminary

MICHELLE CLIFTON-SODERSTROM
    Associate Professor of Theology and Ethics, North Park Theological Seminary

JO ANN DEASY
    Senior pastor, Sojourner Covenant Church

DENNIS EDWARDS
    Senior pastor, The Sanctuary Covenant Church

JACK LUNDBOM
    Visiting Professor of Old Testament, Garrett-Evangelical Theological Seminary

LUKE POWERY
    Dean of Duke Chapel, Duke University

ERICA OLSON-BANG
    PhD Candidate and Research Fellow, Fordham University

EX AUDITU

Volumes Available

Vol. 1 (1985) consists of selected articles presenting the issues inherent in the theological interpretation of Scripture.

Vol. 2 (1986) discusses the theme: "Church and State Relationship." In addition, there are two lead articles: one by Peter Stuhlmacher on "EX AUDITU and the Theological Interpretation of Holy Scripture," and the second by Ben F. Meyer on "The Primacy of Consent and the Uses of Suspicion."

Vol. 3 (1987) "Creation."
Vol. 4 (1988) "The Church and Israel (Romans 9–11)."
Vol. 5 (1989) "What is Salvation?"
Vol. 6 (1990) "Prophetic and/or Apocalyptic Eschatology."
Vol. 7 (1991) "Christology and Incarnation"
Vol. 8 (1992) "Worship."
Vol. 9 (1993) "Resurrection."
Vol. 10 (1994) "The Church."
Vol. 11 (1995) "Biblical Law and Liberty."
Vol. 12 (1996) "Holy Spirit."
Vol. 13 (1997) "What is a Human?"
Vol. 14 (1998) "The Theological Significance of the Earthly Jesus."
Vol. 15 (1999) "Idolatry and the Understanding of God."
Vol. 16 (2000) "The Task of Interpreting Scripture Theologically."
Vol. 17 (2001) "Biblical Ethics."
Vol. 18 (2002) "Spiritual Formation."
Vol. 19 (2003) "The Authority and Function of Scripture."
Vol. 20 (2004) "Judgment."
Vol. 21 (2005) "Health and Healing."
Vol. 22 (2006) "Justice."
Vol. 23 (2007) "Christianity's Engagement with Culture."
Vol. 24 (2008) "The Idolatry of Security."
Vol. 25 (2009) "Conversion."
Vol. 26 (2010) "Atonement."
Vol. 27 (2011) "Wealth and Possessions."
Vol. 28 (2012) "Family"

Pickwick Publications
An Imprint of Wipf and Stock Publishers
199 West 8th Avenue, Ste. 3
Eugene OR 97401
www.wipfandstock.com
twitter.com/wipfandstock
www.facebook.com/wipfandstock
www.runningheads.net (editors' blog)

www.ingramcontent.com/pod-product-compliance
Lightning Source LLC
Chambersburg PA
CBHW081352230426
43667CB00017B/2803